GLOBAL MELTDOWN

*Immigration, Multiculturalism,
and National Breakdown
in the New World Disorder*

Joseph Wayne Smith,
Graham Lyons,
and Evonne Moore

Westport, Connecticut
London

Library of Congress Cataloging-in-Publication Data

Smith, Joseph Wayne.
  Global meltdown : immigration, multiculturalism, and national
breakdown in the New World disorder / Joseph Wayne Smith, Graham
Lyons, and Evonne Moore.
      p.   cm.
  Includes bibliographical references and index.
  ISBN 0–275–95600–8 (alk. paper)
  1. Sustainable development. 2. Environmentalism.
3. Overpopulation. 4. Civilization, Modern. I. Lyons, Graham,
1936– . II. Moore, Evonne. III. Title.
HC79.E5S5357   1998
363.9'1—dc21   97–33226

British Library Cataloguing in Publication Data is available.

Library of Congress Catalog Card Number: 97–33226
ISBN: 0–275–95600–8

First published in 1998

Praeger Publishers, 88 Post Road West, Westport, CT 06881
An imprint of Greenwood Publishing Group, Inc.

Printed in the United States of America

The paper used in this book complies with the
Permanent Paper Standard issued by the National
Information Standards Organization (Z39.48–1984).

10 9 8 7 6 5 4 3 2 1

Contents

Preface

> Now, as never before, the prospects for a human future are exceptionally dismal. Most probably, the human race will soon and swiftly, but certainly not painlessly, be committed to suicide through use of extant nuclear weaponry. Even if this does not happen, every human being remains in peril of a slow death through poisoning and desiccating the environment in which he lives and by which he is sustained. Even if, just in time, humans should somehow impose a check on their blind and unbelievably stupid conduct, they still remain threatened by a progressive decline of all those attributes and attainments that constitute their humanity. (Lorenz, 1989,3)

This book, although self-contained, develops the argument advanced in our book *Healing a Wounded World: Economics, Ecology and Health for a Sustainable Life* (Smith et al., 1997). That book was concerned with the environmental crisis and the sustainability of human civilization in the light of a number of biophysical limits to growth. We argued in support of the thesis that human demands on the global ecosystem have already reached a point of critical overload and that humanity has already overshot the carrying capacity of the planet. Hence we are living on ecological credit, stolen from future generations ("future-eating"). The entire human race is therefore living on borrowed time and the ecological horsemen of the apocalypse will soon catch up with us. This argument was defended in some detail against the cornucopians and technological optimists who believe that technology, like a *deus ex machina*, will save us in the nick of time. We argued that technology alone cannot be the answer to human *hubris* and cannot in itself prevent an environmental *nemesis* or downfall. Furthermore, the types of economic, social, and lifestyle changes required to avert ecological disaster are too difficult to implement in the time frame of decades, which is essentially all the time humanity has. Therefore we concluded our previous book, asserting that our ecologically wounded world is likely to be "healed," if at all, only by an environmental catastrophe or series of catastrophes that eliminates the human species *in toto* or reduces our numbers substantially.

This book continues this theme, although this time we broaden our analysis to consider many other variables, not just ecological ones. In particular we focus on the breakdown of civilization—of organized social life—that will occur in humankind's ecological nemesis. We will argue here that even apart from the environmental crisis there is good reason to believe that civilization as we know it will not last and that even if the human race does survive as a species, it will do so for however long it does endure in a state of barbarism. Some of the social, political, and philosophical ramifications of this vision will be explored here.

The Coming Anarchy: The Collapse of Civilization and the Coming of Hell on Earth

We need to learn to love our differences. But in the meantime, and for a long time, we are going to be faced with chaos and political disintegration—both at levels which will make the ideal of democratic capitalism seem laughable. The process has already begun with ethnic violence, unprovoked crime, ruthless regimes and the migration of millions of permanent refugees. Central governments have begun to wither, regional and tribal identities are being revived, and fundamentalism of every stripe is becoming ever more obvious and more strident. Under the pressure of environmental and demographic stress, we are watching the old order crack and fragment into city states, shanty states and rag-tag private armies belonging to a whole new generation of local warlords. . . . What we are seeing is the rebirth of warrior societies, the reprivatising of mankind into smaller, more ruthless communities in which the radius of trust is being limited once again to immediate kin and close comrades. We are being retribalized, closing the genetic gates; but with nature breaking down and clean water in dangerously short supply, our biological roots can no longer provide us with the moral nourishment we need. (Watson, 1995, 250–51)

Man never has really loved humanity all of a piece—all its races, its people, its religions—but only those creatures he feels are his kin, a part of his clan, no matter how vast. As far as the rest are concerned, he forces himself, and lets the world force him. And then, when he does, when the damage is done, he himself falls apart. In this curious war taking shape, those who loved themselves best were the ones who would triumph. (Raspail, 1975, 16;1995)

The world is not run by skeptics and ironists but by gunmen and true believers and the new world they are bequeathing to the next century already seems a more violent and desperate place that I could ever have imagined. If I had supposed, as the Cold War came to an end, that the new world might be ruled by philosophers and poets, it was because I believed, foolishly, that the precarious civility and order of the states in which I live must be what all people rationally desire. Now I am not so sure. I began the journey as a liberal, and I end as one, but I cannot help thinking that liberal civilization—the rule of laws, not men, of argument in place of force, of compromise in place of violence—runs deeply against the human grain and is only achieved and sustained by the most unremitting struggle against human nature. (Ignatieff, 1993, 189)

THE COMING ANARCHY OF THE CLASH OF CIVILIZATIONS

A meltdown of a nuclear reactor occurs when the fuel rods melt because of a defect in the cooling system, leading to the possibility of a violent escape of radiation into the surrounding environment. It is the thesis of this book that the modern world is just like a nuclear reactor undergoing the process of meltdown—*global meltdown*. The interaction of the forces of environmental destruction and ecological scarcity, economic rationalism, globalization, and the technological revolution are interacting with a wide array of other social problems—immigration, multiculturalism, racial and ethnic conflict, the loss of personal, spiritual, and religious meaning and so on—to produce a heavy burden of problems facing humanity. Even the most optimistic cornucopian does not deny the existence of such problems; such folk believe that all will be well in the end. Humanity will survive. Civilization will endure. Human ingenuity will find a way. We do not believe that this is so. In the short term, barring cosmic and manmade catastrophes, perhaps the human race may survive, but we doubt whether our modern globalized techno-industrial civilization will survive. In our book *Healing a Wounded World* (Smith et al.,1997), we examined one aspect of the global meltdown thesis—the environmental crisis—and concluded that this crisis in itself was sufficient to destroy modernity because of ecological scarcity. We shall have more to say about the limits to growth argument in this book. Here we shall presuppose that the argument of our previous book is essentially satisfactory and proceed further. The global meltdown thesis is a generalization of a thesis advanced by Roberto Vacca (among others) in his book *The Coming Dark Age*: "our great technological systems of human organization and association are continuously outgrowing ordered control: they are now reaching critical dimensions of instability" (Vacca, 1973, 4). Large systems, due to their complexity, are highly vulnerable and are subject to systems-breakdown. There will be, in Vacca's opinion, an era of disorder and destruction, followed by a rebirth. We agree with Vacca right up to the last point. There will be no rebirth of an environmentally sensitive civilization as the environmental damage produced by modern techno-industrial civilization will be too great to sustain any great "civilization" (Smith et al., 1997, 153–54). Humanity will ultimately return to barbarism. Indeed, we have already entered a new dark age, as Shawcross notes: "The modern world that was invented around [A.D.]1500 is coming to an end. We are back to the medieval world of beggars, plagues, conflagration and *superstitions*" (Shawcross, 1994, 23). The modern age has been dominated by the activities of states, in particular, nation-states (Van Creveld, 1991, 49). We see economic globalization breaking down and weakening such nation-states and the forces of ecological scarcity and racial and ethnic conflict finally breaking up such nation-states. This will ultimately lead to the self-destruction of civilization as depicted in the United Kingdom documentary *Pulp Future* (1995).

Before we elaborate the global meltdown thesis we need to clarify our views on the collapse of civilizations and societies. This can be done by discussing briefly some theories of the rise and fall of civilizations, and outlining our own position. It is not arbitrary to start with the positions of Oswald Spengler and Arnold Toynbee, whose respective works, *The Decline of the West* (Spengler, 1926) and *A Study of History* (Toynbee, 1949), have been highly influential in this field of study. Let us begin with Spengler. Spengler held that human society was a social organism; he held to a strong form of social holism that saw society as a perfectly intelligible whole where the individual as a part of this whole cannot exist independently. Spengler saw civilizations arising out of the "void" and returning to it. As he puts it in *Der Untergang des Abendlandes*:

A civilization [*Kultur*] is born at the moment when, out of the primitive psychic conditions of a perpetually infantile [raw] humanity, a mighty soul awakes and extricates itself: a form out of the formless, a bounded and transitory existence out of the boundless and persistent. This soul comes to flower on the soil of a country with precise boundaries, to which it remains attached like a plant. Conversely a civilization dies once this soul has realized the complete sum of its possibilities in the shape of people, languages, creeds, arts, states and sciences, and thereupon goes back into the primitive psyche from which it originally emerged. (quoted from Toynbee, 1949, 210–11)

In the English version of *The Decline of the West*, Spengler describes the rise and fall of civilizations as the "waxing and waning of organic forms":

I see, in place of that empty figment of *one* linear history which can only be kept up by shutting one's eyes to the overwhelming multitude of the facts, the drama of a *number* of mighty Cultures, each springing with primitive strength from the soil of a mother-region to which it remains firmly bound throughout its whole life-cycle; each stamping its material, its mankind, in *its own* image; each having *its own* idea, *its own* passions, *its own* life, will and feeling, *its own* death. Here indeed are colors, lights, movements, that no intellectual eye has yet discovered. Here the Cultures, peoples, languages, truths, gods, landscapes bloom and age as the oaks and the stone-pines, the blossoms, twigs and leaves—but there is no aging "Mankind." Each Culture has its own new possibilities of self-expression which arise, ripen, decay, and never return. There is not *one* sculpture, *one* painting, *one* mathematics, *one* physics, but many, each in its deepest essence different from the others, each limited in duration and self-contained, just as each species of plant has its peculiar blossom or fruit, its special type of growth and decline. These cultures, sublimated life-essences, grow with the same superb aimlessness as the flowers of the field. They belong, like the plants and the animals, to the living nature of Goethe, and not to the dead nature of Newton. I see world-history as a picture of endless formations and transformations, of the marvelous waxing and waning of organic forms. The professional historian, on the contrary, sees it as a sort of tapeworm industriously adding on to itself one epoch after another. (Spengler, 1926, 21–22)

Toynbee by contrast sees the matter as such: society is a field of action, but the individuals composing it are the source of action. Human societies are systems of relationships between individuals. These individuals are *social* animals in the sense that their identity depends upon relationships to others. A society arises from "the coincidence of their individual fields of action" (Toynbee, 1949, 211). According to Toynbee, civilizations grow as follows:

Growth is achieved when an individual or a minority or a whole society replies to a challenge by a response which not only answers that challenge but also exposes the respondent to a fresh challenge which demands a further response on his part. . . . Each successive challenge thus produces differentiation within the society, and the longer the series of challenges the more sharply pronounced will this differentiation become. Moreover, if the process of growth thus gives rise to differentiation within a single growing society where the challenges are the same for all, then *a fortiori*, the same process must differentiate one growing society from another where the challenges themselves differ in character. (Toynbee, 1949, 241)

Disintegrating civilizations in their last stage of decline often purchase a reprieve by submitting to political unification in a universal state (Toynbee, 1949, 244). For example, Hellenic society was gathered up into the Roman empire; Orthodox Christianity in the Ottoman Empire; Hindu civilization in the Mughal Empire and then the British Raj; Far Eastern Civilization in the Mongol empire and then the Manchus; Japan in the Tokugawa Shogunate (Toynbee, 1949, 244–45). Such a universal state is a prelude to decline. Civilizations break down internally before they are broken down by outsiders.

Three points are made by Toynbee with respect to the nature and breakdown of civilizations:

(1) there is a failure of creative power in a minority which becomes a dominant minority maintaining its position by force;
(2) the "proletariat"/people/majority "no longer admires and imitates its rulers and revolts against its servitude" (Toynbee, 1949, 246);
(3) a loss of social unity in society as a whole occurs.

The simile used to describe this breakdown is that of climbers who fall to their death (Toynbee, 1949, 245).

Toynbee rejects the idea that civilizations are predestined or deterministically caused to disintegrate; Spengler maintains that every civilization passes through the same succession of ages as a human being so that every society has a predestined time-span. Toynbee also rejects the idea that civilizations are "organic" entities with a "biological life-span" (Toynbee, 1949, 248). Rather, Toynbee sees the breakdown of civilizations as coming from "within." He quotes from Meredith's *Love's Grave*:

In tragic life, God wot,
No villain need be! Passions spin the plot:
We are betrayed by what is false within.

What is this weakness? Leaders cease to lead and abuse their power:

This secession of the led from the leaders may be regarded as a loss of harmony between the parts which make up the whole ensemble of the society. In any whole consisting of parts a loss of harmony between the parts is paid for by the whole in a corresponding loss of self-determination. This loss of self-determination is the ultimate criterion of break-down. (Toynbee, 1949, 279)

For Toynbee the growth of civilization is linked to a mechanism of challenge-and-response—challenges are answered, bringing forth new challenges, which are in turn answered. In disintegration the challenges are not responded to, or are responded to and the attempt fails. The unanswered challenge "receives some tardy and imperfect answer or else brings about the destruction of the society" (Toynbee, 1949, 364). He observes that "the destruction which has overtaken a number of civilizations in the past has never been the work of any external agency, but has always been in the nature of an act of suicide" (Toynbee, 1949, 419).

There are, of course, many other explanations of the rise and, particularly, the decline of civilizations, from both poets and more scientifically minded thinkers. Lord Byron (1788–1824), in his major poetic work *Childe Harold's Pilgrimage*, wrote:

There is the moral of all human tales:
'Tis but the same rehearsal of the past,
First freedom, and then glory—when that fails,
Wealth—Vice—Corruption—Barbarism at last.

A well-known quotation from Voltaire (1694–1778) has it that "History is only the patter of silken slippers descending the stairs—to the clatter of hobnail boots coming up." Nations and civilizations grow soft as they become successful. Environmental causes have also been cited as leading to the decline and fall of civilizations (for a review see Smith et al., 1997). The supporting agriculture fails and soils may be destroyed as occurred in ancient Mesopotamia. Overpopulation also can have a destructive impact, especially in civilizations heavily dependent upon irrigation, such as Mesopotamia, beginning 4000 B.C.; Egypt, beginning 3000 B.C.; the Indus Valley, beginning about 2500 B.C.; and China, beginning about 1500 B.C. Joseph Tainter, in his book *The Collapse of Complex Societies* (Tainter, 1988), recognizes that all of these factors play a part, but he sees the *ultimate* cause of the collapse of complex societies linked to the operation of the law of diminishing returns to imperial social organization. His argument in summary is as follows:

(1) human societies are problem-solving organizations;
(2) sociopolitical systems require energy for their maintenance;
(3) increased complexity carries with it increased costs per capita; and
(4) investment in sociopolitical complexity as a problem-solving response often reaches a point of declining marginal returns. (Tainter, 1988, 118)

Thus: "At some point in the evolution of a society, continued investment in complexity as a problem-solving strategy yields a declining marginal return" (Tainter, 1988, 119–20).

Tainter's theory, like all the theories of collapse discussed here, has its merits and limits. The merits of each theory of collapse lie in the theory in question being able to explain the collapse of certain civilizations and societies. However, critics are usually able to give counterexamples, showing that the theory cannot be a *general* theory of collapse. Stated almost paradoxically, it is generally true that most general theories (excluding this meta-theoretical proposition—theories are taken to be systems of propositions) are strictly false or only approximately true. It is more likely that civilizations and societies collapse for a variety of reasons, such as internal decay of social cohesion, genetic deterioration (Lynn, 1996), environmental destruction, treason, entropy, and declining marginal returns. Rather than attempt to aim to construct any general theory of social collapse, we believe that it is more fruitful to investigate the plurality of forces leading to social and civilization disintegration. With very limited space, the best way of doing this is by a series of book reviews. Here is author X_1 who has argued that force F_1 is socially disruptive and author X_2 ... and so on. Proceeding in this way, putting the contents of the various works together in a coherent picture (and this must involve a fair but selective citation) eventually results in an image coming into focus, an image of death and destruction.

Let us begin with Zbigniew Brzezinski's book *Out of Control: Global Turmoil on the Eve of the 21st Century* (Brzezinski, 1993). His subjective interpretation is that global change is out of control. A collapse of established moral values has occurred with consumerism masquerading as a substitute for such values. Although humanity's technological power has been increasing, "our societal criteria of moral discernment and of self-control have become increasingly vague" (Brzezinski, 1993, x). The tendency in the West to link liberal democracy with "permissive cornucopia" and individual self-gratification is also a disintegrative force (Bzezinski, 1993, xii). While the potential exists for global community, Brzezinski doubts that American culture can supply it because of its moral emptiness. As well, mass immigration of non-European people into America, the high "colored" birth rate, and the below replacement level birth rate of European America will mean that by 2050 the European component will drop from 60 percent to around 40 percent. This will result in a very different America, "one more likely to mirror the cultural and philosophical cleavages that already divide the world" (Brzezinski, 1993, 114). Brzezinski elaborates on this problem:

The transformation of America from a society dominated—and shaped—by a white Anglo-Saxon Protestant culture into a global mosaic inevitably will involve a profound shift in values and perhaps some further loss of social cohesion. While such change may generate new creativity and dynamism—and its intellectual and human benefits are undeniable—it is also likely to be disruptive, even potentially divisive, especially if in the process the unifying function of a common language and of an inculcated common political philosophy are deliberately down-graded. A shared language and a shared constitutional commitment produce the common foundation on which a nation's cultural consensus rests, and without them cultural diversity could become incapable of sustaining social tolerance. The American society could then face the threat of disintegration.

It is easy to label such a concern as racist but to do so is to evade—and even to precipitate—the resulting problems. One simply cannot ignore the high probability that the recreation of the global cultural and ethnic mosaic within a very differentiated America will actually make it more difficult to address the social and cultural dilemmas that the country confronts. Indeed, in the absence of major progress in dealing compassionately with these dilemmas, the new mosaic could generate within America even escalating urban guerrilla warfare. (Brzezinski, 1993, 115)

America's shortcomings include indebtedness; the trade deficit; low savings and investment, industrial noncompetitiveness; low productivity and growth rates; inadequate health care; poor-quality secondary education; deteriorating social infrastructure and widespread urban decay; a greedy wealthy upper class; a parasitic obsession with litigation; a deepening race and poverty problem; widespread crime and violence; the spread of a massive drug culture; the inbreeding of social helplessness; the profusion of sexual license; the massive propagation of moral corruption by the visual media ("Hollywood movie and TV producers have become cultural subverters who—cynically exploiting the shield offered by the First Amendment—have been propagating a self-destructive social ethic" [Brzezinski, 1993, 71–72]); a decline in civic consciousness; the emergence of potentially divisive multiculturalism; the emerging gridlock in the political system; and an increasingly pervasive sense of spiritual emptiness. Smaller problems than these have destroyed nations. Further, the fate of America reflects in many ways the fate of most nations. Brzezinski agrees with James Schlesinger's 1992 conclusion that "The world order of the future . . . will be marked by power politics, national rivalries, and ethnic tensions" (Brzezinski, 1993, 166), and further—*"the dilemmas of global disorder may become the defining determinants of the new age"* (Brzezinski, 1993, 200, emphasis added).

Paul Kennedy, in his book *Preparing for the Twenty-First Century* (Kennedy, 1993), discusses many of the issues featured in Brzezinki's *Out of Control*, as well as offering a detailed examination of the environmental crisis. As we have critically evaluated Kennedy's useful contribution in *Healing a Wounded World* (Smith et al., 1997), we will not outline Kennedy's arguments here. Let us instead go to the heart of the matter, his conclusion about the human prospect:

In sum, we need to be concerned about the condition of our planet as a whole not simply because we face a new agenda of security risks such as global warming and mass migration, but also because these phenomena could interact with and exacerbate older threats to international stability such as regional wars, hostage-taking, and closure of sealanes. (Kennedy, 1993, 347–48)

These forces constitute additional sources of social conflict (Kennedy, 1993, 348). Kennedy then says in a revealing passage:

Given this array of problems, it may seem that our merely human political leadership has no chance of doing much; that instead we ought to brace ourselves for a continuation of jolts and jars and smashes in the social life of humanity—and on an increasingly global and intense scale. If so, it would be foolish for any country—or social class—to assume that it can isolate itself from future changes, some of which may be unexpected and perhaps dramatic. . . . We also ought to be aware that interventions . . . could produce their own unforeseen and unintended changes. Nothing is certain except that we face innumerable uncertainties. (Kennedy, 1993, 348)

As we cannot predict the future, Kennedy does not conclude in either an optimistic or a pessimistic note: "What is clear is that as the Cold War fades away, we face not a 'new world order' but a troubled and fractured planet, whose problems deserve the serious attention of politicians and publics alike" (Kennedy, 1993, 349). Kennedy gives no final assessment of whether our "troubled and fractured planet" will overcome its problems.

J. D. Davidson and W. Rees-Mogg in their work *The Great Reckoning* (Davidson and Rees-Mogg, 1992) believe that a financial armageddon will occur, most likely due to the compounding debt of the United States. In a globalized economic system, it takes only one major player to collapse for the entire system itself to collapse. We will have more to say about this below. Here we note that Davidson and Rees-Mogg also predict that multi-national, multi-racial countries will break apart, including Canada, India, South Africa, Israel, and Ethiopia. They also believe that Islam will replace Marxism as the main challenge to liberal-democratic ideologies.

Robert D. Kaplan has also offered a tempestuous vision of the twenty-first century, both in his justly famous February 1994 *The Atlantic Monthly* article "The Coming Anarchy: How Scarcity, Crime, Overpopulation, Tribalism, and Disease are Rapidly Destroying the Social Fabric of Our Planet" (Kaplan, 1994) and his book *The Ends of the Earth* (Kaplan, 1996a). Kaplan's February 1994 article in *The Atlantic Monthly* was advertised on the front cover of the magazine thus:

The coming anarchy: nations break up under the tidal flow of refugees from environmental and social disaster. As borders crumble, another type of boundary is erected—a wall of disease. Wars are fought over scarce resources, especially water, and war itself becomes continuous with crime, as armed bands of stateless marauders clash with the private security forces of the elites.

Kaplan's article is concerned primarily with West Africa and the Third World because West Africa is *the* symbol of a region facing demographic, ecological, and socio-political stress:

Africa may be as relevant to the future character of world politics as the Balkans were a hundred years ago, prior to the two Balkan wars and the First World War. Then the threat was the collapse of empires and the birth of nations based solely on tribe. Now the threat is more elemental: *nature unchecked*. Africa's immediate future could be very bad. The coming upheaval, in which foreign embassies are shut down, states collapse, and contact with the outside world takes place through dangerous, disease-ridden coastal trading posts, will loom large in the century we are entering. (Nine of twenty-one U.S. foreign-aid missions to be closed over the next three years are in Africa—a prologue to a consolidation of U.S. embassies themselves.) Precisely because much of Africa is set to go over the edge at a time when the Cold War has ended, when environmental and demographic stress in other parts of the globe is becoming critical, and when the post–First World War system of nation-states—not just in the Balkans but perhaps also in the Middle East—is about to be toppled, Africa suggests what war, borders, and ethnic politics will be like a few decades hence. (Kaplan, 1994, 54)

Kaplan develops these themes in his book *The Ends of the Earth*, a travel book that attempts to illustrate the issues discussed by Paul Kennedy in his work *Preparing for the Twenty-First Century* (Kennedy, 1993). Kaplan's book details his "unsentimental journey" through Africa—through tribal war in Liberia (although he falsely notes that "violence has nothing to do with race" [Kaplan, 1996a, 14]); social breakdown in Sierra Leone; strife and instability in the Gulf of Guinea; and various degrees of disintegration and violence in Egypt, Central Asia, India, Pakistan, and Southeast Asia. There is much empirical evidence to support Kaplan's thesis of "the coming anarchy." Here is a brief litany of woe from across the globe.

The famine and war in Somalia, the genocide in Rwanda, the exodus of Rwandan refugees to Zaire, the civil war in the Southern Sudan—these are all events familiar to us from the evening news (Schofield, 1996). Images of putrid, decaying corpses littering streets, of poorly buried corpses with limbs sticking out from the soil, fingers reaching for the sky in the agony of death, and heads, decapitated from their bodies and placed on poles—are frequently encountered images of chaos in Africa (Schofield, 1996, 2–3). At no time since 1979 has the greater Horn of Africa (and many regions beyond this) been free of both drought and civil strife (Anderson, 1996; Anonymous, 1996a). Over the past six years, civil war and famine have led to the deaths of over 350,000 Somalis. This torn country faces a battle between 16 warring factions, each with a rival warlord. The most powerful was Mohammed Farrah Aidid, who died after a gun battle in early August 1996. His son, Hussein Mohammed Aidid, an American citizen and member of the United States Marine Corps, returned to Somalia from the United States to continue his father's rule. Rampaging gang members and the MFA army murdered scores of United Nations' peacekeepers in 1993, leading to the beaten United Nations force retreating in 1995.

In Burundi, the government of Hutu President Sylvester Ntibantungaya collapsed in July 25, 1996. He took refuge in the United States Ambassador's residence. Tutsi youths armed with nail-studded clubs took over the streets of Bujumbura. The toppling of the previous Hutu president of Burundi also led to inter-ethnic slaughter between Hutus and Tutsis. Already 150,000 Burundians have died in ethnic warfare since 1993. In Rwanda, in 1994, one million Tutsis and moderate Hutus were killed by hardline Hutu (Anonymous a, 1996).

In Liberia, April 1996, drugged gangs of gunmen rampaged in the capital of Monrovia. Even the warlords had lost control of their troops and peacekeepers, particularly Nigerians, joined in the rampage of violence and looting (Griffith, 1996). Over 150,000 people have died in the seven-year war between seven rebel factions.

Zaire remains in a state of perpetual turmoil. On October 31, 1996, an exchange of artillery fire occurred across the border of Zaire and Rwanda and in December 1996 further conflict occurred between Zaire and Uganda. Ethnic warfare has led to half a million people, mainly Rwandan refugees, to be left roaming the bush. Four hundred thousand refugees were in Mugunga Camp, near Goma on the border with Rwanda as of October 1996. Tutsi rebels massacred over 300 Hutu refugees at a camp near the regional capital of Bukavu on November 17, 1996. Early, on October 29, 1996, both soldiers and civilians went on a looting rampage in Bukavu. On May 17, 1997, Laurent Kabila's rebel troops entered the capital of Zaire, Kinshasa. The former president, Mobutu Sese Seko, fled to Morocco. The country has been renamed the *Democratic Republic of Congo*. The victory of Laurent Kabila has been looked upon by much of the Western media as a step in the right direction for the resolution of Zaire's national crisis. The hope has been expressed that Kabila will encourage stability and economic growth. However, separatist urges and ethnic hatred have been suppressed to depose the dictator Mobutu. The replacement of one corrupt dictator by another would ensure anarchy in Zaire. Kabila's power base would shatter, leading to a battle for power and a breakup of Zaire. Disorder and turmoil seem destined to be Zaire's future.

Countries may become destabilized very quickly and just as quickly pull back from the abyss of anarchy and destruction. For example, Papua New Guinea destabilized on March 17, 1997, but regained order quickly. The problem was caused by former Papua New Guinea Prime Minister Sir Julius Chan, who employed 70 mercenaries through the British company Sandline International to end the secessionist war on Bougainville. The island of Bougainville is a land where war and social anarchy has "turned back the clock" (Marshall, 1997). The military did not support bringing in mercenaries. The exposure of secret dealings between Chan and the mercenaries led to widespread revolt against Chan. Brigadier Jerry Singirok launched Operation *Rausim Kwik* ("get them out quick") on March 17, 1997. This involved the arrest of the mercenaries, the termination of their contract, and a demand for Chan's resignation. A military coup threatened. When Singirok was sacked, the country destabilized and riots and looting occurred. Shops belonging to Chinese merchants were targeted in particular because of the Chinese wealth and Chan's Chinese ancestry (O'Callaghan and Scott, 1997, 1; McKenzie, 1997, 4). Fearing a complete breakdown of civil order, many Australians left Papua New Guinea, and Australian troops in Townsville were put on alert in case mass evacuation of Australians was necessary. The crisis ended on March 26, 1997, when Chan resigned as Prime Minister. Problems remain. A hint of the level of disillusion with the existing government and even with the concept of the nation-state was given by many Papua New Guineans interviewed in the Australian Channel 7 TV program *Witness*, shown on July 9, 1996. Many Papuans favored a return to colonial rule by Australia and even Sir Julius Chan hinted at this prospect in an interview in this program. Papua New Guinea is another country that stands on the edge of chaos.

Albania is a country that toppled into the abyss of anarchy and destruction in 1997. However, violence has gripped Albania for over five years since the military-backed government cancelled the second round of elections in January 1992 that the now-banned Salvation Front was set to win. Since that time 50,000 people have been killed in the resulting conflict (Walker, 1997a, b). The 1997 conflict was initiated by the collapse of the bogus Vefa pyramid investment scheme in mid-January 1997. This left thousands beggared and anti-government protests, beginning on January 15, 1997, with riots in Tirana, eventually escalated to all-out revolt. The turning point was on February 27, 1997, when the ruling Democratic Party re-elected President Berisha. Protesters then began raiding police and military armories in a large-scale pattern, and what were once protesters emerged as a rebel army who defined themselves, without a recognized leader, as freedom fighters. They soon dominated the south of Albania and began conducting "treason trials" (Behrakis, 1997). Albania, one of Europe's poorest countries, rests on the economic foundation of the profits of organized crime, in particular arms and drugs smuggling. The British newspaper *The Independent* has described the Albanian government as a "gangster regime," and noted that "It will be almost impossible for any government to reassert control over a restive, angry population that is now armed to the teeth" (Gumbel, 1997). Indeed, one theory about the Albanian revolt asserts, observing that many of the towns that are in rebel hands are controlled by Mafia clans, that the revolt had been initiated by the Mafia clans who wished to operate without police interference (Malone, 1997). There is also another element at work here. As Michael Ignatieff notes in his book *Blood and Belonging* (Ignatieff, 1993), there is a strong male resentment toward the over-civilization of modernity and the relative softness of modern life, an existential resentment that liberals have ignored. This pacification of male aggression by civilization has been detested by a hard-core of men in all societies. At times when countries destabilize, the gods of war are seemingly released, and young men can once more enjoy the sexual thrill of having the power of life or death in their hands (Ignatieff, 1993, 187). One elderly Albanian observer said, about the summary execution of suspected government agents at roadsides by the rebels, "These people are criminals. We want peace, but these people will not give up their arms. Why? Because they have never had guns before and they like the power" (Malone, 1997, 6). Tribal tensions will also ensure that the present conflict may diminish but will not be easily resolved. Albania is split north/south along a "tribal" fault line, where traditionally the Ghegs live in the north and the Tosqs in the south. The division is based largely on language differences.

Bulgaria also seems to be sliding toward political and economic chaos. Runaway inflation, the plunging value of the lev, the national currency, food shortages, and organized crime eat away at Bulgaria's social fabric. This is a common tale throughout Eastern Europe, and economic deprivation is increasingly being met by mass protests and demonstrations by tens of millions of people who have been reduced to poverty. It is not unreasonable to speculate that Russia could face an Albanian situation some time in the future if economic conditions continue to deteriorate. The possibility then exists of nuclear-armed missiles falling into the hands of resentful males longing for revenge and destruction. Any cities in the West could be their targets.

In South Africa, even under "black" rule, race riots continue. On February 7, 1997, race riots occurred in Johannesburg's mixed race suburbs of Westbury and Eldorado Park. Two people were killed and 200 injured. The riots began as a protest against municipal rates but degenerated into violence. South Africa's minority colored population feel that "black" majority rule has not improved the conditions they experienced under apartheid and that this is because of their mixed race. "We are not black enough," one rioter said on a TV news report we saw on February 7, 1997. In Cape Town, August 1996, a war began between young gangsters and fundamentalist Muslims following a vigilante killing of a supposed drug lord, Rashaad Staggie. He was shot and set on fire on August 4, 1996. With rapidly escalating murder rates, this is but one example of South Africa's slow but inevitable slide toward turmoil. The death of President Mandela will be a crisis point for this troubled land.

Across the world in Indonesia, ethnic strife is erupting in a multicultural and multiracial nation that is held together by the dual forces of economic growth and military might (Earl, 1997). On March 7, 1997, President Suharto warned that he would crush any political dissent that created unrest. Authorities proved their point by arresting ex-MP and leading anti-government critic Sri Bintang Pamungkas on subversion charges. A book criticizing President Suharto was banned. Suharto observed the existence of groups in Indonesian society, which if they had their way could produce "national disintegration." Suharto would flatten or smash ("gebuk") anyone who tried to unseat him unconstitutionally (Walters, 1997a).

The President will have his hands full. Dayaks in Indonesia's West Kalimantan province, for example, have mobilized against an influx of Moslem migrants from Madura, a small island north of Java. In the past the Dayaks were a headhunting community and in many respects they have returned to that tradition in confronting the Madurese. This "clash of cultures" has already led to about 5,000 deaths. Hundreds of Madurese have been beheaded and their hearts and livers have been cut out and eaten. In late December 1996, thousands of Dayaks attacked the Madurese and burnt their homes leading to five people dead and 21 people missing. On February 4, 1997, 50 masked men torched a Catholic dormitory containing Dayaks. They then raided a Dayak home, stabbing two Dayak women. A battle then erupted between the Dayaks and the Madurese in a number of towns, leading to two Dayak men dying. Earlier, on February 1, 1997, in Salatiga in Kalimantan, Dayak tribesmen armed with shotguns, spears, and machetes expelled 300 or more Madurese inhabitants and then torched their homes. A Javanese woman, Ibu Titi, saw a Dayak man walking along a road in Salatiga carrying a severed head on a pole. He had on his shoulders a basket with a mutilated body in it, the legs dangling over the side (Walters, 1997b, 1). Patrick Walters, the Jakarta correspondent for *The Australian*, describes what he saw at Salatiga at that time:

In Salatiga the marketplace is now a charred mass of corrugated iron. All that's left of a substantial Madurese house nearby are the fake Corinthian pillars that supported the front porch. There is a burnt sewing machine and the skeletons of a couple of bicycles. A large satellite dish lies on its side, bent and buckled by the fierce heat that has scorched surrounding coconut palms. On the main road leading out of Salatiga for kilometer after kilometer, virtually every house has been razed, the blackened ruins contrasting with the sharp green of surrounding banana groves and vegetable gardens. Madurese families, who over several generations prospered in this district as traders and businessmen, have fled enmasse to Pontianak, 50 km south. Dayak vigilantes, armed to the teeth, patrol the roads on motorbikes and in the back of utility trucks. Off the road they stalk through the abandoned dwellings, shotguns at the ready, on the lookout for the enemy. You can identify a Madurese, say the Dayaks, by the smell of their bodies as well as the color of their skin. (Walters, 1997b, 1)

Ethnic riots are occurring more frequently in Indonesia. In November 1995 hundreds of people rioted in the Javanese town of Pekalongan against ethnic Chinese. The riot was sparked by a rumor that an ethnic Chinese had torn pages from the *Koran*. Shops were attacked and cars set alight. Also in November 1995 another riot occurred against the Chinese in Purwakarta in West Java. Thousands rioted in Tasikmalaya on December 26, 1996, killing four people and damaging 100 buildings. On January 31, 1997, in the West Javanese town of Rengasdengklok, thousands of Muslims rioted, targeting ethnic Chinese properties. (Ethnic Chinese constitute four percent of Indonesia's population but control more than 80 percent of the country's wealth.) Six thousand people rioted in East Timor on February 21, 1997, leading to one person dead and numerous buildings and vehicles destroyed. This riot occurred in Ambeno, on the northern coast of West Timor province about 150 kilometers southwest of the East Timor capital Dili. The riot was initiated when a migrant from the largely Muslim Bugis ethnic group of southern Sulawesi province insulted a local Catholic priest. All in all, there is in Indonesia, in the words of Nobel prize winner Jose Ramos Horta, "an explosive cocktail of political repression, social and economic injustice that have reached a boiling point" (Anonymous j, 1997, 8). This could lead to the disintegration of Indonesia: "Many people fear the worst now, and that unless the regime changes course and adopts a more humane and wise strategy in dealing with grievances, the country could disintegrate, and no amount of force will be enough to control the anger of the population" (Anonymous j, 1997, 8). Horta has raised a real problem here. In 1966 when Suharto was a 44-year-old Major General, he was ordered by President Sukarno to ensure "security, calm and stability." Suharto saved Indonesia from civil war by a unique integration of the army into all aspects of Indonesian life, from the bureaucracy to State-owned companies (Walters, 1997c). The problem remains: what happens to Indonesia after Suharto? How can a stable transition be made to a new political system— one better suited to the needs of economic globalization—when the present system, the New Order Government, has the army at its core? (Lowry, 1996)

North East Asia also has its share of "the coming anarchy." In North Korea, March 1997, Chinese truck drivers carting grain into this hungry land have seen starved children's corpses lying abandoned and the bodies of dead children stacked on the backs of trucks (Pringle, 1997). Floods and crop failures over the last two years have contributed to these conditions of starvation, but the main factor is economic and agricultural mismanagement in the world's last remaining Stalinist state. Catherine Bertini, Head of the United Nations World Food Program, stated in March 1997 that she thought, based on her observations, that North Korea faced imminent starvation. At the time of writing, there is no food on the market and the government is distributing rations of 100 grams of rice, a below starvation level diet. This meager diet has been supplemented with roots, bark, and leaves scrounged from the countryside (Pringle, 1997). United States intelligence officials predicted a collapse of North Korea in 1996, and United Nations' food expert David Chikvaidze thought that starvation was on the horizon. If such a collapse does occur, it will almost certainly lead to a mass exodus of North Koreans across the border into South Korea, resulting in a "social explosion" (Shuja, 1995). Alternatively, North Korea could implode, as the CIA warned in February 1997, in turn engaging in a war for food and resources with South Korea (Anonymous b, 1997). South Korea itself, like many other Asian economies, is beginning to face social discontent about economic reforms essential for economic globalization (Smith and Sheridan, 1997). For example, President Kim's new labor laws led to street riots in January 1997. Moving for a moment on a necessary tangent from our North Korean discussion, South Korea's problem is a common one throughout Asia. The "Asian Miracle" was produced by cheap compliant labor, internal protection, and closed domestic markets. Economic growth and success in the context of the globalized economy produces new economic and social circumstances that ironically erode the very structure that made the miracle possible in the first place. Increased economic growth and wealth means that labor may no longer wish to be cheap and compliant; hence the resistance to President Kim's creation of a "flexible labor market" in South Korea. At the same time the logic of economic globalization in a post–Cold War world results in increasing international pressure being placed upon countries such as South Korea to open up their markets. Internal economic unrest, meeting head-on with an external threat from either an imploding or an exploding North Korea, could easily shatter social order in South Korea and send shock waves throughout the entire Asian region. We will have more to say about the future of the "Asian miracle" later in this book, and we will look more closely at the prospects of anarchy and social chaos arising from the forces of economic globalization later as well.

Let us turn now, albeit briefly, to China, thought by many to be on the verge of becoming the economic center of the world in the twenty-first century. We will challenge this view on economic, resource, and environmental grounds, arguing that a more likely fate for China is implosion and destruction, rather than economic greatness. Concentrating here only on social forces, it is possible to see already the seeds of "the coming anarchy" in China. First a crime wave is said to be sweeping the country and thousands of criminals a year are being executed in an attempt to deal with it. Although the actual number of executions is a state secret, it is believed that 1,865 death sentences and 1,313 executions occurred during the first half of 1995 alone (Hutchings, 1996).

China is also far from free of ethnic unrest. Radical Muslim separatists, for example, killed at least 10 Han Chinese and injured 100 others in rioting in the city of Yining, in China's Xinjiang Province on February 5 and 6, 1997. One thousand ethnic Uighurs, demanding a separate state, rioted and looted. All of their victims were Han Chinese. Uighur and other Muslim groups have been struggling for centuries to free themselves from the Han Chinese (Anonymous c, 1997). China extracted swift retribution, executing approximately one hundred Muslim separatists after summary trials. China's Muslim population has a greater loyalty to neighboring Central Asian states than it does to the Chinese nation-state and many ethnic Uighur "will attack their Chinese rulers whenever they have a chance" (Anonymous d, 1997, 9). Three terrorist bombs, planted by Islamic terrorists, detonated simultaneously in Urumqi, the regional capital of the far-western Xinjiang Province in late February 1997, killing five people and injuring scores of others. In early March 1997, two bombs exploded in Beijing itself, and these were also thought to have been planted by Islamic terrorists. Inner Mongolia and Tibet are also hotspots for China, which could result in waves of terrorism. In March 1997, the Dalai Lama accused China of "cultural genocide" in Tibet and he stated that isolated violence could spread (Anonymous e, 1997). The real possibility therefore exists of China facing its own version of Northern Ireland. In itself, this is hardly sufficient to threaten the Chinese nation-state, but it will be a force, adding to others to produce instability.

For China to become the world's number one economic superpower, the highly inefficient state-owned enterprises, which constitute about half of China's industry, must be closed. These enterprises usually run at a loss and produce inferior goods that sell poorly. Yet to do this will instantly produce at least another one hundred million unemployed to be added to the free-floating millions who already roam China searching for work. China observer Robert Elegant sees all of these various forces—including the lack of a powerful leader equal to Deng Xiaoping—as contributing toward a destabilized China (Elegant, 1997). The "best prospect" in Elegant's opinion is "open violence"; the worst prospect is a series of civil wars with units of the People's Liberation Army being pitched against each other. Regional sentiment is stronger than national sentiment in China. The army itself is fragmented because of private enterprise, as most members of the army are engaged in some legal or illegal activity from meat production, to arms exports, to prostitution. This factor also produces commitment to a region rather than a social whole. As Elegant notes, "Gangs claiming to be units of the army have risen in the west-central Shanxi Province, complete with their own munitions factories and representatives to civilian administrations" (Elegant, 1997, 11). Growing social disarray will, Elegant believes, lead to a return to quasi-warlord control in China's provinces:

This modern warlordism will be far more complicated, perhaps even more destructive than the predatory rule of the warlords who tormented China from 1916 to 1930. It will be highly organized chaos if the army splinters as the generals, all active in private commerce, place personal and local interests above the national interest.

The most likely outcome of scattered violence is a situation resembling that which has prevailed at the end of almost every one of the more than 20 imperial dynasties that have ruled China for the past two millenniums and two centuries. Groups of provinces moved by common interests will make common cause against the central government, as did the groups of provinces called vice-royalties in the past.

In Beijing the facade of centralized power will endure, as it did in the declining days of each imperial dynasty and even during the warlord era. But the Central Committee of the Communist Party and the Central People's Government will exercise very little power. . . . Communism according to Mao sought to fill the vacuum of belief left by the collapse of Confucianism. But communism has failed. Neither entrepreneurship nor consumerism will provide such an ideological foundation. China today is a vast nation in search of a reason for being. (Elegant, 1997, 11)

Our tour of "the coming anarchy" around the world could easily be extended—for thousands of pages if necessary. For example, peace in the Middle East is as far away as ever. In September 1996 the worst violence seen for thirty years in Palestinian-ruled areas occurred. Massacres seemingly occur daily; suicide bombings are regular in this torn land.[1] IRA bombs continue to shatter any prospect of peace in Northern Ireland. For example, on October 8, 1996, two car bombs exploded in Lisburn, Northern Ireland, near Belfast. The first bomb blasted the barracks of the British military headquarters. The second bomb exploded ten minutes later near the British army headquarters medical center, so that victims of the first bomb attack were also subjected to the blast of the second bomb. This same "double whammy" pattern was attempted in the failed April 3, 1997, bomb plot on the M6 in the West Midlands. The detonator of one of the two explosive devices had fired but the main charge had not exploded. The other device had been found. If the primary bomb had exploded it would have brought down the fly-over and caused a massive loss of life.

Misery and wretchedness are therefore not in short supply in the world today (De Silva and May, eds. 1991; Howard, 1995). Bosnia-Herzegovina requires an international security presence to prevent this torn state from sliding back into social chaos (Higgins, 1996) and it is doubtful whether such globalist strategies for maintaining the peace are sustainable in the long term. Nicaragua's "economy has collapsed with no indication of imminent revival. . . . [The country is on] a downward spiral into anarchy" (Isbester, 1996, 476). But the empiricist approach of Robert Kaplan, and our approach as well to date, does not allow us to infer (inductively) any generally justified conclusion about the breakdown of civilized order. Particular regions of the world may be facing social chaos or anarchy, but this in itself does not tell us much at all about the *really* important regions of the world—where the bulk of the readers of this book live—namely the civilized highly developed West! It is easy to forget about human misery if it is simply "over there." It is a major criticism of Kaplan's work that he takes certain highly vulnerable regions of the world as an overall image of the nature of the twenty-first century. The inside dust jacket of his book takes Kaplan's empiricism as a virtue: "Kaplan's ground-level experiences allow him to avoid grandiose generalizations about the clash of civilizations," even though chapter 17 of his book *The End of the Earth* (Kaplan, 1996a) is entitled "Pre-Byzantine Turks and Civilization Clashes." Kaplan has, however, made "grandiose generalizations" that need also to be supported by theoretical arguments enriched by empirical considerations. Having given the reader a general outline of the global meltdown thesis, we will now attempt to support this thesis by theoretical considerations. In particular, we need to give good reasons to demonstrate that the West is not immune to the global pandemic of social chaos, breakdown, and anarchy.

THE SUICIDE OF THE WEST: BREAKUP AND BREAKDOWN

The breakup and breakdown of the nation-state is not restricted to the non-Western world. Paradoxically, as the economies of the world become increasingly integrated, the world is also becoming increasingly fragmented. Dr. Boutros Boutros-Ghali, the (then) United Nations Secretary-General, said in a keynote address to the Global Cultural Diversity Conference in Sydney, April 1995, that the "explosion of micro-nationalism" is a "new troubling phenomenon." Speaking as a committed internationalist he said:

Ethnic religious and cultural separatism threatens a return to some of the worst problems of the past: intolerance or antagonism towards other cultures; opposition to practices unlike one's own; and an inability to conduct productive dialogue across the global range of diverse cultures. When a culture walls itself off from others, the only outcome can be sterility and antagonism. The cause of co-operation and progress on a global scale cannot but be set back by this phenomenon. (O'Neill, 1995)

A brief glance around the West and in particular Europe, indicates that *devolution* movements are widespread (Sale, 1980; 1985).

- After war and conflict, Scotland became a part of England in 1707. Today, the Scottish National Party is fighting for the independence of Scotland.
- Cornwall, an ancient Celtic nation in the southwest of England, lost its independence in the 10th century. Its language was replaced by English early last century. The militant Sons of Cornwall are struggling for a Cornish assembly with autonomous powers, as well as bilingual education for Cornish students.
- The ethnic Manx population on the Isle of Man, through the Nationalist Party, Mec Vannin, strives for full political autonomy from England, as do various other political organizations in Northumbria.
- Andalusia was once a Moorish kingdom, being conquered largely by Castile in the thirteenth century and in turn becoming part of Spain. Independence of Andalusia from Spanish rule is advocated by the Andalusian Socialist Party.
- Catalonia did not formally join Spain until 1714. The organization Terre Lliur has adopted terrorism as a mechanism for gaining independence for Catalonia.
- Terrorism has been used by the group ETA against the Spanish government in an attempt to unite the Basques in Spain with those in France to form a Basque state. Spain's three Basque provinces have been more or less independent, but this situation is inadequate in the opinion of ETA.
- The Galicians were conquered by Castile in the Middle Ages. An independence movement arose after about 400 years in the nineteenth century, but was stopped by Franco in 1936. The Spanish government allowed a Galician parliament to form in 1981 and the Galician language has become an official language.
- Manuel Fraga, the founding member of the Popular Party that won the Spanish general election in March 1996, warned that Spain may disintegrate because of growing inequality between regions, the same sort of inequality that led to civil war 60 years ago (Owen, 1996).
- France has not been free of terrorism by separatist groups. Many Corsican independent movements have used terrorism, as has the Front for the Liberation of Brittany and the Breton Republican Army.

- Alsace is a French province with a high proportion of German speakers; Alsatians wish to obtain independence from France.
- Jura became part of France in the eighteenth century, but went back to Switzerland in 1813. A battle for relative autonomy resulted in the northern part of Jura becoming Switzerland's twenty-sixth canton in 1975. However, the French-speaking Catholic Jurans oppose their southern territory remaining part of the German-speaking canton of Bern.
- Savoy was a duchy that once included part of southern Switzerland, northern Italy, and southeast France, but it was absorbed into France in 1860. An independence movement seeks to reconstruct Savoy and gain recognition.
- Ancient Lapland was divided between Norway, Sweden, Finland, and the former Soviet Union. The Sami Rights Movement hopes to gain independence for Sami-land.
- Friesland was deprived of its sovereignty in the sixteenth century and four centuries later was absorbed by the Netherlands and West Germany. Now an independence movement aims for the reconstruction of Friesland.
- Scania was annexed by Sweden in the late seventeenth century and the Scanian language disappeared in the early twentieth century. These people are also striving to recreate their heritage.
- The Flemish, constituting about half the population of Belgium, have full language rights and their own provincial parliament. The Flemish culturally identify with Holland. The Walloons identify with France, comprising the French-speaking half of Belgium (Sale, 1985, 155).
- Although Sicilian separatists succeeded in the 1940s in having the Italian government recognize the island as an autonomous region with its own parliament, many Sicilians want full independence. A number of separatist movements are backed by the Mafia.
- Italy's separatist Northern League continues to fight for the creation of Padania, an independent Republic of the North. The possibility of the separatist political battle degenerating into armed conflict and an Italian civil war is a concern (Anonymous f, g, 1996). According to the Northern League leader Umberto Bossi, Italy should formally divide because Italy is already divided: "There are two economies, north and south, and so there should be two treasuries, and two central banks" (Anonymous f, 1996, 13).

With the retribalization of Europe (Slattery, 1996; Kelly, 1997), it is ironic to find Jacques Delors, President of the European Commission since 1985, arguing that as Japan and America "explode" Europe will endure:

We have substantial problems with rural development, increasing criminality in the cities, drug abuse, social exclusion, youth crime and so on. These are enormous challenges, and it remains to be seen whether Europe can meet them and still retain its distinctiveness. With its culture and social model, Europe has the requisites for handling problems in a humane and civilized manner. The other two models, I believe, will explode in the face of this technocultural revolution.

The Japanese model will explode because the Japanese will no longer be able to sustain guardianship, and economically they won't be able to guarantee everyone the right to remain within one and the same firm for his entire life.

In the US, that kind of accepted social cruelty, which is represented by the frenetic competition among individuals, will lead to ever increasing violence in the cities and other kinds of wretchedness. This cannot go on. I continue to feel not that we are better than others, but that our model and our historical inheritance permit us to find better solutions. (Delors, 1995, 26–27)

Canada faces the prospect of dissolution, splitting into two or more states by early next century (Lamont, 1994). Opinion polls indicate the majority of Canadians believe that Canada cannot survive as a national entity (Lamont, 1994, 24) as it fractures "along the faultlines of race and regionalism" (Lamont, 1994, 25). The Quebec separatism vote in November 1995 resulted in 50.6 percent for the no side, 49.4 for the yes side, the difference being a mere 53,000 votes out of 4.8 million cast. Sixty percent of French-speaking Quebeckers, making up 82 percent of Quebec's seven million people, voted to leave Canada. However, this trend has further fragmenting consequences, Lamont notes in his book *Breakup*:

Quebec's independentist trend has rekindled other frictions that are abrading the thin fabric of national unity: the stubborn resentments nurtured by the country's besetting regionalism; the vying demands of Canada's other powerful provinces; the insistent claims and sometimes ugly protests of its aboriginal peoples; the know-it-all arrogance of its nannying federal bureaucracy in distant Ottawa, coupled with collapsing public confidence in political institutions; and, always, the specter of an embracing United States threatening Canada with further loss of identity through its invasive culture and the inexorable pull of trade currents toward some unwanted, homogenizing continentalism. (Lamont, 1994, 24)

Canada's "aggressive commitment to multiculturalism," is, as Lamont points out on the backcover flap of *Breakup*, "a further step in the disintegrative process." Canada's multiculturalism model has been used as a model for multiculturalism in Australia and, like a lethal virus introduced into a computer program, it is having highly destructive effects (Rimmer, 1991).

Sir James Goldsmith in *The Trap* (Goldsmith, 1994) observes that the proliferation of conflict in the post–Cold War era—represented by the fact that around 30 wars are now being fought—is due to the desire of people who believe that they constitute a nation to escape from the political bounds of artificial states. Goldsmith defines a nation as "a land whose citizens, in their overwhelming majority, share a common culture, sense of identity, heritage and traditional roots" (Goldsmith, 1994, 50). Nations differ from mere populated spaces, Goldsmith argues, because a populated space is composed of people of a variety of cultures, races, and ethnicities mixed in an area, while nations are much more homogeneous. Nations can only absorb a limited amount of "new blood" at a time and they "cannot allow themselves to be overwhelmed by immigration otherwise they will lose their identity and cease to be nations" (Goldsmith, 1994, 53). In Goldsmith's opinion, immigrants "who are welcomed into a nation should want to honor and respect the customs of their new home. They must not step on shore or over the border and reject the national culture. If they do, the inevitable results are hostility, intolerance and conflict" (Goldsmith, 1994, 53–54).

A similar argument has also been made by Walker Connor in his book *Ethnonationalism: The Quest for Understanding* (Connor, 1994). Connor adopts a definition of nationalism that recognizes the racial origins of the term. *Nation* is derived from the past participle of the Latin verb *nasci,* meaning "to be born." The Latin noun *nationem,* means *race* (Connor, 1994, 94). Consequently, the nation is a group of people who believe that they are ancestrally related; it is the largest group commanding a person's loyalty because of perceived kinship ties, being essentially an extension of the family, the family-nation. Connor also quotes with sympathy Rupert Emerson's definition of the nation as "the largest community which, when the chips are down, effectively commands men's loyalty, overriding the claims of both lesser communities within it and those which cut across it or potentially enfold it within a still greater society" (Emerson, 1960, 95–96). Connor believes that there are limits to the rational understanding of group identity: "In sharpest contrast with most academic analysts of nationalism, those who have successfully mobilized nations have understood that at the core of ethno-psychology is the sense of shared blood" (Connor, 1994, 197). The nation itself is something of a "work-in-progress," an "imagined community" (Anderson, 1991).

Jackson (1997) has noted that these theoretical considerations by Connor cast doubt upon the very legitimacy of the United States even though this was not Connor's overt intention. According to Connor, the majority of political units claiming to be nations are not, they are merely multiethnic states. The equation of "nation" and "state" is so common that Connor coined the term "ethnonationalism" to emphasize the kinship element that has been lost from the modern theory of nationalism (Brimelow, 1995). Jackson recognizes that to admit common ancestry as the "necessary glue of nations" is also to admit that the United States, Canada, and Australia, for example, are not nations and cannot become nations. Moreover: "Nationalist conflict usually has simple causes: state and national borders that do not coincide. National sentiment is sure to arise when a nation feels that its sacred land is being invaded by strangers or when a nation chafes under alien rule. As history has repeatedly shown, local autonomy or even outright separation are the most reliable cures for national conflict" (Jackson, 1997, 9).[2]

The possibility of the breakup of the United States has been discussed in passing from time to time, but is seldom given the serious attention it deserves, especially by American writers.[3] But William Rees-Mogg, writing in the British Newspaper *The Independent*, has said:

Yet at present, the United States is unwinding strand by strand, rather like the Soviet Union, Yugoslavia or Northern Ireland. South Africa now seems to be the only rich country that is not moving towards a social, economic and ethnic apartheid. In 1992 the Los Angeles riots and the IRA bomb in the City of London—where 100 lbs of Semtex did one billion pounds of damage—alike show the strength of the forces of disintegration and the vulnerability of our modern society to them. (Rees-Mogg, 1992, 17, quoted from Moynihan, 1993, 24)

Charles Krauthammer is equally as pessimistic about America's survival:

Canada has an escape. By accident of geography, separation is a real option because the different cultures inhabit different territories. For a country like America, where the different cultures are thoroughly intermixed, there is no such answer. Canada can break up cleanly; the U.S. cannot.

America is proceeding blithely down the path of diversity and ethnic separatism. America's destination, however, is not Canada, which will find some civil way out of its dilemma. America's destination is the Balkans. (Krauthammer, 1995)

On April 29, 1997, Texan Republican Separatists were locked in siege with the FBI, an incident that may be the shape of things to come in the United States.

Sir James Goldsmith has concerns about "vast, centralized, multicultural nations" such as the former Soviet Union and the United States, as they have not "demonstrated that their structures are viable" (Goldsmith, 1994, 83). The Soviet Union collapsed and the United States "has become a leviathan, partially paralyzed by its centralization" (Goldsmith, 1994, 82). Further, the racial and ethnic transformation of the United States, by virtue of mass immigration from non-European sources after the Immigration and Nationality Act Amendments were passed in 1965, is leading to an America where people of European descent will be a racial minority by 2050 (Oppenheimer, 1996). This radical and rapid social experiment will inevitably lead to social torment in Goldsmith's opinion: "The destabilization and in some cases social breakdown of the cities, the multiethnic, multi-tongued population, the rapid geographic mobility which has resulted in uprooted nuclear or broken families, have all contributed to widespread disorientation" (Goldsmith, 1994, 61–62). These conflicts are certain to intensify as migration flows have the tendency to become self-perpetuating (Weiner, 1995) and global migration from the Third World to the West continues (Castles and Miller, 1993; Pick, 1993; Stahl et al., 1993).

Matthew Connelly and Paul Kennedy, in a challenging essay entitled "Must it be the Rest Against the West?", published in *The Atlanic Monthly* in December 1994, base their article around Jean Raspail's novel *The Camp of the Saints* (Raspail, 1995) in addressing the controversial question of racial balance (Connelly and Kennedy, 1994). Raspail's novel is about the mass migration of Third World "boat people" to the West. The novel is about the imbalance between wealth and resources, demographic trends, and the relationship between the two (Connelly and Kennedy, 1994, 62). Raspail expresses a vision of a polarized world in which "the rich will have to fight and the poor will have to die if mass migration is not to overwhelm us all" (Connelly and Kennedy, 1994, 62). It is a vision that is gaining acceptance in the "North" as people confront the issue of white racial suicide or the doom of the white race. Raspail's stark message is that "race, not class or ideology, determines everything, and the wretched of the earth will see no distinction between unfriendly, fascistic Frenchmen on the one hand and liberal-minded bishops and yuppies on the other. All have enjoyed too large a share of the world's wealth for too long, and their common fate is now at hand" (Connelly and Kennedy, 1994, 66). Raspail, in his 1982 preface to his novel, said, "Our hypersensitive and totally blind West . . . has not yet understood that whites, in a world becoming too small for its inhabitants, are now a minority and that the proliferation of other races dooms our race, my race, irretrievably to extinction in the century to come, if we hold fast to our present moral principles" (Connelly and Kennedy, 1994, 66).

Connelly and Kennedy recognize that Raspail's views may not be politically correct, and his language "vicious and repulsive," but they accept the core message of *The Camp of the Saints* of the bifurcation of the world into a rich West (including Japan) with an aging population and below replacement level birthrates, and a poor "the rest" where populations double at least every twenty-five years.[4] Cornucopian theorists, they note, concentrate upon the high tech business world of the world's winners, but they devote little time to the world's losers. Globalizers are keen about the liberalization of capital flows but not about the liberalization of labor: "behind the ostensible philanthropic concern about world demographic trends lies a deep fear that the white races of the world will be steadily overwhelmed by everyone else" (Connelly and Kennedy, 1994, 72). This is a difficult fact for the liberal West to admit. Kishore Mahbubani, who in 1994 was Deputy Secretary of Singapore's Foreign Ministry, has said: "Simple arithmetic demonstrates Western folly. The West has 800 million people; the rest make up almost 4.7 billion. . . . No Western society would accept a situation where 15 percent of its population legislated for the remaining 85 percent" (Connelly and Kennedy, 1994, 76). The West, in Mahbubani's opinion, has a "fatal flaw," "an inability to conceive that [it] may have developed structural weaknesses in its core value systems and institutions. The West is bringing about its relative decline by its own hand" (Connelly and Kennedy, 1994, 76). These remarks are addressed to the United States in particular.

It is interesting in this context to consider the remarks made by the Malaysian Prime Minster, Dr. Mahathir, in his keynote address to the Inaugural Southern African International Dialogue in Botswana on May 5, 1997. Dr. Mahathir proposed that Asian and African countries should swamp Europe and the United States with legal and illegal migration, if developing nations were "not allowed to prosper" (Stewart, 1997, 10). "People mobility" would be, he proposed, the ultimate weapon against the developed world. The developed world was intent upon recolonizing the developing world through "globalization," the "breaking down of national borders," If the developing world was not allowed "a piece of the action" then, according to Mahathir, "We should migrate North in the millions, legally or illegally, if we are going to be global citizens." (Stewart, 1997, 10). Can one blame the ordinary Australian people for not wanting to "integrate" with Asia, if this *Camp of the Saints* scenario is the ultimate price to be paid? Demographic warfare may prove in the future to be as much a threat to national security as conventional warfare.

What is to be done? Connelly and Kennedy dismiss the idea of the Finland eco-fascist philosopher, Pentti Linkola (Milbank, 1994), who welcomes the elimination of billions of humans and the destruction of America. The United States, in Linkola's opinion, "symbolizes the worst ideologies in the world: growth and freedom" (Milbank, 1994, A1). Despite Linkola's extremism, the proposal that the West should use whatever it takes to survive leads to this, Connelly and Kennedy believe. Their solution is the predictable one that economic development via economic aid from the West will solve the problem of Third World population growth. Virginia Abernethy (1994), in a reply to Connelly and Kennedy, criticized their reliance on the demographic transition theory (Smith et al., 1997) and their implicit globalism:

Let the globalists step aside. One-world solutions do not work. Local solutions will. Everywhere people act in accord with their perception of their best interests. People are adept at interpreting *local* signs to find the *next* move needed. In many countries and communities today, where social, economic, and environmental conditions are indubitably worsening, the demand for modern contraceptions rising, marriage and sexual initiation are delayed, and family size is contracting. Individuals responding with low fertility to signs of limits are the local solution. One prays that the hucksters of inappropriate development do not mess this up. (Abernethy, 1994, 91)

There is, however, every indication that the "hucksters of inappropriate development" are messing it up, and will continue to do so, bringing the planet to the brink of destruction (Smith et al., 1997).

Even if the United States were able to insulate itself from the external forces of social chaos, internal pressures are also sufficient to produce what John Lyons has described as a "crumbling of America," an imminent death on the fault lines of race and economic decline (Lyons, 1994). "White flight" has meant that many large United States cities are virtually bankrupt, as whites fleeing to the suburbs have deprived the darkening city core of a tax base. Washington D.C., for example, has the highest murder rate in the world. The city is on the brink of financial collapse unless the federal government moves to prevent it, according to a 46 page report by the city's financial control board released in 1996. Washington D.C.'s population has fallen from 800,000 in the 1950s to 554,00 in 1995 and is still dropping due to the "white flight" of the white middle class. Streets fall into disrepair, water mains leak, buildings are burnt-out and abandoned, and only a few blocks from the United States Senate, gunshots can be heard. This is an emerging dangerous America, ruled by the law of the jungle. Paxton Quigley observes this in her book *Armed and Female*:

If you are over the age of twelve and female, be prepared to be criminally assaulted some time in your life. If you are about thirty years old now, there's a fifty-fifty chance of your being raped, robbed, or attacked. . . . Across our nation, one out of every four families will be victims of serious crimes like burglary, rape, robbery, or murder. Our cities are citadels of crime. And there is no such thing anymore as safe rural America. . . . A Gallup poll [found] that six out of ten women in this country are afraid to walk at night in their own neighborhoods. (Quigley, 1990, 4)

Race riots in America have the potential to happen at any time—such is the level of antagonism between blacks and whites and blacks and the rest. In October 1996 in St. Petersburg Florida, a race-riot resulted in the torching of businesses. The cause of the riot was this incident. Police stopped two blacks who were speeding in a Pontiac LeMans. They ordered the driver to get out of the car; he refused, and attempted to flee. The car lurched towards an officer who shot and killed the driver. Word quickly spread that the shooting was allegedly unprovoked. A crowd swarmed around the officers who radioed for help. The violence escalated from there. Even the Greek playwrights of antiquity would have difficulty depicting a more poignant picture of pathos. The possibility of racial conflict escalating into a full scale race war has been discussed by a number of black American writers. One of the characters in Richard Delgado's *The Coming Race War?* says:

It's not a conspiracy, exactly. Rather I think there is a general sense that it's time to pick a fight. Caucasians will cease being a majority in this country about midway in the next century. At that point, numerical and voting power should, logically shift to groups of color—blacks, Asians, and Latinos. White opinion-makers don't want this to happen. So, they're gearing up for a fight. It's one of the oldest tricks in the world—provoke your enemy until he responds, then slap him down decisively. You get to impose your regime and sleep well nights too, because you can maintain that it was all his fault. (Delgado, 1996, 120)

Carl T. Rowan's book *The Coming Race War in America* (Rowan, 1996) also has as its central thesis that crime, greed, economic decline, and social decay is producing a fertile breeding ground for racism and resentment: "One senses that our nation is split irrevocably and that there is no one to bring us together again" (Rowan, 1996, 6). The end result is a race war, started by the white racists and then spreading:

The conflict that I foresee will be as crazily complex as it will be violent, cruel, and heinous. We now see the skinheads and Ku Klux Klansmen emboldened in their campaigns against blacks, Jews, Catholics. We see the Muslims at war not only against Jews, but against the Italian Mayor of New York, Rudolph Giuliani, and against America as a whole, as reflected in terrorist bombings. We hear black students talk about "the basis of truth" in a speech full of anti-Semitic invective by Nation of Islam minister Khalid Muhammad at Kean College in New Jersey. We see blacks in political struggle with Hispanics. And from Los Angeles to Detroit to New York, we see a growing underclass at war against "the establishment." (Rowan, 1996, 16)

The fault, of course, lies with white and Jewish America, in Rowan's opinion.[5] There are other opinions (Taylor, 1992). In a series of articles in Australia's *The Sydney Morning Herald* newspaper, under the main headline "Four Stories the US Media Refuse to Tell," Paul Sheehan observes that for the past 30 years "a large segment of black America has waged a war of violent retribution against white America" (Sheehan, 1995, 1A). This dirty war has already claimed over 25 million victims and is getting worse. Young blacks under the age of 18 years are 12 times more likely to be arrested for murder than young whites. Violent crime over the past two decades has increased four times faster than the American population. Here are some statistics quoted by Sheehan:

- According to the latest US Department of Justice survey of crime victims, more than 6.6 million violent crimes (murder, rape, assault and robbery) are committed in the US each year, of which about 20 per cent, or 1.3 million, are inter-racial crimes.
- Most victims of race crime—about 90 per cent—are white, according to the survey "Highlights from 20 Years of Surveying Crime Victims", published in 1993.

- Almost 1 million white Americans were murdered, robbed, assaulted or raped by black Americans in 1992, compared with about 132,000 blacks who were murdered, robbed, assaulted or raped by whites, according to the same survey.
- Blacks thus committed 7.5 times more violent inter-racial crimes than whites even though the black population is only one-seventh the size of the white population. When these figures are adjusted on a per capita basis, they reveal an extraordinary disparity: blacks are committing more than 50 times the number of violent racial crimes of whites.
- According to the latest annual report on murder by the Federal Bureau of Investigation, most inter-racial murders involve black assailants and white victims, with blacks murdering whites at 18 times the rate that whites murder blacks. (Sheehan, 1995, 1A)

A sharp increase in black crime against whites in America corresponds perfectly, Sheehan notes, with the start of the civil rights movement. Between 1964 and 1994, according to Justice Department and FBI statistics, over 25 million violent inter-racial crimes were committed "overwhelmingly involving black offenders and white victims" (Sheehan, 1995, 1A). Over 45,000 people have been killed in inter-racial murders (compared to 58,000 Americans in the Vietnam War and 34,000 in the Korean War), again predominantly by blacks against whites. According to Bureau of Justice statistics, 27 million nonviolent crimes (such as personal theft, car theft, larceny, and burglary) were committed in the United States in 1992. Thirty-one percent of the robberies involved white victims who were preyed upon by blacks. There was only two percent in the reverse. All in all, black Americans have committed at least 170 million crimes against white Americans over the past 30 years (Sheehan, 1995, 1A).

Sheehan goes on in his article to argue against the obvious rejoinder that would be made to his argument, namely that black racism is a product of economic deprivation. This argument and the cause of black crime does not concern us here. The orthodox view that racism and economic deprivation are causally related—such that economic deprivation builds up a culture of resentment and violence, in turn leading to racism—does, in fact, support the global meltdown thesis. We will argue later in this chapter that economic deprivation and the economic decline of America and the West are virtually inevitable. Consequently, the race war between white and black America will intensify. Further, this race war will become increasingly complex as black Americans, their culture destroyed through drugs, crime, unemployment, and poverty, lash out with bottomless contempt at an economic system that has rendered all but an elite strata of their race economically redundant (Rifkin, 1995).

The global meltdown thesis, that "the coming anarchy" of social breakdown and chaos, precipitated from economic and environmental destruction, is supported by the worldwide rise of terrorism, a phenomenon from which both the United States and Australia cannot escape (Crown, 1986). CIA Director John Deutsch predicted a worldwide increase in terrorism over the next decade (Anonymous h, 1995). Former FBI special agent Robert Ressler predicts a rise in serial killings over the same period (Fife-Yeoman, 1995)—which adds some sociological support to the key premise of the television series *Millennium*, that as the clock ticks down to the year 2000 deranged sociopaths and psychopaths emerge from the shadows to unleash terror against the population through seemingly random massacres (Chester, 1993). The Martin Bryant massacre in Tasmania Australia, in 1996, had enormous political consequences. It led to a ban on certain types of firearms, and enormous popular resentment resulted. More recent examples can be given. Six people were killed when a gunman went on a rampage in the New Zealand North Island town of Raurimu on February 8, 1997. Also in February 1997, Ali Hassan Abu Kamal, an English professor at Gaza University, shot a Danish tourist and wounded six others, after firing a rifle from the eighty-sixth floor observation deck of the Empire State Building before shooting himself. The Palestinian had a document in English entitled *A Charter of Honor*, in which he expressed his intent to kill as many Zionists as possible at the Empire State Building: "My restless aspiration is to murder as many of them as possible, and I have decided to strike at their own den in New York, and at the very Empire State building in particular" (Stead, 1997, 26).

Guns are probably the least effective of the terrorist's weapons. Food terrorism—involving actual or threatened poisoning of various supermarket food products—has been used in extortionist bids frequently in both Australia and the United States (Meade and Fife-Yeoman, 1997). For example, in February 1997 in Australia, an extortionist threatened to poison Arnott's biscuits, leading to thousands of packs of biscuits being withdrawn from supermarket shelves. At the time of writing the extortionist has not been apprehended and the poisoning has not been carried out.

Bombs are the terrorist's main weapon of destruction. A lengthy book could be written describing in detail terrorist bomb attacks across the world, based only on the last two years. Here we shall mention, albeit briefly, incidents relevant to the United States. One of the most bloody bombings in United States history occurred at 9:02 A.M. April 19, 1995, in Oklahoma City, when the Alfred P. Murrah Federal Building was destroyed by a truck bomb of about two tons of ammonium nitrate fertilizer and fuel oil. The blast killed 168 people—149 adults and 19 children. Timothy McVeigh and Terry Nichols have both been found guilty of this crime. Despite the horror of this act of terrorism, the prosecution case indicated that these bombers were amateurs. This is also so for Arizona's "Viper Militia," an underground organization arrested in early July 1996 for plotting to blow up several Phoenix Federal offices.[6] These acts of terrorism also appear to be the work of amateurs; professional terrorists are capable of repeated atrocities because they are seldom caught.

On June 25, 1996, in Dahran, Saudi Arabia, a fuel tanker converted into a truck bomb destroyed an eight-floor apartment building housing United States and foreign troops. In this tragedy 19 United States service officers were killed and 386 others injured. On July 17, 1996, an explosion on board TWA Flight 800 from New York killed 230 passengers and crew. At the time of writing this disaster appears to have been caused by an electrical fault in the fuel tank, but for some time the explosion was conjectured to have been due to a terrorist bomb or missile. Significantly, the internal-defect theory was only accepted after the possibility of terrorism was discounted. A pipe bomb exploded at Atlanta's Olympic Centennial Park on July 27, 1996, during the 1996 Olympic Games, killing two people (one of the people being a Turkish cameraman who died of a heart attack as he filmed the event) and injuring 111 other people. The prime suspect at the time, Richard Jewell, an Atlanta security guard, has been completely cleared. In Atlanta alone, up to February 1997, four bombs have exploded in the past seven months indicating that a serial bomber may be operating. All of the crimes discussed in this paragraph remain unsolved. The alarming thing that can be observed about all of these crimes, from our relative safety in Australia, is that they can be easily replicated. To begin to deal with them will require police surveillance that American citizens will not tolerate. Yet even the extensive use of camera surveillance practiced in Britain (and to some degree in Australia) has proved to be inadequate in dealing with IRA bombings.

The terrorist story, however, gets much worse. Gordon Oehler, Director of the CIA's Nonproliferation Center, told a United States Senate Armed Services Committee Hearing in early 1996 that the threat of nuclear, chemical, and biological attacks by terrorist groups has never been greater:

The chilling reality is that nuclear materials and technologies are more accessible now than at any other time in history—due primarily to the dissolution of the former Soviet Union and the region's worsening economic conditions. . . . Extremist groups worldwide are increasingly learning how to manufacture chemical and biological agents and the potential for additional chemical and biological attacks by such groups continues to grow. . . . A few countries whose interests are inimical to the United States are attempting to acquire nuclear weapons—Iraq and Iran being two of our greatest concerns. Should one of these countries, or a terrorist group, acquire one or more nuclear weapons, they could enormously complicate US political or military activity, threaten or attack deployed US or allied forces, or possibly conduct an attack against the United States. (Anonymous i, 1996)

Iran has acquired an arsenal of biological weapons and is prepared to use them, according to a CIA report sent to the United States Senate Intelligence Committee in August 1996. Israeli intelligence has linked Iran to the crash of TWA Flight 800, but United States intelligence sources view this with skepticism. Israeli intelligence sources have also claimed that Iran would respond to United States attacks by poisoning water resources in Western Europe and the United States (Mahnaimi and Adams, 1996). A meeting of the leaders of the G7 nations in Lyon, France on June 27, 1996, recognized that terrorist groups would increasingly resort to nuclear, biological, and chemical warfare (Cole, 1997; Pearson, 1996).

The fear of the terrorist use of nuclear weapons has also been expressed in Australia by the Canberra Commission on the Elimination of Nuclear Weapons. Australian commission member and Oxford University history of war professor Robert O'Neill believes that it is "only a matter of time before terrorists steal a nuclear warhead and detonate it in the US" (Steketee, 1996, 3; see also Nuckolls, 1995; Kleiner, 1996b; Williams and Woessner, 1996). The smuggling of weapons of mass destruction into the United States is a reality. In May 1996 seven people were arrested in San Francisco in connection with smuggling fully automatic AK-47 assault rifles from China into the United States. Howard Ku, a Taiwanese who lived in Soquel, California, was at the time of his arrest arranging purchase of anti-tank rockets and shoulder-fired anti-aircraft systems capable of shooting airplanes out of the sky (Sanger, 1996).

Terrorist attacks need not necessarily come from hostile nations. Shoko Asahara, leader of Aum Shinrikyo, the Aum Supreme Truth sect, instigated a sarin nerve gas attack on Tokyo's subway system, killing 10 people and sickening 5,500 others. Preparing for the apocalypse, in which they would allegedly actively participate, the sect had accumulated enough dangerous chemicals to kill around 10 million people. Shoko Asahara's own vision was that Japan would be destroyed by a gas attack by the United States, which he believed is run by Jews and Freemasons who want to destroy the Japanese race (van Biema, 1995, 29). Presumably, Shoko Asahara wished to destroy Japanese society first. In a story almost bordering on science fiction, he recruited alienated young scientists to experiment with laser and particle beam weapons. Stockpiles of biological and chemical weapons were made including cyanide, sarin, anthrax, and botulism. Some Aum Shinrikyo missionaries even traveled to Zaire to obtain the Ebola virus. Automatic rifles and high explosives were manufactured in secret factories. Negotiations were underway to obtain an atomic bomb. Sect members were also planning to spray the Japanese parliament with neurotoxin. David Kaplan and Andrew Marshall, in their book *The Cult at the End of the World* (Kaplan and Marshall, 1996), observe that Shoko Asahara intended to become a world dictator. He was fascinated by Hitler, whom young sect members were taught to admire (Kaplan and Marshall, 1996, 63). The anti-Semitism of this group tapped into the soil of "a long reactionary tradition of xenophobia in Japan" (Kaplan and Marshall, 1996, 220). Kaplan and Marshall note: "Most Japanese . . . have never met a Jew: that has not stopped them from buying shelves of best-selling anti-Semitic books on how Jews run the world and secretly subvert Japan" (Kaplan and Marshall, 1996, 219; Brackett, 1996). If such an organization could develop in an ordered society such as Japan it would be dangerously foolish to suppose that it could not happen elsewhere in the world, particularly the United States. Robert Kupperman, a terrorism expert at Washington's Center for Strategic and International Studies, has said: "Nightmares are coming true. I think we're in for deep trouble" (Nelan, 1995, 33). Technical sophistication is not necessary for this terror. A "metaphysical terrorist" such as the Unabomber, a hater of technology and the modern world, although mechanically unsophisticated, was still able to construct bombs, usually involving crude wood and handmade components and explosives made out of available chemicals (Gibbs, 1996). The rise of "third wave terrorism" further contributes to the increasing irrelevance of the nation-state in our globalized world, Alvin Toffler believes:

The sarin attack in Japan was qualitatively different from the old forms of terrorism that cause havoc but kill or maim only 30 or 50 people. Remember that this Japanese attack was very crude—a briefcase, bag or box left on the subway train. When a greater sophistication evolves on the part of terrorists in the use of chemical and biological weapons, including remote detonation devices for binary weapons, thousands upon thousands of people can be felled in one blow.

This is a momentous development because it signals . . . the failure of the state system itself, which was founded on the ability of the governing elite, or the gang in power as the case may be, to enforce its authority with organized violence and to control alternative means of violence, no less mass violence, in its own territory.

This doesn't mean the end of the nation state, as some suggest, but that it will become just one player among many others of relatively comparative power in varying realms. As the power of the state fragments, the number of players is multiplying—all of whom are potentially capable of laying their hands on weaponry. (Toffler, 1995, 4)

One of the major challengers to the monopoly of mass violence, that was once the exclusive domain of the nation-state, is globalized organized crime. Claire Sterling, in her book *Crime Without Frontiers* (Sterling, 1994), documents the emergence of a Pax Mafiosa, an international Mafia involving the Sicilian Mafia, American Cosa Nostra, Columbian drug cartels, Japanese Yakuza, Chinese Triads, and Russian Mafia. This is confirmed by the United States State Department Office of Diplomatic Security. Criminal leaders met in Warsaw in 1991, Prague in 1992, and Berlin in 1993 where "they agreed to apply strategic planning and market development policies for the newly emerging free markets, to program legitimate investments much as corporations do, and to develop and expand extremely illegal activities" (Sterling, 1994, 1) including narcotics trafficking, conventional arms, and weapons of mass destruction. Italy's parliamentary anti-Mafia Commission, in a report to the United Nations Assembly, March 20, 1990, also recognized this:

International criminal organizations have reached agreements and understanding to divide up geographical areas, develop new market strategies, work out forms of mutual assistance and the settlement of conflicts . . . and this on a planetary level.

We are faced with a genuine criminal counter-power, capable of imposing its will on legitimate states, of undermining institutions and forces of law and order, of upsetting delicate economic and financial equilibrium and destroying democratic life. (Sterling, 1994, 55)

As Western nation-states break down, the warlords seem almost certain to be ready to move into the power vacuum as has occurred in West Africa and parts of South America (Varese, 1994; Farah and Robberson, 1995; Shelley, 1995; Kleiner, 1996b).

CONCLUSION: THE STATE OF THE ARGUMENT

Let us summarize our argument in this section. We have attempted to show that the breakup and breakdown of the nation-state, and more broadly of social order, is not restricted to the non-Western world: social chaos and "the coming anarchy," a global meltdown, also threatens Western society. We have looked very briefly at separatist movements, racial, ethnic, and national tensions, and terrorism as forces challenging the social coherence of Western societies. But our argument is unsatisfactory and incomplete at this point because we have not shown that the forces discussed so far in this book are sufficient to produce the type of cataclysmic chaos that will lead to a collapse of civilization and a veritable return to the "law of the jungle." We must therefore push our eschatological analysis further, examining the mechanisms for the collapse of civilization.

NOTES

1. Israel is not free from race riots and internal ethnic tension. For example, on January 29, 1996, thousands of Ethiopian Jews attempted to storm the Prime Minister's office, struggled with police, and then pelted them with bottles and stones. Twenty-two protesters and 40 police were injured. The riots occurred because of a story in the newspaper *Maariv*, which said that bags of blood donated by Ethiopian Jews had been routinely disposed of without informing donors because of a fear of AIDS. The then Health Minister, Ephraim Sneh, defended the action, saying that the HIV virus was 50 times higher in the Ethiopian community than among the general population. The action was not politically correct but was widely supported by many non-Ethiopian Israelis (Walker, 1996).

2. Brimelow (1995) has asserted that there is no example of a multicultural, multiracial society which has been sustainable. William H. McNeill, in the Donald G. Creighton Lectures of 1985, *Polyethnicity and National Unity in World History* (McNeill, 1986), defends the idea that the historical record shows that, according to the backcover of his book, "ethnic homogeneity was a barbarian trait; civilized societies mingled peoples of diverse backgrounds into ethnically plural and hierarchically ordered polities." The exception, McNeill notes, was northwestern Europe, which had national unity while civilization developed, but now the mingling of cultures and genes is occurring in the West. Now if this were true, miscegenation would have long-ago eliminated races, leading to the creation of a coffee-colored man—which would in turn constitute a new homogeneity. Cultures would also have merged, leading to a new universal culture, rather than ethnic plurality. In fact McNeill's own *Plagues and Peoples* (McNeill, 1976) shows that the mingling of people is a major source of disease transmission and has devastated entire races and civilizations. McNeill himself has also said: "Political resistance to intermingling of peoples and skills across state boundaries is . . . far from negligible and may well increase in time to come as the difficulties of living in polyethnic societies become more widely apparent" (McNeill, 1986, 81). Isaacs, we believe, has more accurately described the fate of polyethnic societies than McNeill:

We are experiencing on a massively universal scale a convulsive ingathering of people in their numberless grouping of kinds—tribal, racial, linguistic, religious, national. It is a great clustering into separateness that will, it is thought, improve, assure, or extend each group's power or place, or keep it safe or safer from the power, threat, or hostility of others. This is obviously no new tradition, only the latest and by far the most inclusive chapter of the old story in which after failing again to find how they can co-exist in sight of each other without tearing each other limb from limb, Isaac and Ishmael clash and part in panic and retreat once more into their caves. (Isaacs, 1989, 1)

Further, even if McNeill were correct, that is, that polyethnicity can produce great civilizations, polyethnicity can also destroy them:

A hundred years before its fall Rome was a world power, defended by a mighty military. Growing ethnic diversity—a strength for so long—eventually helped to undermine Rome. As it entered its final century, the empire was a place of decaying cities, a threatened middle class, terrorists, and lawyers who paralyzed government through unending legal challenges. The classicist Michael Grant wrote in *The Fall of the Roman Empire* that the configurations of settlement of the Visigoths and other immigrant minorities within the Roman Empire "formed an important part of the process by which the ancient world gradually developed the new national patterns characteristic of the Middle Ages." From one undivided polity came many smaller ones. (Kaplan, 1996b, 88)

3. An exception to this rule of American silence on the breakup of the Union is the eminent American statesman, George Kennan. He supports regionalization in the United States, involving highly autonomous units because the United States has become too diverse for effective government (Abernethy, 1995). Former Australian Senator John Button has also noted that other unnamed, but influential Americans also believe that America may be ungovernable: "A former US senator and presidential aspirant told me that he feared the country had become ungovernable. 'In Los Angeles,' he kept saying, 'the Korean community has a well-equipped private army. How do you govern a country like that?' " (Button, 1993, 19).

4. Amartya Sen (1994) has addressed the racial suicide of the West thesis. He rightly observes that before the European industrial revolution and the rise of European population levels, the share of Asia and Africa in world population in 1650 was about 78.4 percent. The UN prediction that this share will again reach 78.5 percent by the year 2050 indicates that the idea of a racial imbalance in the world is somewhat arbitrary in Sen's opinion. This may be so, but Raspail and others are concerned with the distribution of "racial units" so to speak. Further, although the point of Sen's article is to argue against environmental pessimists, if limitationism is correct (Smith et al., 1997), the situation depicted by Raspail will ensure a bloody battle for scarce resources occurs that will inevitably become racial and tribal.

5. Rowan (1996) is critical of anti-Semitism at a number of points in his book. However in chapter 5, after again condemning anti-Semitism, he tells the story of neo-Nazi killer Larry Wayne Shoemake of Jackson, Mississippi, who killed one black and wounded 10 others in a shooting rampage. Rowan then says:

Yes, I can understand the murderous behavior of this crazy man. His philosophy was clear: the subhumans should be eliminated. What I cannot understand are the self-styled Christian and Jewish intellectuals and the unthreatened political leaders who are driving this society to a race war even when they cannot answer the question "What is race?" Are these celebrated columnists, talk-show hosts, and supposed statesmen really more enlightened than Shoemake, or the other whites who inspire race murders? (Rowan, 1996, 142–43)

The claim appears to be made here by Rowan that Jewish intellectuals (and others) are inspiring a race war, a claim which is surely offensive to American Jewry and anti-Semitic in itself (Friedman, 1995).

6. Timothy McVeigh wrote, in a letter now in police possession: "Is civil war imminent? Do we have to shed blood to reform the system? I hope it doesn't come to that! But it might." Twenty-seven percent of Americans believe that they live in a police state and that civil war is indeed imminent (Wark, 1995, 51).

2

The Ecology of Collapse: Technological and Ecological Mechanisms for the Destruction of Civilization

Prejudice is an organic truth, false in itself but accumulated by generations and transmitted: we cannot rid ourselves of it with impunity. The nation that renounces it heedlessly will then renounce itself until it has nothing left to give up. The duration of a collectivity and its consistency coincide with the duration and consistency of its prejudices. The Oriental nations owe their everlastingness to their loyalty to themselves: having failed to "develop," they have not betrayed themselves; and they have not *lived* in the sense in which life is conceived by civilizations *on the run*, the only ones history is concerned with; for history, discipline of dawns and of gasping deathbeds—history is a novel laying claim to rigor and which draws its substance from the archives of the blood. (Cioran, 1975, 116)

Today we find a vigorous revival of ethnic, cultural and racial particularism in the "advanced" societies of the West. Whether in the form of a peaceful cultural revival or as a violent demand for political autonomy, such movements are now under way everywhere. In the North there is a nostalgia for the old days when people shared common values, when immigrants could be counted on to disappear into the melting pot and become assimilated. There is a fear of social fractionation. (Boulding, 1988, 57)

Behind all the great climactic struggles of history we will find symptoms of an expanding population. Whenever people have been ingenious so that the quality of their lives has improved they have let their numbers rise. The demand for more resources for the better life has always been more than the prevailing political systems could provide. And the grand themes of history have been the result: repressions, revolutions, liberations and always, in the end, aggressive war. (Colinvaux, 1980, 17)

DOOMSDAY: A SHORT HISTORY OF DECAY

In this chapter we will discuss some of the technological and ecological forces we believe will lead to a breakdown of the established world order and lead us into a "new world disorder," and to the breakdown of techno-industrial civilization itself. Given that this is a vision of "doomsday," it is apt to organize the argument of this section of the chapter around an argument known simply as the "doomsday argument."

The "doomsday argument" was first advanced by the cosmologist Brandon Carter at a meeting of the Royal Society in London in 1983 (Carter, 1983) and has been developed by the Canadian philosopher John Leslie in a number of publications (Leslie, 1989, 1992, 1994), including his recent book *The End of the World: The Science and Ethics of Human Extinction* (Leslie, 1996). According to Leslie: *"We ought to have some reluctance to believe that we are very exceptionally early, for instance in the earliest 0.001 per cent, among all humans who have ever lived.* This would be some reason for thinking that humankind will not survive for many more centuries, let alone colonize the galaxy" (Leslie, 1996, 1). Paul Davies, a theoretical physicist at the University of Adelaide, has given the following clear account of the Carter-Leslie doomsday argument:

Imagine all the human beings who will ever have lived. . . . If humanity survives its present troubles and thrives for thousands or even millions of years, nearly all the people who ever live will live a long time in our future. So *we* would be very untypical humans, living as we do at the end of the twentieth century. But what reason have we to suppose that we late-twentieth-century folk—mere random human beings in the vastness of human history—are so *special*? None. Hence: the assumption that humanity will thrive for a long duration is suspect. If we are typical, then humanity is doomed, and destined for imminent annihilation. (Davies, 1995, 259–60)

In terms of probability theory, if there are n unlikely steps in human development, then the greater n is, the closer will be doomsday, the end of the trial (Davies, 1995, 263). Most biologists believe that n is a large number. Consequently, we would be, by Carter's reasoning, quite close to doomsday. Just how close is calculated by dividing the sun's total life expectancy of about eight billion years by $n + 1$ (Davies, 1995, 263). John Leslie concludes that the "doomsday argument aims to show that we ought to feel *some* reluctance to accept any theory which made us very exceptionally early among all humans who would ever have been born. The sheer fact that such a theory made us very exceptionally early would at least strengthen any reasons we had for rejecting it" (Leslie, 1996, 3). How much it would strengthen these reasons for rejecting it would depend upon the strength of the competing reasons, namely that the human race will survive for centuries and colonize the galaxy. The Carter-Leslie doomsday argument does not itself give specific risk-estimates of our doom, but is a reason for revising risk-estimates when various threats to human survival are considered. The risks to our survival are not negligible and Leslie provides a useful litany of dangers facing humanity. These threats include: nuclear war; nuclear terrorism, perhaps resulting in an ecological catastrophe such as nuclear winter; biological warfare; chemical warfare; destruction of the ozone layer by chlorofluorocarbons or other chemicals; the enhanced greenhouse effect and runaway global warming leading to a Venus-effect on Earth, raising temperatures sufficient to kill most life; poisoning by pollution; disease epidemics; volcanic eruptions leading to a "volcanic winter," asteroid, and comet strikes; a new ice-age produced by passage through an interstellar cloud; radiation damage caused by supernova explosions, or other astronomical explosions such as black hole evaporation or the merger of two black holes, two neutron stars, or a black hole and a neutron star; the chaotic and unpredictable breakdown of complex systems due to chaotic behavior, such as the breakdown of the planetary motions of the solar system; an array of manmade disasters, such as the unwillingness to bear children; disasters from genetic engineering and nanotechnology; computing disasters, such as computer-initiated global thermo-nuclear war or the breakdown of global computer networks; the replacement of humans by superior thinking machines; the destruction of agricultural potential due to biodiversity decline; the production of a new Big Bang in the laboratory; the production of an all-destroying phase transition or a vacuum metastability danger involving high-energy physics experiments; and annihilation by extraterrestrials.

Leslie also considers various risks to human survival based on philosophy and ideology such as Schopenhauerian pessimism, ethical relativism, emotivism, prescriptivism, and other doctrines denying objective meaning and moral right-ness. These skeptical and nihilistic doctrines could lead to a breakdown of order at the social level or they may support movements that thrive in such an envi-ronment, such as neo-Nazism. Any of these doctrines defuses the moral serious-ness of actions. Leslie's example is the Holocaust: what is *really* bad about burning people alive for fun?" (Leslie, 1996, 11). *Ethical relativism* maintains that the Holocaust is bad only relative to particular moral codes, but these are not objectively or universally correct. *Emotivism* holds that describing burning peo-ple as bad describes no fact about burning people, but merely expresses emotions of disapproval or disgust because there are no moral facts. *Prescriptivism* also holds that there are no moral facts. "Burning people alive is bad" simply means "I prescribe that nobody is to burn anybody." On the basis of any of these doc-trines, there is nothing *really* wrong in sending millions of people to their deaths (Leslie, 1996, 12). Another ethical doctrine, that of *negative utilitarianism*, is concerned with reducing evils rather than maximizing goods. One way of doing this, Leslie argues elsewhere (Leslie, 1983), may be to eliminate the human race. In summary then, the doomsday argument claims that, considering the above threats, one would be more inclined than not to believe in the imminent extinc-tion of the human race.

Martin Krieger (1987, 1989, 1995) has advanced an argument for the prob-ability of doom being either zero, or one. Doom is viewed as a limit of a series of actions, a path to doom. Doom is taken to be a "tail event, an event which is sta-tistically independent of any finite number of steps made on the way to it. The probability of a tail event is determined by the 'infinite tail of the sequence' and not by the probability of any finite number of steps" (Krieger, 1995, 384). The steps remain statistically independent of each other. This assumption may be rejected by ecologists who see nature as a unity, whole, or system, and see the environmental crisis as being comprised of synergistically related problems. The assumption best fits cornucopianism, and the orthodox technologically optimistic philosophy of economic globalism and growthism. In any case, the assumption that doom is independent of any finite set of actions amounts to the claim that "we cannot be sure what are the ultimate consequences given any finite set of our actions" (Krieger, 1995, 383). Using the Kolmogorov zero-or-one theorem (if A is a tail event, then the probability of A is zero or one), the probability of doom must be zero or one. Now, the proposition that the probability of doom is zero, is false on the basis of our best available evidence (Smith et al., 1997). There is *some* risk of human extinction—it is not absolutely certain that human beings will survive to colonize the galaxy. Indeed, from a cosmological point of view, the universe itself may end in a "big crunch" (Davies, 1994). Hence the probability of doom must be one—we are certainly doomed.

The Carter-Leslie doomsday argument is primarily concerned with the probability of human survival or extinction. Nothing prevents the argument from being used for more modest purposes, such as considering the probability of the survival or collapse of modern civilization—of our global, techno-industrial modern order. We contend that if the doomsday argument has any power with respect to the larger question of the fate of the human species, the doomsday argument is irresistible when applied to the question of the survival of civilized order. To see this let us consider some of the threats Leslie has considered.

First, and most dramatic, is the prospect of global destruction by a doomsday asteroid. An asteroid named Toutatis, measuring 2 kilometers by 6 kilometers, passed 5.3 million kilometers from Earth on December 1 1996. This distance is a very close astronomical distance. The asteroid passes the Earth every four years according to Dr. Viktor Sokolov of the Institute of Theoretical Astronomy in Russia. If Toutatis collided with Earth, it could destroy life by causing an ecological catastrophe. On May 19, 1996, a 304 meter–wide asteroid 1996 JA1 missed Earth by 450,520 kilometers. Traveling at 92,000 kilometers per hour, 1996 JA1 would have had an impact energy of 3–4 billion tons of TNT and would have had the capacity to end human civilization if it struck. A much larger asteroid, 433 Eros, with a diameter greater than 22 kilometers, may impact with the Earth after about 1.14 million years. Eros, the second largest near-Earth asteroid, has an orbital resonance with Mars. Mars has the potential to perturb the asteroid's orbit, placing it in Earth-crossing orbits. In a paper published by P. Michael, P. Farinella, and Ch. Froeschlé in 1996 in the British scientific journal *Nature* (Michael et al., 1996), it was observed that in eight computer simulated orbits, three are Earth-crossing in the next two million years and one impacts with the Earth after 1.14 million years. Eros is at least twice as big as the asteroid that caused the "Chickxulub" crater, a gigantic crater 177 kilometers across, located off the coast of Mexico. This asteroid is thought to have resulted in the extinction of the dinosaurs when it struck the Earth 65 million years ago. Cosmic catastrophes do not occur often; the last one was 100,000 years ago. However, when such collisions occur they are enormously destructive. Dr. Duncan Steel of Adelaide University and the Spaceguard Foundation (SGF) in Rome maintains that the probability of an arbitrary individual dying by a cosmic collision is higher than that of an airplane crash (Matthews, 1996). More than 200 stray asteroids, many greater than 1 kilometer in diameter, roam the solar system and may collide with Earth in the future. The asteroids come from the Trojan swarm, two groups of asteroids that orbit the sun at about the same distance as Jupiter, which have been forced from their previous location because of the gravitational pull of the planet Saturn. The probability of a giant meteorite or small asteroid (less than one kilometer diameter) striking the Earth in the not-too-distant future is an event regarded by the experts as highly probable (Farinella and Davis, 1996). It is technologically possible to deal with a *known* asteroid on a collision course with the Earth, deflecting it from its collision course by exploding a nuclear bomb near the asteroid (exploding the asteroid itself would merely result in a shot gun–like hit on the Earth). Ironically, the main danger humanity may face is not so much cosmic annihilation by a large asteroid, but local destruction by a giant meteorite, small asteroid, or other Near Earth Object (NEO) located in the asteroid belt between Mars and Jupiter. Two thousand or more of these objects are thought to be undetected and they will prove more difficult to detect in time, leaving us with the prospect of the Earth being "shot in the back," unprepared.

Dr. Victor Clube, a senior research fellow in astrophysics at the University of Oxford believes that debris from giant comets has caused the collapse of past civilizations on Earth (Press Association, 1997). Clube's hypothesis is that the collapse of a number of past civilizations is correlated with meteorite activity and cosmic storms, which strike the Earth every 2,500 years as the Little Bull comet orbits the sun. Two such calamities occurred between 2200–2000 B.C. and A.D. 400–600, the former coinciding with the fall of Bronze Age civilizations in 40 cities across the world and the latter with the fall of Rome and the arrival of the Dark Ages in Europe. Clube believes that large meteorites could have obliterated communities as depicted in the Book of Genesis description of the destruction of Sodom and Gomorrah. The next upheaval is due in 1,000 years as the Taurid meteorite stream arrives in the area. The result, Clube predicts, will be terror: "If it happened again we would see people desperately trying to understand what was going on and the more they knew about it the worse it would be. First to go would be the advanced civilizations. As people became more frightened they would try to hide up in mountains, disappear into deserts, and throw themselves off cliffs in despair. It would be the most terrifying thing imaginable to mankind" (Press Association, 1997, 17). A sample of some of the bizarre things that can be done when gripped by cosmic cultism was seen by the suicide of 39 members of the Heaven's Gate cult on March 27, 1997, in the exclusive Rancho Sante Fe district, 50 kilometers north of San Diego. The members, under guru Marshall Applewhite, believed that a UFO was hiding in the tail of the Hale-Bopp comet and they hoped to "hitch a ride to heaven" by committing suicide. One can imagine the degree of social dislocation that will occur in the scenario sketched by Clube.

A second force that may threaten the sustainability of civilized order is human technology itself. It is difficult for us in the West to conceive that our own technology, by some Faustian twist, could lead to negative effects, let alone act like an acid upon civilized order (Glendinning, 1990; Regis, 1992). M. T. Savage, in his book *The Millennial Project: Colonizing the Galaxy in Eight Easy Steps* (Savage, 1994), is in general a technological optimist, believing that "The stars are our destiny. They are our legacy" (Savage, 1994, 18). He accepts, though, that humanity is on an "accelerating slide toward disaster" (Savage, 1994, 19) and that humanity is in a Faustian dilemma:

The same unleashed powers that enable us to enliven the universe are now, ironically, causing us to destroy the Earth. The longer we delay, the further we may slip into a pit of our own digging. If we wait too long, we will be swept into a world so poisoned by pollution, so overrun by masses of starving people, so stripped of surplus resources, that there will be no chance to ever leave this planet. (Savage, 1994, 18)

On this point, ironically, a debris belt is being created around the Earth that may make manned space flights too dangerous; as Harris observes "collisions between payloads, rocket bodies and bits of debris in orbit about 1,000 kilometers above the Earth may lead to that region becoming a veritable shooting gallery within a century or so" (Harris, 1995, 212). Space flight leads to a situation where, in the longer run, space flight (at least manned space flight) becomes impossible. Edward Tenner, in his book *Why Things Bite Back: Technology and the Revenge of Unintended Consequences* (Tenner, 1996), has given the name "the revenge effect" to the bitter irony that technological breakthroughs create problems that tend to defeat the original point of developing the technology in the first place: "in controlling the catastrophic problems we are exposing ourselves to more elusive chronic ones that are even harder to address" (Tenner, 1996, xi). As an example, the electronic office led to a worldwide escalation in paper prices because the new office machinery led to the printing of multiple copies of documents. A more important example of "the revenge effect" is given by Conway (1985) in his discussion of the Green Revolution. The Green Revolution in the Third World involved new crops and the increased use of irrigation and fertilizers. Even though a dramatic increase in yields occurred, the "new technologies have also been accompanied by a number of serious short-and medium-term problems. These include increasing incidence of pest, disease, and weed problems, sometimes aggravated by pesticide use, deterioration in soil structure and fertility, increased indebtedness, and inequity (Conway, 1985, 32). These problems have been tackled individually. Conway argues that they are systematic and interrelated, so that the productivity of the system as a whole may be unsustainable:

As a consequence problems that were initially viewed as side-effects often, it turns out, threaten directly the main objectives of development. Moreover, even where agricultural production is increased, this success may be short lived if attention is not diverted to side effects which threaten other equally important development goals. (Conway, 1985, 32)

The new technologies and the Green Revolution supplied an artificial prop to already unsustainable population growth in the Third World.

Revenge effects arise from the unintended consequences of technological developments and from Garrett Hardin's ecological law *that we can never do only one thing* (Hardin, 1993). The existence of revenge effects clearly demonstrates that it is foolish to believe that technology will mechanically save modern civilization from collapse. It could very well contribute, either directly or indirectly, to the disruption of established civilized order. To support this allegation we will now consider some typical examples of technological revenge effects that are likely to have disrupting influences at the social level.

By way of an initial example, consider the science of *nanotechnology* (Drexler, 1990; Drexler et al., 1991). Nanotechnology is molecular technology, the idea of structuring matter atom by atom. This idea was originally expressed by the physicist Richard Feynman, who gave a talk entitled "There's Plenty of Room at the Bottom" on December 29, 1959, at the annual meeting of the American Physical Society. There Feynman said that the principles of physics "do not speak against the possibility of maneuvering things atom by atom" (Drexler, 1990, 40). Drexler, in his books, discusses the possibility of restoring species (atom by atom) and even using molecular assemblers (nanobots) to build large technological objects such as rocket ships and robots (in types of "chemical baths"). All of this, Drexler admits, is futuristic speculation, light years ahead of present technological development (Heath, 1995; Kaiser, 1995; Ball, 1996; Black, 1996; Coghlan, 1996b; Debreczeny, 1996; Hogan, 1996; Schmidt, 1996). If Drexler's wildest dreams in nanotechnology were fulfilled, humanity would have an enormous capacity for both creation and destruction. As Drexler warns:

Replicating assemblers and thinking machines pose basic threats to people and to life on Earth. Today's organisms have abilities far from the limits of the possible, and our machines are evolving faster than we are. Within a few decades they seem likely to surpass us. Unless we learn to live with them in safety, our future will likely be both exciting and short. (Drexler, 1990, 171)

Even if the creations of nanotechnology do not replace us, the prospects of warfare and terrorism are chilling:

Replicators can be more potent than nuclear weapons: to devastate Earth with bombs would require masses of exotic hardware and rare isotopes, but to destroy all life with replicators would require only a single speck made of ordinary elements. Replicators give nuclear war some company as a potential cause of extinction, giving a broader context to extinction as a moral concern. (Drexler, 1990, 174)

The nanotechnological developments and dangers discussed by Drexler may be thought to lie too far off in the future to concern us. It is necessary, therefore, to give some examples of technological revenge effects more relevant to the future.

Our next example relates to modern computer technology. In the previous section of this chapter, we considered arguments about the alleged devastating effects computer technology will, and is, having upon employment prospects in the West. Other criticisms of the high tech society have and can be made (Levidow and Robins, eds., 1989; Hayes, 1990). Joseph Weizenbaum, a key-developer of computer technology, has recognized that revenge-like effects arise in a computerized society:

The computer—logical, linear, rule-governed—encourages a certain kind of thought process. Call it scientific rationality. The introduction of the computer has driven man to an ever more highly rationalist view of his society, and an ever more mechanistic view of himself. We are now, as a society, close to the point of trusting only modern science to give reliable knowledge of the world. I think this is terribly dangerous. The dependence on computers is merely the most recent—and most extreme—example of how man relies on technology in order to escape the burden of acting as an independent agent; it helps him avoid the task of giving meaning to his life, of deciding and pursuing what is truly valuable. . . .

Now what we have to fear is that inherently human problems—for example, social and political problems—will increasingly be turned over to computers for solutions. And because computers cannot, in principle, ask value laden questions, the most important questions will never be asked. . . . I think we are absolutely intoxicated with science and technology. Massively distorted perceptions of reality are everywhere. We euphorically embrace every technological fix as a solution to every human problem, which we have, of course, first converted to a technological problem. (quoted from Milbrath, 1989, 257)

The ultimate ramification of this technological world view is that humans will became redundant in the scheme of things. Ken Warwick, professor of cybernetics at Reading University, gives the following assessment of our creation of a post-biological world of thinking machines:

The creatures we create might not like the human race as much as we do. The obvious danger is that we might not be around much longer or we might lead just a slave-type existence. People who say it will never happen are not being realistic. If something is more intelligent than us, we will not be top dogs on Earth anymore. This is the logical conclusion of current work in the field of robotics and artificial intelligence. It is frightening. I don't like to think about it. But if machines can be made as intelligent as humans, then that's really it for the human race. (quoted from Berry, 1995, 101)

This example may be thought to be fanciful or fantastic, or if realistic, then a possibility too far off in the future to concern us now. But even if we grant this claim, less esoteric examples of revenge effects can be readily found in the realm of high technology (Stoll, 1995). Consider the Internet or information super-highway, widely promoted as being the information nexus of the twenty-first century and ultimately leading to the end of the paper book (Moorhouse, 1996; Wilson, R., 1996). Yet, as anyone who has regularly "surfed the net" knows, there are at times painfully long delays on the net, primarily due to congestion from user traffic. Traffic through the net has been doubling every six months, but the number of subscribers has been doubling every twelve months. As well, the transmission of music and video uses up a proportionately greater amount of band-width than simple text transmissions. The demand for the web may lead to an implosion of the web or to its loss of efficiency, defeating its key point of promotion. George Kelly of Morgan Stanley, a leading Wall Street analyst of network companies, believes that a meltdown of the Internet is coming, as does Eric Blachno of the company Bear Stearns, who sees a "Chernobyl on the net" occurring (Yakal, 1996, 51). Robert Metcalfe, inventor of Ethernet and founder of the network company 3Com, believes that a breakdown of the net has already occurred, as seen in times when the net has been slow or when the system would not operate at all, due to lack of capacity, equipment outage, software bugs, or hacker sabotage. He sees the ultimate collapse of the net involving hundreds of thousands of people, possibly for days, resulting in an enormous economic cost.

Apart from the problems of the self-generated inefficiencies of the Internet, there are also great dangers from an efficiently operating Internet. The Internet is providing a new venue for hackers and organized crime and is leading to a rise in information warfare and terrorism. Information warfare is a problem for anyone whose business relies upon computer networks or electronic trading and who uses information databases and the Internet (McIntosh, 1996). In a conference on information warfare held in Sydney in the last week of November 1996, Glenn Wahlert, security analyst with the Australian Federal Government's Office of Strategic Crime Assessments, delivered a paper entitled "Crime in Cyberspace." Wahlert noted that organized crime is seeing opportunities for money laundering using digital cash: "there are no laws that limit the balance of electronic currency that can be loaded on to a smart card and, if e-cash can transcend international borders, it would not be affected by present international currency exchange efforts" (McIntosh, 1996, 52). E-cash may be offered by organizations other than banks, the non-bank purveyors of e-cash including insurance companies, software manufacturers, and telecommunications carriers. Wahlert claims that sophisticated computer hackers could break into e-cash systems and steal money: "Should they also crack the encryption devices guarding such systems—as recently occurred in France with one of Netscape's products—the successful hacker may be able to literally 'print' his own money" (McIntosh, 1996, 53).

Computer Associates chief executive, Charles Wang, spoke to 18,000 developers and business people on this topic at CA World in New Orleans, in September 1996. He argued that not all technological innovations produce a better world: some technological advances can send society backwards (Wilson, E., 1996). Wang had in mind, specifically, ActiveX and Java-based technologies. The Java wallet allows Internet commerce on a completely open market of official and unofficial currencies. The wallet technology is distributed by netscape in its Navigator 4 web browser. The Java wallet, when connected to the banking system, allows every personal computer to be an automatic teller machine. Hence, one can send money to other Java wallets over the Internet. Vast sums of money can be transferred in complete anonymity, making money laundering a near-perfect crime. Wang believes that ActiveX has potential hazards that must be addressed: "an ActiveX application on a Web page can have all the low-level control over the desktop that viruses use, and could possibly send information anywhere in the world. Using DCOM or standard network services, it could look around a corporate network, utilizing the user's own rights and privileges. It is inevitable that twisted virus writers will catch on to the power of ActiveX to tempt end users to download Trojan horses" (Wilson, E., 1996, 3). This, in Wang's opinion "could result in the China syndrome, an uncontrollable chain reaction burning through the economy, as clouds of anarchy, leaking from compromised systems, enter daily life" (Wilson, E., 1996, 3).

Cyber-crime and cyber-terrorism are major problems for both governments and businesses. These problems are neatly summarized (at least in the business context) by a full-page advertisement placed by IBM in the October 1996 edition of *The Atlantic Monthly*: "Will a 14-year-old Sociopath Bring My Company to Its Knees?" The question is a good one. Financial institutions in the City of London paid ransom in 1996 to a gang of cyber-terrorists who threatened to wipe out computer systems (*Sunday Times* Insight Team, 1996). The gang received $US 777 million, including money from banks, broking firms, and investment houses in the United States. According to the United States National Security Agency (NSA), the terrorists used advanced information warfare techniques such as electromagnetic pulses, high emission radio frequency guns, and "logic bombs," remotely detonated coded devices. The prospects of cyber-terrorism are very real and alarming. Eli Biham of Technion, the Israel Institute of Technology in Haifa, and Adi Shamir of the Weizmann Institute in Rehovot have discovered a code-breaking technique that can crack virtually any encryption system (Matthews, 1996). The technique is called differential fault analysis (DFA) and can be used to break encryption systems, such as the Data Encryption Standard (DES), which all banks use for commercial transnational communications and transactions.

In September 1996 a hacker closed down a thousand web sites on the Internet, in an attack aimed at the provider Panix (Brake, 1996). The attack involved firing hundreds of requests per second for information to nonexistent addresses. As each request was treated as "innocent until proven guilty," the computer "clogged up". William Cheswick of Bell Labs in Murray Hill, New Jersey, believes that there is no satisfactory way at present of dealing with this difficulty given the way the Internet now is organized. It will have to be dealt with by the adoption of a new version of the Internet's protocol (Brake, 1996). According to the United States established squad of counter-cyber-terrorism, Cyber Security Assurance Group, hackers had entered unclassified Pentagon computer systems 250,000 times in 1995 and were successful 162,500 times (Casey, 1996). Jim Settle, former head of the FBI's computer security section, believes that a dedicated band of cyber-terrorists could bring the United States to its knees (Casey, 1996). Steve Orlowski, Special Advisor in Information Technology at the Australian Attorney-General's Department, has said, "It is now becoming recognized that the threat cyber warfare poses to non-military infrastructures is as great, if not greater, than the traditional military threat" (McIntosh, 1996, 53). Orlowski goes on to say in his interview that "One nation can obtain advantage over another by destroying confidence in either the technology itself, thus reducing the rate of development of that technology and any economic advantages of it, or the uptake of the technology, often the subject of massive investment, with similar consequences" (McIntosh, 1996, 53).

Information technology, which was supposed to be able to supply us with a secure exchange of information, is generating its own critical instabilities. G.J.E. Rawlins, in his book *Moths to the Flame: The Seductions of Computer Technology* (Rawlins, 1996), observes that Murphy's Law operates with respect to computer technology because "our largest systems are too complex for us to completely predict their behavior. We've lost control" (Rawlins, 1996, 143). Rawlins goes on to write:

In a complex system too many things can interact, and so too many things can go wrong. No programmer can predict them all. Today's computers can't help us either, because they don't understand what we want—because we don't understand what we want. Nor can they tell us we're bungling a program because—so far—they can only do what we tell them to do, and we don't see the error. If we did, we would simply fix it. (Rawlins, 1996, 144)

This problem is inescapable because, as Brian Medlin has observed, "every brain is too 'small' to solve all the problems that it is 'big' enough to generate," which is "an easy consequence of a simple theorem known as the Map Paradox" (Medlin, 1992, 36).

Murphy's Law operates not only with complexity, but also with simplicity. Consider for example the Y2K problem, or "millennium bomb." An article in *The Guardian Weekly* of Britain on this topic begins as follows:

Crazed members of bizarre millennium cults no longer have a monopoly on the belief that the end may be nigh. Some of the most respectable and earnest folk in the land, from city bosses and captains of industry to politicians and civil servants, are all uniting in a warning chorus that the Western world faces meltdown—economic chaos, social disorder and political upheaval—the nanosecond 1999 becomes 2000.

It is one of the 20th century's most brutal ironies. January 1, 2000 is essentially an arbitrary convention, neither 2,000 years from Jesus's birth nor an obvious indicator of any cosmic happening. Yet we have imbued it with a kind of mythical power that has produced a global feeling of anxiety, self-reflection and doom. Now, like a self-fulfilling prophecy, the millennium could bring chaos to the Western world because of one problem: the inability of computers to distinguish 2000 from 1900.

The problem is embarrassing in its simplicity; but more embarrassing still in its potential consequences. If dates are muddled then computer systems will churn out wrong numbers. For banks, governments, factories, shops, hospitals, air traffic control systems—in fact, every business that uses a microchip—this could precipitate a total collapse. "The very best outcome is severe economic depression," says Peter de Jager, a Canadian consultant who has been preaching about the so-called Millennium Bomb for the past six years. (Bellos, 1997, 27)

It is easy to find similar predictions of computer catastrophe on the Internet and in the computer sections of most daily papers. An article in Australia's *The Age* newspaper quotes an unnamed "American programmer" who tongue-in-cheek predicts the end of the computerized global economy: "Buy a cabin in the country and stock up on plenty of beer and ammunition. Then sit tight and wait for civilization to evolve again" (van Niekerk, 1996, A17). If this prediction were accurate, then the "global meltdown" thesis would be established at this point.

We are not computer experts, but we doubt whether the Y2K problem itself could bring down civilization. Nevertheless, dealing with the problem is difficult, messy, and expensive because there is no immediate and cheap technical fix. Businesses and institutions will have to painstakingly survey lines of computer code and look for instances where the data is operative and then discard or re-write it. The cost to globally correct the problem is about $US1.2 trillion (Bellos, 1997, 27). If the doomsday predictions of social chaos and "digital disaster" (Jinman, 1996) do not occur, then Y2K will still be "the biggest, most costly and absurd mistake in the history of the industrialized world" (Reeve et al., 1996, 53).

It has been our aim in this discussion to show that modern civilization is not immune to collapse because of its technological sophistication; indeed because of "revenge effects" our very technological sophistication may lead to our de-struction. In developing this argument we have given examples from the infor-mation sciences. Another interesting example of a technological revenge effect comes from the field of biochemistry. T. Colborn, J. P. Myers, and D. Duma-noski, in their book *Our Stolen Future. Are We Threatening Our Fertility, Intel-ligence and Survival? A Scientific Detective Story* (Colborn et al., 1996) show an array of manmade chemicals that disrupt the hormonal systems of organisms, including humans, producing aberrant sexual development and reproductive problems (Kleiner, 1996a; Stokstad, 1996; Pearce, 1996). Their book begins as a detective story with the observation of events such as:

(i) the sterility of Florida's Gulf Coast bald eagle population in the 1950s;

(ii) in the late 1950s—the decline of England's otter population;

(iii) in the mid-1960s at Lake Michigan—the decline in mink numbers;

(iv) 1970: Lake Ontario—deformities and wasting in herring gull colonies;

(v) early 1970s: the Channel Islands and Southern California—females nesting with other females among western gull populations;

(vi) the 1980s: Lake Apopka, Florida—reproductive faults observed in alligators. Usually 90 percent of all alligator eggs hatch; here the hatching rate was 18 per-cent, and one half of the baby alligators that did hatch died within the first ten days (Colborn et al., 1996, 6). Males were deformed and at least 60 percent had abnormally small penises.

(vii) 1988: Northern Europe—a seal die-off occurs. Although this is generally thought to have been caused by infectious disease, some environmentalists think that the deaths may have had an environmental component, as fewer deaths oc-curred on the fewer polluted shores of Scotland (Colborn et al., 1996, 7).

(viii) the early 1990s: the Mediterranean Sea—a striped dolphin die-off. This is thought to have been caused by a virus in the distemper family, although con-tamination may have played a part (Colborn et al., 1996, 8).

(ix) 1992: Copenhagen, Denmark. Niels Skakkebaek, a reproductive researcher at the University of Copenhagen, observes a worldwide trend, that human sperm counts have dropped by almost 50 percent between 1938 and 1990. Testicular cancer rates have increased, as have genital abnormalities in young boys (Chilvers et al., 1984; Carsen et al., 1992; Sharpe and Skakkebaek, 1993; Keid-ing et al., 1994; Hutson et al., 1994; Auger et al., 1995).

Colborn and colleagues document other cases of wildlife reports involving defective sexual organs, behavioral abnormalities, and even the extinction of entire animal populations. The common cause is the mega-exposure of animals to hundreds of chemicals, the long-term effects of which are unknown. Michael Fry, a wildlife toxicologist at the University of California at Davis, also investigated the effects of synthetic chemicals in disrupting the sexual development of birds. He found that DDT could disrupt the sexual development of male western gulls and California gulls, acting like the hormone estrogen, resulting in the feminization of the male reproductive tract (Colborn et al., 1996, 21). PCBs also behave like hormone mimics, disrupting biological activities. PCB concentrations are highest in top-of-the-food chain feeders, becoming concentrated by a process of bio-magnification. PCB concentrations are so low in the Great Lakes that they cannot be measured using standard water tests. However, such chemicals concentrate in body tissue and increase exponentially up the food chain. Thus, PCBs can be magnified up to 25 million times in top level feeders such as herring gulls (Colborn et al., 1996, 27).

If it is true that certain synthetic chemicals that are released into the environment as a normal part of the metabolism of modern techno-industrial society can act as hormonal mimics and blockers, it is not difficult to see some alarming ramifications for the future of the human race. Robert Moore of the School of Pharmacy and the Environmental Toxicology Center at the University of Wisconsin believes that the human sperm count is in general "borderline pathological" for many individuals. "Humans . . . are inefficient breeders, who tend to produce barely the number of sperm required for successful fertilization" (Colborn, et al., 1996, 120–21). Colborn and coworkers observe that "If Moore is correct and if long-term declines in human sperm count continue, our species faces a troubling prospect. Such a drop could have a devastating impact on human fertility" (Colborn et al., 1996, 121). Given the problem of overpopulation, this may be thought to be a good thing; however, these problems are distinct. The bio-chemical disruption problem may lead to the "insidious erosion of the human species" (Colborn et al., 1996, 234), including intelligence (Colborn et al., 1996, 236). As these writers observe: "humans in their restless quest for dominance over nature may be inadvertently undermining their own ability to reproduce or to learn and think" (Colborn et al., 1996, 238). This erosion of the basic biological potential of the human species would, in the long-term, solve the problem of human overpopulation, but it will solve this problem in a much too drastic fashion—by eroding human biological potential in such a way that the species may be faced with extinction. Professor Dennis Lincoln of Griffith University, Queensland Australia, has observed that human sperm counts in a number of countries are falling at a rate of 2.5 per cent per annum. Post mortem studies of predominantly middle-aged Finnish men showed that human sperm production fell from 56.4 per cent in 1981 to 26.9 per cent in 1991. This has led Professor Lincoln to speculate that by 2020 successful conception may only occur in the laboratory, not the bedroom (Hammond, 1997).

Critics often point out that studies involving the testing of the carcinogenic potential of DDT usually involve very high doses, often 800 times higher than the doses humans would normally receive. This argument is of little relevance to the issue of hormone-disrupting chemicals. The knowledge of the mechanisms inducing cancer is poor compared to hormone knowledge. Further, hormones guide development in basically the same way in all mammals. The hormone response curve is an inverted U-shaped curve, the response increasing with the dose and then diminishing with higher doses. Consequently hormone systems

do not conform to the assumptions that underlie classical toxicology—that a biological response always increases with dose. It means that testing with very high doses will miss some effects that would show up if the animals were given lower doses. The inverted U is another example of how the action of endocrine disrupters challenges prevailing notions about toxic chemicals. Extrapolation from high-dose tests to lower doses may in some cases seriously underestimate risks rather than exaggerate them. (Colborn et al., 1996, 170)

In summary:

The dilemma is simply stated: the Earth did not come with a blueprint or an instruction book. When we conduct experiments on a global scale by releasing billions of pounds of synthetic chemicals, we are tinkering with immensely complex systems that we will never fully comprehend. If there is a lesson in the ozone hole and our experience with hormone-disrupting chemicals, it is this: as we speed toward the future, we are flying blind. (Colborn et al., 1996, 242–43)

Let us now draw together the argument of this section to date. We began by considering the doomsday argument of Brandon Carter and John Leslie and suggested that the argument would have even greater power directed not merely at the large question of the survival of the human species itself, but more modestly directed at the question of the survival of techno-industrial civilization. For example, it would take a smaller killer asteroid to wipe out modernity than it would to annihilate the human race, and the probability of this modernity-destroying event occurring is much greater. In contemplating the destruction of the modern world, we are likely to have our concerns dismissed by technological optimists who, while accepting that all previous great civilizations have fallen, believe that modern technology will save modernity from such a fate. We then set out to show by way of examples that modern technology is a double-edged sword that often has hidden revenge effects. Examples of this potential for chaos and destruction were seen in nanotechnology, advanced computer technology, and biochemistry. On this basis, we now reject the claim that the modern world is immune to breakdown and collapse, because of its technological sophistication. On the contrary, breakdown, collapse and chaos may occur because of the technological complexity of the modern world.

In our book *Healing a Wounded World* (Smith et al., 1997), we gave a detailed argument, based upon the limits to growth position, why humanity will not "solve" the environmental crisis and why the modern world is doomed.[1] We believe that on the basis of present trends, a great die-back in human population numbers will occur; however, we remain agnostic about the "long"-term survival of the human race itself. We remain optimistic in the "moderate"-term: after a time of massive death and destruction, some people will survive living unhealthy lives in a severely polluted environment. The key to this vision is the limits to growth position—that there are biophysical limits to the matter-energy through-puts of the modern economy—and that the environmental crisis indicates that modern economies have already "overshot" their limits and are now living on scarce ecological capital (Douthwaite, 1992; Smith et al., 1997). There is no real debate about whether, in the short-run, resources are limited. Even a cornucopian such as Julian Simon accepts this. If his message is one of "receding limits and increasing resources and possibilities" (Simon and Zinsmeister, 1995, 79), then logically he must accept that in the short-term some limits must exist, or else there would be nothing from which to recede. Simon believes that human inge-nuity and technology will enable us to solve the environmental crisis; we do not.

There is also little controversy about the proposition that severe ecological damage can lead to an intensification of inequalities within societies and an in-tensification of international conflicts. Gurr has argued that "the greater the rela-tive increases in scarcity, and the more rapid its onset, the greater are its negative political consequences" (Gurr, 1985, 54). Further, "if economic effects occur rapidly and in circumstances of uncertainty, the potential for inequities, conflict, and crisis pressures on governments are substantial" (Gurr, 1985, 55). Dr. Marc Latham, Director-General of the International Board for Soil Research and Man-agement, also believes that land and water degradation could lead to food short-ages, political destabilization, war, and floods of environmental refugees (Cribb, 1994). Similar points have also been made about the "ecology of violence" (Robins and Pye-Smith, 1997) by Thomas Homer-Dixon, head of the Project on Environment, Population, and Scarcity at the University of Toronto in Canada (Homer-Dixon, 1991; Homer-Dixon et al., 1993) and many others (Brown, 1989; Gleick, 1989; Myers, 1989). Homer-Dixon has recognized that for poorer coun-tries, resource scarcity can produce an "ingenuity gap" impeding the supply of solutions: "Social improvements such as better markets and resources distribu-tion, which are products of ingenuity, often alleviate scarcity. But a society's capacity to make these improvements will be partly determined by scarcity itself, which is powerfully influenced by the society's physical context" (Homer-Dixon, 1995, 605). The view of Homer-Dixon and coworkers is that although resource scarcity has been with humanity since the dawn of biological time, resource scarcities in the next 50 years will occur with a speed, complexity, and magni-tude that has not been previously experienced (Homer-Dixon et al., 1993).

Norman Myers is in agreement with Homer-Dixon about the destabilizing effects that ecological scarcity can and will have on the security of nations. In his book with J. Kent, *Environmental Exodus* (Myers and Kent, 1995), it is observed that at least 25 million environmental refugees exist in the world (in 1995), com-pared to 22 million nonenvironmental refugees. They are located in sub-Saharan Africa (the Sahel and the Horn), the Indian sub-continent, China, Mexico, and Central America. This figure is expected to double by the year 2010, and numbers will be even greater if global warming's dire consequences are realized, leaving up to 200 million people displaced. This is a conservative estimate as "there are already 135 million people threatened by severe desertification, and 550 million people subject to chronic water shortages" (Myers and Kent, 1995, 1). Many of these people migrate without strictly being environmental refugees—environmental refugees being people who can no longer sustain themselves in their usual homelands because of environmental degradation (Myers and Kent, 1995, 1). An even larger pool of potential migrants comes from people living in marginal environments, "around 900 million of the 1.3 billion people who endure absolute poverty with an average cash income of $1 or less per day" (Myers and Kent, 1995, 1). Over 70 percent of these 900 million people live in areas that are of low agricultural potential and 57 percent of these live in areas that have a vulnerable environment. They will also contribute environmental refugees over and above the 25 million figure. The mixture of environmental degradation and poverty is a particularly dangerous one, as Myers and Kent describe:

The plight of these destitute drives them to seek a livelihood wherever they can, often in marginal environments, or environments that are too wet, too dry or too steep for sustainable agriculture of conventional kind. Hence these people account for much deforestation, desertification and soil erosion, and they aggravate the environmental decline caused by other factors. It is estimated that in Africa, 51 percent of the poorest people occupy marginal lands; in Asia, 60 percent; and in Latin America, 80 percent. Of the one billion additional people projected to be added to the global population during the 1990s, the majority are expected to be among impoverished communities, precisely the ones who are likely to migrate into marginal environments. In Sub-Saharan Africa, these environments may need to support an extra 225 million people, and in India an extra 190 million during the 1990s. (Myers and Kent, 1995, 2; Weiner, 1995)

The worst-case scenario for 2010, with respect to food and agriculture, sees Africa's malnourished reaching 300 million, with 100 million people requiring international aid. In India, the stable functioning of the monsoon is needed for 70 percent of its rainfall. A mere 0.5°C rise in temperature could reduce the wheat crop by 10 percent (Myers and Kent, 1995, 3). One billion people worldwide already face water shortages. In northern China, most water stocks are already being used to capacity, in a region where half a billion people live and where a quarter of the nation's food is produced. Climatic effects could be devastating. Myers and Kent estimate that by 2010, 500 million people will be experiencing absolute shortages in firewood and 180 million people will be affected by desertification. Urbanization trends in the developing world will intensify. China's urban population will reach 600 million by 2010, which will greatly increase the demand for water. Already China's agriculture takes 87 percent of all available water (Myers and Kent, 1995, 4). By 2025, on the worst-case scenario all of these stresses will intensify: "The urban total of developing countries is expected to reach four billion people. In the wake of a 2.4-times increase in the total since 1995, much urban infrastructure may be increasingly unable to cope, with systems breakdown becoming widespread" (Myers and Kent, 1995, 6). The end result —strife and social chaos.

Myers and Kent's position gains support from a United Nations Population Fund report released on May 29, 1996 (UN Press Release, May 29, 1996), which predicts that by 2015 3.2 billion people will live in the cities of the developing world and there will be 4.1 billion city-dwellers world-wide. In 1950 there were 83 cities with populations of more than a million people, with 34 of these in developing countries. Now there are more than 280 cities with such population numbers, and this figure will double by 2015. Cities with projected growth rates of more than 3 percent in the period 1990–2000 include Kinshasa and Lagos in Africa, Karachi and Lahore in Pakistan, Jakarta in Indonesia, Istanbul in Turkey, Dhaka in Bangladesh, and Bangalore, Bombay, Delhi, and Hyderabad in India. One third of all people living in cities live in poverty, totaling 600 million people worldwide. The UN Population Fund recognizes that by "the very nature of large cities as concentrations of human creativity and the highest forms of social organization," "new avenues for human development" will be opened up; however, "It carries many risks—such as the possibility of the collapse of basic services, intolerable environmental degradation and escalating social conflict" (UN Press Release, May 29, 1996). For example, according to a World Bank study, 40,000 people a year die from air pollution–related causes in 36 Indian cities and there are 20 million hospital admissions (Patel, 1996a, b). The annual death toll from air pollution in Delhi alone is 7,500 people (Patel, 1996a, b; Hiscock, 1996).

Most cities in the developing world will face extreme water shortages by 2010 (Pearce, 1997). At the United Nations Human Settlement Conference, Habitat II, the UN Habitat secretary-general acknowledged that "water is going to be the most hotly contested urban issue facing the world community in the twenty-first century. The water crisis is coming about not only because of a lack of water in some regions, but also from the inability of governments to make the necessary investments in a timely manner to ensure that water is available in all cities" (Erdem, 1996).

Lester Brown, viewed as something of a professional prophet of doom by the cornucopians and technological optimists, believes that at the international level "the population-driven environmental deterioration /political disintegration scenario described by Robert Kaplan is not only possible; indeed, it is likely in a business-as-usual world" (Brown and Kane, 1995, 33). Of this business-as-usual world, Brown has more recently said:

The pace of change in the world is speeding up, accelerating to the point where it threatens to overwhelm the management capacity of political leaders. This acceleration of history comes not only from advancing technology, but also from unprecedented world population growth, even faster economic growth, and the increasingly frequent collisions between expanding human demands and the limits of the earth's natural systems. (Brown, 1996, 3)

Since 1950 grain demand has almost tripled and water use has tripled. Fossil fuel use has increased almost fourfold (Brown, 1996, 4). Oceanic fisheries and rangelands, in Brown's opinion, are reaching their sustainable yield limits.

Emerging food scarcity is seen, he believes, in falling grainstocks, rising grain prices, and rising seafood prices (Brown, 1996, 7). The world-grain-carry-over-stocks, calculated as days of consumption, is declining and has been declining since about 1993 (Brown, 1996,8). The decline in the world's grain harvested has been from 732 million hectares in 1981 to 669 million hectares in 1995, due to land erosion in the former Soviet Union, the loss of cropland to industrialization in Asia, and the reversion of highly eroded cropland back into grassland in the United States (Brown, 1996, 9). In the United States and elsewhere, increases in land productivity seem to be subjected to the operation of the law of diminishing returns. In the United States land productivity was raised by more than 40 percent in the 1950s and 1960s compared to the 1940s. This fell to 20 percent in the 1970s, 10 percent in the 1980s, and will fall further in Brown's opinion in the 1990s (Brown, 1996, 10).

Brown believes that the official food projections by the World Bank and the United Nations Food and Agriculture Organization (FAO), being extrapolations of past trends, fail to account for factors such as the effect of soil erosion on land productivity, the depletion of water resources (especially aquifers), and of heat waves and climate change caused by global warming on harvests (Brown, 1996, 17). A looming food shortage will arise because of (a) the lack of growth of world grain harvests since 1990, (b) crop-damage from heat waves in the time to come, and (c) the growth in world population (Brown, 1996, 18). Ecological overshoot has already occurred: "The demands of our generation now exceed the income, the sustainable yield, of the earth's ecological endowment" (Brown, 1996, 4). Brown believes that if humanity fails to act in time

our future will spiral out of control as the acceleration of history overwhelms political institutions. It will almost guarantee a future of starvation, economic insecurity, and political instability. It will bring political conflict between societies and among ethnic and religious groups within societies. As these forces are unleashed, they will leave social disintegration in their wake. (Brown, 1996, 18)

Conflicts over shared river systems are already occurring: Bangladesh protests against India's excessive use of the Ganges, there is a conflict between Israel and Palestine over water resources, the United States and Mexico over the Rio Grande's water, and conflicts in Central Asia over the Amu Dar'ya and Syr Dar'ya rivers (Brown, 1996, 6).

Brown's most controversial recent work is his book *Who Will Feed China?* (Brown, 1995b). There Brown argues that the prospects of China as an importer of massive quantities of grain will cause an economic earthquake that will spread throughout the world. Further, China is only the first of scores of countries in this situation. Brown notes that in countries that are densely populated before industrialization, heavy loss of cropland occurs, which typically overrides any rises that might have come from land productivity improvements. This has occurred in Japan, South Korea, and Taiwan. The conversion of grainland to other uses and a decline of multiple-cropping meant that Japan lost 52 percent of its grain area, South Korea 46 percent, and Taiwan 42 percent. Brown notes that as "cropland losses accelerated, they soon exceeded rises in land productivity, leading to steady declines in output" (Brown, 1995b, 25). In Japan, for example, grain production has fallen 32 percent from its peak in 1960, and in both South Korea and Taiwan, output has dropped 24 percent since 1977 (Brown, 1995b, 25). China's industrialization, Brown believes, will show a similar pattern of decline and rising affluence, and changes in diet will further increase China's hunger for grain. China's 1990 area of grain land per person is 0.08 hectares, the same as Japan's was in 1950s. To avoid Japan's decline, China must become more effective in protecting its cropland than Japan, or raise its grain yield per hectare faster than Japan has over a comparable period. China's current yields are high and Japan's achievements have been remarkable, so this will be difficult to do as cropland is lost to industrialization and urbanization. Brown's thesis is that China's grain production will fall *not* as a result of a failure of agriculture, but because of industrial success (Brown, 1995b, 27). Between 1950 and 1994 grain production increased almost fourfold. China's problem is not one of "averting starvation" but one of being able to "maintain price stability in the face of soaring demand for food driven by unprecedented advances in income" (Brown, 1995b, 28)—a genuine technological/ecological revenge effect.

According to Brown, China's population will grow by 490 million people between 1990 and 2030, giving it a population of 1.6 billion. This figure is likely to be regarded by most demographers as too high. Nevertheless, Brown's point remains that the sheer size of China's population means an even slower rate of population growth will translate into a huge population increase by almost four present day Japans. Alarmingly: "Two more beers per person in China would take the entire Norwegian grain harvest. And if the Chinese were to consume seafood at the same rate as the Japanese do, China would need the annual world fish catch" (Brown, 1995b, 30). International free trade cannot by itself feed China. Japan, for example, is able to import grain to account for 72 percent of its total grain consumed. The world market can cope with 120 million people, but 1.2 billion (let alone 1.6 billion) will be too much for grain exporting nations to deal with. If China's grain imports were similar to Japan's, South Korea's, or Taiwan's, then in 2030 China would need to import 333 million tons of grain (Brown, 1995b, 98). Brown quotes Professor Zhou Guangzhao, head of the Chinese Academy of Sciences, who believes that if consumption of grain per person reaches the level of the most affluent provinces, if industrialization continues at the same pace, and if environmental degradation and water resources are degraded at the same rate, then China will need to import 400 million tons of grain and the entire grain output of the United States could not meet this (Brown, 1995b, 99). In an integrated world economy, China becoming an importer of grain will transform the world grain market from a buyer's market to a seller's market. Even if China did have ample foreign exchange to pay for this grain, the problem is that no nation, or group of nations, can meet this demand. As well: "It may . . . force a redefinition of security, a recognition that food scarcity and the associated economic instability are far greater threats to security than military aggression is" (Brown, 1995b, 32).

Brown's thesis has generated great controversy because, if correct, it means the end of the "Asian miracle" and the end of the dream of many ruling class elites in the West, of the eclipse of the dominant power of the West. Chinese leaders, who have always operated on the social Darwinist principle of "might is right" have seen Brown's criticisms as aimed at weakening China (seen as the center of the Earth) and strengthening the West (McGregor, 1996a, b). The Hong Kong Bank's *China Monthly* report for February 1997 states the point of view that China will be able to feed itself, relying in the long-term on "white agriculture," the production of food from micro-organisms, enzymes, algae, and plankton (Bromby, 1997). Vaclav Smil, in his review of Brown's *Who Will Feed China?* in *The New York Review of Books* (Smil, 1996b), notes that Brown is "a professional catastrophist" (Smil, 1996b, 33) who has repeatedly been shown to be mistaken. Brown, for example, was wrong about the world running out of oil: "There is enough crude oil to last us nearly half a century at the 1995 rate of consumption" (Smil, 1996b, 33). We will show below that it is Smil, not Brown, who is wrong about this. Smil makes the point in reply to Brown that China can only continue to modernize if it continues to import costly high tech machinery, which has put China's overall balance of trade in the red during the present period of modernization. He then concludes, "This is hardly a basis for the unlimited purchase of foreign grains, whose prices, according to Brown, are to rise steeply in the tightening global food market" (Smil, 1996b, 33). True, but Brown's thesis is a conditional one: if China's economy is to outstrip the United States' economy, then these things follow, the "things" in question being the propositions of *Who Will Feed China?* Brown's book is essentially a *reductio ad absurdum* of the proposal that the Chinese can sustainably live at the resource consumption levels of present day North Americans. Logically then, China will not be the next economic superpower. From Brown's limitationist perspective, the age of economic superpowers is coming to a close because economic growth and overpopulation have led to ecological overshoot.

Smil himself has documented in a number of works the precarious state of the environmental foundations of China's existence (Smil, 1993, 1996a,b). These basic life-support systems are weak and are deterioriating at a high rate. In Smil's stated opinion, they will deteriorate further given China's high absolute population growth rate and the demand for resources that economic modernization ensures (Smil, 1993, 66). China's environmental crisis is unique because technological remedies are unlikely to solve its problems—the key problem being the magnitude of population expansion:

The odds against harmonizing population growth with both human and environmental well-being may be quite daunting, and endowing the technical fixes with planetwide omnipotence may be crudely arrogant, but discounting our inventive and adaptive capabilities is an equally narrow-minded lapse. The complexity of links among population growth, resource use, and environmental quality invalidates any appealing generalizations, especially those made at the global level. But it repays a close investigation of particulars, revealing almost invariably a mix of depressing trends and hopeful possibilities. (Smil, 1993, 7)

Smil notes, against Julian Simon and with Brown, that China cannot, unlike Japan and South Korea, sell manufactured goods to buy the bulk of its food and natural resources, because of its enormous population size. China cannot import the bulk of its rice or timber because there are simply not enough raw materials traded on the global market to meet China's demand as well as that of all other nations (McGregor, 1996a, b). Smil observes: "The resulting necessity to intensify agricultural output and to overexploit domestic resources cannot but degrade and pollute the environment. Given the country's population density, this environmental deterioration feeds back into the socioeconomic setup by spreading natural disasters, higher costs, reduced productivity, and declining quality of life" (Smil, 1993, 8). Further, from our reading of Smil's *Environmental Problems in China* (Smil, 1996a), we see an emerging picture of ecological catastrophe that may exceed Brown's own prophecies of doom. The degradation of soils and water in China, the destruction of forests, the poisoning of waterways by industrial pollution (e.g., one-third of China's coastal waters are polluted by oil), cannot lead to a happy ending. In the 1996 annual report of the National Environmental Protection Agency of China (NEPA), director Xie Zhenhua stated that China's environment had deteriorated from 1995 and that the situation was "grave" (Hutcheon, 1996, 15). It is only a residual belief in human ingenuity and the technological *deus ex machina* that allows scholars such as Smil (and even Brown) to conclude their works on a note of forlorn optimism, so common to most contemporary books that purport to confront the compelling issues of our time. Such sentiments enable the author to switch off his personal computer (after saving the text)—and the reader to replace the book on the shelf—with a warm fuzzy feeling inside that ultimately all will be well. But such sentiments are in fact separated from reality by a yawning chasm. It is only when the opinions of the experts are placed side-by-side and examined in one view with a critical eye that the genuine horrors that await humanity can be fully grasped. Let us consider, then, some further pieces of the global picture puzzle of emerging ecological disaster.

The agricultural secretary of the Philippines, Roberto Sebastian, believes that the Philippines' population growth will outstrip rice production by the year 2000, primarily because of industrialization using up arable land (Richardson, 1996a). M. Richardson, Asia editor of the *International Herald Tribune*, observes that Indonesia was self-sufficient in rice from 1984 to 1994. It has now begun importing rice because of shortages caused by the industrial encroachment problem, drought, and crop disease. Richardson notes that in the 10 years to 1993, rice production in Java, which itself accounts for 56 percent of the Indonesian total, fell by an annual rate of two percent. During this period 900,000 hectares of rice fields were taken out of production for food due to the previously listed factors. Dr. Per Pinstrup-Andersen, Director-General of the Washington-based International Food Policy Research Institute (IFPRI), said at a food seminar hosted by the Crawford Fund for International Agricultural Research, in May 1996, that: "The carnage wreaked by poverty and hunger is very often out of sight and out of mind. But the tragedy unfolding in the developing world will affect Australia and other industrialized nations. The widespread food insecurity in developing countries today will threaten global stability tomorrow—and undermine the prosperity of all nations" (Dayton, 1996a). This destabilized world of starvation and terrorism will seriously disrupt international markets leading to economic chaos in the Western world as well. This is a view also shared by Nick Cater, one of the writers of the *World Disasters Report 1996*, produced by the International Federation of Red Cross and the Red Crescent Societies, who told the *Sydney Morning Herald* in an interview, "We will see the opening up of a new century of chaos, with food shortages, people on the move, and continuing conflicts, but without the resources or food to even begin patching up the situation" (Dayton, 1996b). Cater also believes that within 35 years China will not be able to feed its population. A study coordinated by the US Environmental Protection Agency and scientists in 25 countries also predicts a decrease in global food production occurring at a time when major increases are needed (Parry and Rosenzweig, 1993). Grain yields are thought to sharply decrease under conventional models of global warming (Pearce, 1992; Nissani, 1996).

A World Bank Discussion Paper, *Toward an Environmental Strategy for Asia* by Carter Brandon and Ramesh Ramankutty (Brandon and Ramankutty, 1993), also recognized the severity of the environmental crisis in Asia, a product of economic growth itself:

Economic growth and population densities have had severe negative impacts on the Asian environment. Pressure on the region's resources is intense and growing. There are serious problems in the areas of urban environmental degradation; industrial pollution; atmospheric emissions; soil erosion and land degradation; water resource degradation; deforestation; and loss of natural habitat. The real costs of environmental degradation are mounting in the form of increasing health costs and mortality, reduced output in resource-based sectors, and the irreversible loss of biodiversity and overall environmental quality. (Brandon & Ramankutty, 1993, ix)[2]

The solution, in Brandon and Ramankutty's opinion, does not lie in restricting economic growth, but increasing the right kinds of growth—"sustainable growth" that will not harm the environment. In *Healing a Wounded World* (Smith et al., 1997), we demonstrated the incoherence of this position and the unlikelihood of achieving sustainable development even if it were a coherent ideal. The central problem here is the sheer size and inertia of the global capitalist system, making it difficult, if not impossible, for any change of economic direction to occur in the short term. The capitalist system is like a bicycle rider with no brakes, riding down a steep mountain track with precipices of economic chaos to either side and a flat hard mountain face of ecological scarcity on the track ahead. The former communist system has proved to be incapable of achieving both economic and ecological sustainablilty.

This bleak picture is supported by reflection on the oil crisis that awaits humanity in the twenty-first century. Brian Fleay has discussed this issue in some depth in his book *The Decline of the Age of Oil* (Fleay, 1995), supporting earlier work (Gever et al., 1991). Sixty percent of the world's oil is consumed by road, rail, water, and air transportation. As Fleay observes:

Infrastructure is about the transport of people and goods, of fluids by pipeline, power in electricity grids and of information by telecommunications.

It has taken two centuries to build this infrastructure that joins and sustains communities, agricultural systems and the global economy. Movement of people and goods is the most indispensable of the transport modes, upon which the other modes are fundamentally dependent. Cheap oil has been the most economically effective of all the fuels because of the high power-weight ratio and ease of transport, storage and use. That is why road and air transport have grown rapidly. (Fleay, 1996, 30)

However oil production in the major producing regions of the world is reaching a peak and beginning to decline:

A fifty-year transition period began in the USA in 1970. The former Soviet Union's (FSU's) oil production peaked in 1989 and has suffered rapid decline since. The remainder of the producing regions outside the Arabian Gulf are expected to peak by the year 2005. The Arabian Gulf region, with two thirds of world oil reserves, is likely to peak last in about 2020. Production of oil in the world as a whole is likely to peak some ten years earlier. (Fleay, 1995, 1)

Oil production, like other forms of production, is subject to the operation of the law of diminishing returns:

The production life cycle of petroleum fuels when graphed has a bell-shaped curve: the peak production rate occurs when about half of the economically extractable oil has been produced. The first half of oil production rising to the peak is the cheapest and most economically effective. . . . The reverse is the case for the second half, with the onset of declining production. The fossil fuels are becoming a constraint to economic activity much sooner than most people think, which is why the world as we know it is undergoing more and more rapid structural change. (Fleay, 1995, 1–2)

C. J. Campbell and J. Laherrere of Petroconsultants, leading consultants to the international petroleum industry, published a report in 1995 entitled *World's Oil Supply 1930–2050*. The report claimed that the production peak and decline of world oil will be much sooner than expected—around the year 2000—and that world production will halve every 25 years after that (Fleay, 1996). Other industry experts, according to Fleay, in responding to Campbell and Laherrere, believe that the peak will be about 2010. The concern here is with cheap oil, in the range of $US2–5 per barrel and up to $US15 per barrel. Oils, shale, and tar-sand are excluded as they will be too expensive to fuel modern global capitalism, in Campbell and Laherrere's opinion. It is important to note that this debate is not an academic one between two schools of thought hoping to win philosophical debating points: it is a private enterprise debate, where fortunes rest on accurate information. Excessive optimism can destroy businesses as easily as excessive pessimism. Further, the debate is not about whether oil reserves will "run out," but rather the extent of oil reserves, how much new oil remains to be discovered, and at what cost. British Petroleum's Paul Appleby believes that proven oil reserves amount to 1,000 billion barrels; however, 30 percent of this, Fleay notes, is merely "political oil" "invented for OPEC quota bargaining." Campbell and Laherrere believe that oil reserves are more likely 838 billion barrels. Appleby believes that about 500 billion barrels of oil remain to be found; Campbell puts the figure at 211 billion barrels. Whereas Appleby is confident that technological innovations will enhance the quantity of oil recoverable from existing fields, Campbell and Leherrere see techniques such as steam injection and in-fill drilling as expensive, massively increasing the cost of oil. Who then are we to believe? Fleay observes that Petroconsultants has a data base encompassing the performance history of every significant oil field in the world and no other company, including British Petroleum, has this. Campbell and Laherrere conclude their report as follows:

The scene is well set for another oil price shock . . . a permanent condition reflecting declining resources and the control by a few countries . . . when oil production will fall and decline to levels not experienced since the first half of the 20th century. This cannot fail but to have colossal political and economic consequences. (Fleay, 1996, 30)

The coming oil crisis spells the end of the Asian century before it is even started. For example, Japan's success in becoming an industrial giant is in part due to oil production from the Arabian Gulf region. The economic boom of the 1950s and 1960s would not have been possible without this relatively cheap oil (Fleay, 1995, 47). Around 60 percent of East Asia's oil for consumption is imported, mostly from the Middle East (Richardson, 1996b, 25). According to John Ferriter, Deputy Executive Director of the International Energy Agency in Paris, most Asian countries have become increasingly dependent upon Middle East oil. China became an importer of oil in 1993, and in 1994 the central authorities allowed everyone to own cars. Thus it is expected that there will be 40 million cars on the road by 2010. This is likely to push China's crude-oil imports to 1.3 million barrels a day by the year 2000. Again, most of this oil will come from the Middle East (Fleay, 1995, 59). The exploration of oil in the South China Sea has not lived up to expectations. Remote areas that may have significant oil reserves, such as the Tarim Basin in northwest China, will be costly to develop, if oil is there at all (Fleay, 1995, 60).

China therefore cannot become another United States, let alone *surpass* the economic might of the United States. Given that renewable sources of energy cannot by themselves sustain a global affluent society (Trainer, 1995), the "decline of the age of oil" problem alone will mean the end of the modern age: the end of the global economy (which is impossible without cheap transport) and the end of the idea of unlimited growth. Fleay sees a new science, a postmodern science, emerging bringing an end to elitism and a re-enchantment with nature (Fleay, 1995, 138–39). In our opinion, this scenario of green new age sustainability, while having its element of appeal, is most unlikely. As Fleay himself admits, it requires nations reducing oil dependence during the next twelve years (Fleay, 1995, 140) and the trend is in the opposite direction. For example, the European motor car giant BMW believes that the first commercial hydrogen-fueled cars will be marketed in 2010 and two percent of all German cars will be fueled with hydrogen by 2025 (Edwards, 1996). This is an optimistic technological scenario, but even this development is too slow to deal with the "decline of the age of oil" problem.

Lewis J. Perelman (1980) has speculated on the social transformations that will occur in the transition to a sustainable energy base. There will be a change from a democratic-republican social system in America to neo-feudalism, a society in which: (1) wealth and power is based on land holdings, (2) political decentralization or balkanization occurs, (3) a quasi-steady state economy is adopted, and (4) social stratification by caste or class is implemented (Perelman, 1980, 395). Throughout history, societies based on solar energy and renewable resources have been feudalistic societies and Perelman expects this to be so in the future. Economic growth and consumerism hold the current democratic-republican capitalist society of America together, but when they are gone, Perelman expects a theocracy to emerge as the social glue of such a society. These are interesting speculations that represent to some degree an alternative scenario to the doomsday vision of the present authors. Neo-feudalism, in Perelman's form, could well be the dominant form of social organization of relatively large populations of people—if there are still relatively large populations of people! In any case, in the short term, the transition away from economic growth and consumerism will not be made in America without racial and ethnic conflict. On this Perelman says:

Centrifugal forces increasingly challenge and strain the centripetal bonds of national and multinational interdependence. Just as dinosaurs were vulnerable to egg snatching by mammalian rodents, physical and social limits make giant organizations ever more vulnerable to the leverage of small groups. In confronting the mighty, the meek aspire to inherit not the whole earth but only small pieces of it: South Malucca, Eritrea, Croatia, Scotland, Quebec, Kurdistan, or (domestically) Maine (Indian lands), Michigan (the Upper Peninsula), Petaluma, or Martha's Vineyard. The way to defuse the destructive potential of irreconcilable paradigm conflict is through division of territory. Historical examples are plentiful: the Biblical exodus, the division of the United States into slave and free states, the division of the Church into Eastern and Western branches, the creation of ghettos, the partitioning of Germany, Ireland, Cyprus, Palestine, India, and so forth. Clearly, territorial division is no panacea for conflict, but in many cases it probably has reduced or deferred some of the destructive consequences of profound conflicts. The impulse to separatism, localism, isolationism, and balkanization seems to be an inevitable feature of the coming transition to sustainable energy. (Perelman, 1980, 406–7)

The vectors of ecological scarcity, environmental destruction, and emerging economic chaos discussed in this section lead us to conclude that the wheels of history are spinning in the direction of anarchy and social chaos—a global meltdown—with a return to social Darwinian values of might is right and the survival of the strongest, most ruthless, and cunning, at an individual, national, racial, and civilizational level. For example, China has already targeted Australia for investment in food, according to Chia Yen, Austrade's Investment Commissioner for East Asia (McGregor, 1996). According to Chia Yen: "When it comes to food, where can they go in the world? Canada and the United States are . . . far less certain politically. Everyone who goes to Australia is bowled over by the climate and the nonpolluted environment" (McGregor, 1996, 18). An unnamed trade official cited by McGregor said that Austrade was trying to formulate joint Chinese and Australian ventures to avoid investments being made on "a guerrilla basis, hitting one industry after another. . . . But if we are complacent about it and let them come to us we may not get the business." However, what starts out as a business venture could in the future lead to the taking of candy from the dumb, blind, and pathetically cringing Australian nation; business-as-usual led to Australian political leaders selling pig iron to the Japanese (by Prime Minister "Pig Iron Bob" Menzies) in the 1930s, iron that was soon used against them in war by the Japanese imperial force. Such realities that would have been of keen and obvious concern to any of the great thinkers of past centuries such as Sun Tzu, Plato, Nietzsche, Hegel, Marx, and Darwin are too painful, too politically incorrect, for public discussion in Australia. To hell with long term survival—all that counts is preserving our economic links with Asia today, is the attitude of Australia's ruling elites (see Hanson, 1997, which generated controversy in Australia in May 1997 on this issue). Only very rarely do scenarios such as the following, by Roger Short, find their way into print:

And what of Australia? Our future will be increasingly determined by events taking place in South East Asia, and particularly in Indonesia, our nearest neighbor. Currently, Indonesia has a population of 181 million, which the World Bank estimates will increase to 206 million by 2000, 265 million by 2025 and will plateau at around 354 million towards the end of the coming century. At that population density, Indonesia's rain forests will have been destroyed in the search for more arable land, and the massive erosion of topsoil from the bare, denuded hillsides, coupled with coastal flooding from the rising sea levels produced by global warming, will result in millions of poor, starving, dispossessed peasants. Their only hope of survival will be to take to their boats and drift south to Australia's northern coastline, where for a time they could eke out a meagre existence. We would be faced by an overwhelming moral and military dilemma if we had to contend with a massive invasion by millions of starving boat people who come in peace— ecological refugees who have fouled their own nest. (Short, 1994, 4)

In Short's paper, entitled "Australia: A Full House," he argues for the limitationist position that Australia is approaching its population carrying capacity. Obviously on these premises, millions of starving boat people cannot be supported. Short believes that this fate can be averted by generous foreign aid. But what if that fails? What then? Presumably on liberal premises, a nation such as Australia should allow itself to be overwhelmed in a *Camp of the Saints* scenario that will bring misery to all. As we shall see, the decadent and politically correct West is ill-prepared for the savage dark age we are about to enter (Tanton et al., eds., 1996).

We now summarize the state of the argument of this section. The discussion began with an outline of the Carter-Leslie doomsday argument, an argument giving reason to believe that the human race is quite close to extinction. We suggested that the doomsday argument gains strength by being redirected against the long-term prospects of survival of modern techno-industrial civilization. The probability of collapse of techno-industrial society is much greater than the probability of the destruction of the entire human race, because the probability of the occurrence of the respective destructive agents is greater (e.g., a smaller asteroid, a lesser nuclear disaster, etc.). The conditional probability of the collapse or destruction of techno-industrial civilization (A), given the present state of the world (E) is given by:

$$Pr(A/E) = \frac{\text{number of ways that A and E can occur}}{\text{number of ways E can occur}}$$

As we have observed elsewhere (Smith et al., forthcoming), the number of ways E can occur is 1 as E is the present state of the world, it is just that which exists. Consequently, $Pr(A/E)$ increases as the number of ways, A, the collapse of techno-industrial civilization, increases. Each of A_1, A_2, A_3, . . . A_n has a non-zero probability that it will alone destroy techno-industrial civilization; however, all of A_1, A_2, A_3, . . . A_n can simultaneously occur so they are not mutually exclusive. Therefore, the probability of the collapse or destruction of techno-industrial civilizations is increasing over time as the number of ways that we can destroy ourselves increases and as ecological scarcity tightens its vice of necessity. This section has attempted to document some of the technological and ecological mechanisms that may lead to the collapse of techno-industrial civilization.

We first argued that mere technological sophistication is not enough in itself to save modernity from the fate faced by all past civilizations—destruction. Technology itself could very well destroy us because of intrinsic "revenge effects" that lie coiled like a Faustian worm within the heart of advanced technology. A number of examples of such "revenge effects" were given, and many more could be cited (Smith et al., 1997). Having done this, we then gave a condensed, but updated, argument originally presented in *Healing a Wounded World* (Smith et al., 1997) as to why we believe techno-industrial society is doomed. We in fact believe more than this, maintaining that both the "developed" and the "developing world" are to meet the same fate, but by different mechanisms. In both cases however, the ultimate cause of collapse is ecological scarcity, and the remaining pages of this section outlined the pathways taken by this grim reaper of scarcity. In particular we have sketched an argument against Asia-Pacific millenarianism (Smith, 1991), the view that the focus of world power in the twenty-first century will be Asia and that China will replace the United States as the world's economic superpower. This, in our opinion, will not occur because China's run to home base is too late. The "decline of the age of oil" argument is sufficient in itself to ensure this, without considering the sustainability of the ecological systems of China—which in turn by a "revenge effect" are being increasingly degraded by increased economic growth. To become the world's largest economy, China must grow at a rate of 9–10 percent a year. The Chinese economy must grow at a rate of 7–8 percent a year merely to maintain the present standard of living in the face of population increase (Gottliebsen, 1996). Robert Gottliebsen observes, in writing about the China question after the World Economic Forum in Davos in 1996:

If China grows at a lesser rate, or even goes into recession—either because the US and Japan freeze it out or because of internal difficulties—then problems there will become similar to those in Russia. So, just as Germany fears that the Russians may one day walk into western Europe, so Japan could be "invaded" by millions of Chinese refugees or boat people. . . . If China's growth was stunted because it could not get access to world markets, the consequences would be serious. There was also the possibility of the country splitting apart, but the Chinese view was that the dream of becoming the world's leading country would overcome most of the internal differences. No one wanted to be responsible for not fulfilling the dream. (Gottliebsen, 1996, 41)

If the argument of this section of the present book is correct, the Chinese dream will not be fulfilled.

In this section we have outlined technological and ecological mechanisms for the collapse of established order and the destruction of modernity, of techno-industrial civilization. However, there are other reasons for believing that the so-called "new world order" will dissolve into a "new world disorder," and these reasons relate to the very success of economic globalization. An economically globalized world has an intrinsic element of social instability. The argument for this claim now follows.

THE NEW WORLD DISORDER: ECONOMIC GLOBALIZATION AND THE BREAKDOWN OF "NATIONS" AND COMMUNITY

At a time in which the world environment is under threat, when both the U.S. National Academy of Science and the British Royal Society see the future of the planet hanging in the balance (see Smith et al., 1997), a major economic revolution is occurring. This is the revolution of economic globalization: the increasingly free movement of capital and labor around the world (see der Derian and Shapiro, 1989; Campbell, 1992a; Daly, 1991, 1993; Drucker, 1993; Lange and Hines, 1993; Taylor, 1993; George, 1994; Sylvester, 1994; Cochran, 1995; Hurrell, 1995, and for excellent bibliographies, used here, see Cochran, 1995; Hurrell, 1995).[3] This revolution is associated with, and justified by, a resurgence of *laissez-faire* or a free market economics. (Canterbery, 1987; Davidson and Davidson, 1988; Hodgson, 1988; Daly and Cobb, 1989; Colander, 1991; Etzioni and Lawrence, 1991; Kuttner, 1991; Ferber and Nelson, 1993; Heilbroner and Milberg, 1995). Kenichi Ohmae, in *The Borderless World: Power and Strategy in the Interlinked Economy* (Ohmae, 1990), describes this alleged new world order in these terms:

In recent decades we have watched the free flow of ideas, individuals, and industries grow into an organic bond among developed economies. Not only are traditionally traded goods and securities freely exchanged in the interlinked economy, but so too are such crucial assets as land, companies, software, commercial rights (patents, memberships, and brands), art objects, and expertise.

Inevitably the emergence of the interlinked economy brings with it an erosion of national sovereignty as the power of information directly touches local communities; academic, professional, and social institutions; corporations and individuals. It is this borderless world that will give participating economies the capacity for boundless prosperity. (Ohmae, 1990)

Gregory Stock, in his book *Metaman: Humans, Machines, and the Birth of a Global Super-Organism* (Stock, 1993), sees human society becoming a living being, a global super-organism, with humans like cells linked by the nerves of modern technology and communication (Hardison, 1989). This new organism, Stock calls "Metaman," meaning "beyond and transcending humans." This idea is something of an economist's revenge on James Lovelock's idea of Gaia (Lovelock, 1979, 1988), Gaia being the idea that life on Earth constitutes in itself an organic and connected whole or "superorganism." Stock, like Ohmae, believes that a complete integration of the world's economies is inevitable:

Today . . . many countries are being forced to consider whether it is possible for them to thrive over the long term if they isolate themselves economically. Examining the dynamics of Metaman suggests that this is not possible, and that any economic policies which do not allow for expanding international trade are seriously flawed because worldwide economic integration is inevitable. The concept of Metaman further implies that humankind has before it a long and vital future in a world where the natural environment will be managed, where the nation state will lose its dominance in world affairs, where technology will penetrate into virtually all aspects of human life, where human reproduction and biology will be managed, and where local cultural traditions will merge to form a rich global culture. (Stock, 1993, 6)

The General Agreement on Tariffs and Trade (GATT) is an organization that, since it came into operation in January 1948, has promoted the expansion of international trade through the removal of tariffs and other restrictions on international commerce. GATT operates along with the International Monetary Fund, the World Bank, and the formation of various free trade blocs and associations— such as Asian-Pacific Economic Cooperation (APEC), Association of South-East Asian Nations (ASEAN), European Union (EU), North American Free Trade Agreement (NAFTA), and the proposed Free Trade Area of the Americas (FTAA)—to produce the sort of world described by Ohmae and Stock in the citations given above, where transnational corporations (TNC) are free to roam the world in search of labor and environments that offer maximum profitability for their enterprises. All of these organizations and agreements exist to ensure that markets are deregulated and that nations are open to the penetration of the transnational corporations. An editorial (March 11, 1995) in the generally economic rationalist *Sydney Morning Herald* sums up this situation accurately:

The IMF and the World Bank are not democratic organizations. The interests they serve are primarily the interests of investment capital. And the outcome they typically seek, especially in developing countries, are those conducive to the operation of foreign traders and investors. Not surprisingly, while the World Bank and IMF were getting a caning in Copenhagen (World Summit on Social Development), their officials were applying the same old austerity screws to the Argentine Government. (Quotation from *TOES* [The Other Economic Summit], 1995, 13)

We argue in this section that trade liberalization, economic globalization, and the increasing domination of economic criteria over all aspects of life (*economic rationalism* or *economic reductionism*) will have a disastrous impact upon the environment and the security and freedom of people.

Government of the so-called Western democratic nations can be controlled, to some degree, by the citizens of those nations by either lobbying, the law, or the ballot box. But it is very difficult if not impossible for citizens to control transnational corporations and globalist economic agencies such as GATT, APEC, or NAFTA. They are highly undemocratic. Although they affect our lives and destinies, and indeed the fate of life on Earth, we the ordinary people have not and will not be given a chance to vote on their existence. For this reason we support the principle of *national sovereignty*: nations and states should have national independence and legal and political autonomy. Powerful nations and states should not be able to force less powerful nations and states to adopt policies contrary to the general will of the citizenry of those less-powerful nations.

In a globalized world, however, all of this is changed. Samuel Francis (1994) has noted that the World Trade Organization's (WTO) "Dispute Settlement Panels," composed of WTO experts, will have the final authority to overturn U.S. laws and policies (and the laws and policies of other signatory nations) if they violate WTO rules. Both NAFTA and APEC will have the power to review state and federal laws to ensure that they do not pose any barrier to free trade. The NAFTA agreement means that U.S. companies can take legal action against many Canadian social and environmental policies on the grounds that they restrict free trade by constituting unfair competition. There must be no discrimination against foreign investment and no preference arrangements to assist local industries and employment. Subsidies for development of renewable energy, by definition based upon local resources, are forbidden.

John Wiseman (1995) has noted that corporations have used NAFTA to overcome controls on the introduction of rBGH genetically engineered hormones in dairy cattle, a range of recycling measures, food safety regulations, and conservation programs. Even restrictions on tobacco advertising have been challenged. Economic globalization has not improved the economic welfare of the Canadian people. Since the signing of the Free Trade Agreement (FTA) in 1988, over 550,000 Canadian workers have lost their jobs, with new employment being mainly in low-paid, part-time, and casual jobs. This is not due primarily to recession, Wiseman argues, as surveys show that NAFTA has been the real reason why Canadian firms have been relocating to Mexico and the United States. Wiseman also notes that NAFTA has served as an ideological justification for privatization and a wind-down of the Canadian welfare state, with $25 billion being slashed from welfare budgets in the last five years. This attitude of brutal anti-sociality is well summed up by a quotation Wiseman takes from the 1995 Chairman of the Canadian Manufacturers Association:

All Canadian governments must test all their policies to determine whether or not they reinforce or impede competitiveness. If a policy is anti-competitive, dump it. . . . the social programs we've come to depend on . . . we're going to have to abandon. We're going to be shutting down hospitals, like it or lump it. (Wiseman, 1995, 25)

In 1992, the United States passed their Marine Mammal Protection Act. This Act stipulated that tuna caught in dolphin unfriendly nets could not be imported into the United States. Mexico challenged this before the GATT Dispute Resolution Panel on the grounds that it was a non-tariff trade barrier. Mexico won; free trade won over democratic environmental conservation. The European Union is set to challenge a range of U.S. federal and state laws relating to environmental and safety standards as constituting non-tariff trade barriers, such as limits on the lead content of wine and gas guzzler taxes implemented to create incentives for people to buy fuel-efficient cars. The allowable level of pesticide residue in Australian food imports can also be challenged under GATT standards as being too strict and therefore constituting a non-tariff restrictive trade practice. Consequently, Australians must accept imported fruit with higher pesticide levels than deemed satisfactory by the Australian Parliament (Kennedy, 1995).

One would expect the economic merits of globalizaton and free trade to be overwhelming given the Hitlerite power that global organizations have usurped. However, there is an environmental and social case against free trade that we regard as decisive. Herman Daly has noted that more than half of all international trade involves the simultaneous import and export of essentially the same goods (Daly, 1993). Thus we have the absurdity, nay, the economic treason, of Australia being flooded with Brazilian orange concentrate while 3,000 Australian farmers, who could supply fresh local fruit, crash into bankruptcy. Indeed, in Victoria Australia, citrus farmers in December 1996 burnt their "surplus" Valencia orange trees, because Australians (by virtue of product restructuring, not necessarily by way of choice) were drinking seven times more Brazilian orange concentrate than Australian fresh juice. The Brazilian citrus industry does not consist of native farmers making good: it is largely transnationally owned fruit corporations which have planted orchards after extensive clearing of rainforests (Kennedy, 1995).

Ravi Batra, in his book *The Myth of Free Trade* (Batra, 1993), notes that since 1950 the world's population has more than doubled while global economic activity has quadrupled, but between 1950 and 1990, trade grew 1.5 times faster than the pace of the increase in economic activity (Batra, 1993, 220). Trade is therefore a bigger polluter than industrialization. For example, air transport has made international trade in perishable foods possible, but at the cost of dumping millions of tons of jet fuel wastes into the atmosphere. Air borne trade alone emitted into the skies 2.1 million tons of nitrogen oxides in 1990 (Batra, 1993, 223). It makes no environmental sense for one firm to make (steel) nuts in Asia, another bolts in Europe, and a third firm to put them together in the United States (Batra, 1993, 228). Batra, an economist who had previously supported free trade, sums up: "The moral of the story is that international trade is a vast source of pollution, and the environmental costs of global commerce have been totally ignored by orthodox economists." (Batra, 1993, 224). Economic globalization will accelerate the destruction of the biosphere.

Many internationalists and supporters of the concept of a world government and a "new world order" have done so because they believe that internationalism will promote peace. Does free trade promote peace? An argument could be made that this is so in Europe, but then again it could be argued with equal force that it is peace which promotes free trade. However, the realities of APEC are far from the naive view of the Asian region adopted by the former Australian Prime Minister Paul Keating and Senator Gareth Evans, former Foreign Affairs Minister. Brian Toohey (1995) notes that Indonesia still kills dissidents in Aceh, Irian Jaya, and East Timor, and China is using its new-found trading wealth to expand its nuclear arsenal and to produce biological and chemical weapons. Australia even accepts Chinese imports produced with forced prison labor in Chinese gulags. Something of an arms race is developing in the ASEAN region where nations such as Brunei, Indonesia, Malaysia, the Philippines, Singapore, and Thailand are acquiring weapons because of perceived threats from China and Japan (Richardson, 1995). In a free trade world there is nothing wrong with this—even in countries selling nuclear weapons to buyers with the most money—providing the free market rules.

The image of a free trade world is perhaps best captured by this fact: the Textile, Clothing and Footwear Union of Australia estimates that there are more than 300,000 home-based workers in the Australian garment industry, most from non-English speaking backgrounds, working in sweatshops and garages at piece rates. Asian children as young as seven work late at night on sewing machines, in the name of efficiency and global competition (Le Grand, 1995).

Another sorry example of the sort of world the twenty-first century looks like becoming on the "business-as-usual-scenario" is supplied by the Ok Tedi mining disaster in Papua New Guinea. Ralph Nader and many others view this as "the biggest single mining devastation of the environment in the world." (Wilson, 1995, 3). Indeed, the Melbourne law firm of Slater and Gordon filed a $4 billion compensation claim in 1994 on behalf of the Fly and Ok Tedi River communities, against BHP (a 60 percent owner of the mine) in the Victorian Supreme Court. The Papua New Guinean landowners saw their environment as having been destroyed by the 80,000 tonnes of waste a day that had been dumped into the Ok Tedi River. There was no question in this dispute that at least some environmental damage was done. A compensation package of $120 million was prepared for the Fly and Ok Tedi River communities by BHP. The PNG government drafted legislation to make other general compensation claims a criminal offense. The plaintiffs were to be transformed into criminals at the stroke of a computer key. The draft legislation was prepared by BHP lawyers (Hawes, 1995, 2). BHP was found in contempt of court on September 19, 1995, by the Victorian Supreme Court under Justice Cummins because of its involvement in preparing the Eighth Supplemental Agreement covering Ok Tedi.

BHP's point of view has been expressed by its General Manager P. J. Lavers (Lavers, 1995 16). BHP claimed that it was too costly to build a tailing retention system in an earthquake prone area receiving 10 meters of rainfall per annum. So the only option in their opinion was the controlled discharge of tailing. The company recognized that it did not apply the same standards that it would apply in, for example, Australia, but argued that PNG conditions are not Australian conditions. Finally, as BHP's chief executive John Prescott put it: "In the final analysis it is the sovereign government of PNG that has the accountability and responsibility in this matter. They are responsible for determining in the end whether the circumstances are appropriate" (Wilson, 1995, 3). The then PNG Prime Minister, Sir Julius Chan, said that PNG would not allow foreigners "to start setting the price of what Papua New Guinea can afford to pay in compensation because the total future, the whole future, of Papua New Guinea's development strategy is relying on how best we can come up with a format to deal with this sort of situation" (Stevens, 1995; Wilson, 1995).

Peter Fries (1995) has said in commentary on this situation that "With a crumbling economy, foreign exchange reserves depleted (20 per cent of which came from Ok Tedi), the World Bank and the International Monetary Fund on its back, and civil unrest, any change to the revenue stream from the mine would be fatal for PNG" (Fries, 1995). Having adopted a desire to follow Western paths of development, PNG has locked itself into this situation. BHP argues with the impeccable logic of the economic rationalist; all of their actions do make sense from the perspective of profit maximization. In terms, however, of the preservation of human communities and the environment, its actions were appalling. However, there is nothing specifically condemnatory in BHP's activities as it is merely following the inner logic of a transnational corporation. It is a good economic agent.

Another instance in which we can see the deadly working of the logic of economic rationalism is the present privatization of government and community resources that is occurring throughout the world. Although it is not often stated as such, privatization is a form of economic liberalization and deregulation. It is also, by the backdoor, a form of economic globalization—the surrender of local assets and resources to the internationalists and transnational corporations who are nearly always the only buyers of these assets. Privatization is the idea that government assets, functions, and businesses should be sold off or contracted out to private enterprise. Supposedly, any function undertaken by private enterprise in the free market, under conditions of competition, will be done more efficiently so consumers benefit by reduced prices and/or an improved quality of service. This idea has been given a theoretical defense by the Australian economist Fred Hilmer, director of the University of New South Wales Graduate School of Management, a director of Macquarie Bank, Westfield Holdings and deputy chairman of the brewing giant Fosters. We shall consider the Australian examples here because in many respects the Australian examples illustrate the absurdity of economic rationalist principles better than any other examples that one can find in the world. Perhaps because of their massive Australian inferiority complex, Australia's ruling elites feel that they must embrace more absurd doctrines and make bigger mistakes that anyone else in the world. Not content to drag the unwilling public over the edge of the cliff, the elite in Australia compete with each other to hit the bottom first.

Hilmer chaired a Committee of Inquiry, along with Mark Rayner and Geoffrey Taperell, into national competition policy which resulted in the report *National Competition Policy* (Report by the Independent Committee of Inquiry, August, 1993). The idea here was to divide the public sector into "business" and "non-business" activities and then open business activities to competition. This would apply to government boards and departments supplying drinking water, gas, and running railways. Most of these enterprises are owned by the State governments and make substantial profits, which the States use. National competition policy would see the private corporations that came to run essential services, taxed, so that the (Australian) federal government would receive a slice of the profits. This scheme was warmly embraced by big business in Australia. BHP's chief executive John Prescott—whose remarks on the Ok Tedi disaster were quoted previously—said at a joint meeting in Melbourne on March 21, 1995, of ten of Australia's most powerful industry groups, that the Hilmer revolution would help eliminate "the unnecessary costs of doing business in Australia." As for these "unnecessary costs," the (Australian) Industry Commission—a major exponent of economic rationalism in Australia—has estimated that 30 percent of government services will be contracted out to the private sector, including basic instrumentalities such as police, prisons, hospitals, and fire protection agencies.

Australia is embracing the privatization ideal more eagerly than many other countries. For example, it has looked into the privatization of its airports, an idea that has not been widely accepted around the world. The privatization of FAC (Federal Airports Corporation) was announced on May 4, 1994, as part of the federal Labor government's White Paper package *Working Nation*. It was based on the idea that airports in different cities or even the same city can and should *compete*. This absurd assumption is made even though it is widely known by the knowledgeable, that aircraft traffic is driven by *destinations*, not by what an airport can offer by way of services. Airports are complementary, not competitive, serving different sectors of the aviation industry. Privatization will mean that foreign transnational corporations—the only ones with the financial capital to acquire Australian airports—will gain control of all profitable airports and the benefits of investments made by FAC will not be enjoyed by Australians. As profitability rather than community service becomes the criteria for the existence of airports, regional and smaller airports will face huge increases in charges or be forced to close down. Environmental, security, and safety standards may be compromised in the name of profitability.

Australia may also adopt the Hilmer-style revolution in the university system. Hilmer himself has suggested applying national competition policies to Australian universities so that universities would directly compete against each other for students. The so-called "Hoare Report," submitted to the (then) Minister for Employment Education and Training on December 12, 1995, recommends giving universities more power to make enterprise bargaining agreements and to overhaul awards to remove tenure ratios.

Hilmer reforms were supported by the (Australian) Industry Commission Report, *The Growth and Revenue Implications of the Hilmer Reforms* (1995), which made the unjustified claim that consumers would benefit by "an increase in average household income of $1,500." These estimates were for a ten year period, the base year for many sectors being 1990, so that much of the supposed reform has already occurred. The economist John Quiggin (1995) has shown that the Industry Commission has overestimated economic benefits without including any of the costs. However, even on the Industry Commission's own model, it was shown that reforms would result in a 20 percent rise in water prices for city residents and a 19 percent rise in rail fares over a ten year period. On self-interest considerations alone, there is no reason for Australian consumers to accept these privatization measures.

The most radical changes with respect to privatization in Australia have come with the Jeff Kennett government in the state of Victoria. To deal with the state debt, accumulated because of mismanagement of the State Bank (a situation that also occurred, "conspiracy theorists," note, in South Australia as well), 40,000 government employees have been retrenched along with thousands more in other government enterprises. Jeff Kennett said in his speech to the Italian Chamber of Commerce in August 1992 that: "Approximately 300,000 are employed in the Victorian public sector for public service. On top of that there's all the councils around the state, that's another 200,000 employed. So in real terms we have 500,000 people working for us . . . who don't produce a dollar of wealth. . . . We can't afford them" (Office of the Premier, Victoria Australia, 1992). The Olsen government in South Australia is following this advice, cutting spending on hospitals and health services, slashing education and police budgets, reducing public transport, and selling off state assets accumulated at great cost over generations, in a great fire sale.

Water privatization is underway or is being proposed in most developed and less developed countries in the world. First-world transnational corporations are falling over each other to own or manage the drinking water of less developed Asian and South American countries. This trend is supported by globalist entities such as the World Bank, which uses nongovernment investment as a criterion for approving loans for water development projects. The World Bank also supports privatization in the First World: it actively pushed for the privatization of South Australia's water management. Why have the internationalists and globalists moved to snap up water utilities? The reason is, in economic jargon, that consumers have a perfectly inelastic demand curve, meaning that they are not able to greatly alter their level of consumption in response to price rises. Controlling water resources is, in the long term, a license for printing money.

The privatization of water utilities in the United Kingdom came through the U.K. Water Act 1989. Friends of the Earth (FOE) and Greenpeace have publicly campaigned against the privatization of Britain's water, their criticisms centering upon water quality and the discharge of domestic and industrial wastes into rivers. The European Court of Justice ruled in 1992 that the British Government had failed to bring British drinking water up to the European Community standard for nitrates. FOE and Greenpeace claim that the British Government has shielded the water industry from prosecution for not meeting EU water quality standards. Even so, the big privatized water companies have been prosecuted 157 times for river pollution since privatization in 1989.

A deterioration in British river quality has occurred. In 1980, 3,900 kilometers of rivers were classified as badly polluted; by 1990 it was 4,680 kilometers.

In 1981, 12,600 water pollution incidents in England and Wales were reported; in 1991 there were 28,143 incidents with only 282 resulting in prosecution. Greenpeace has also noted that 5,046 tonnes of toxic pollutants a year flow from factories into the seas through more than 12,000 government-licensed discharge pipes. Greenpeace has also publicized the fact that a government environment white paper has stated that "the rivers have to be used for waste disposal by industry." And indeed they are. The British Government's own figures, quoted in Greenpeace literature, show that 40 percent of toxic metals entering the northeast Atlantic come from British rivers with 84 percent of this being polychlorinated biphenyls (PCBs), toxic chemicals that endanger marine life.

Research by the University of New South Wales indicates that since the privatization of water services in the United Kingdom in 1989, domestic water charges are up an average of 67 percent with increases of up to 122 percent for sewage and 108 percent for water. Disconnections because people cannot pay their bills were up 50 percent, and infrastructural investment levels have not kept pace with the agreed schedules. Companies have passed to consumers the burden of these (inadequate) future investment costs. They have also passed on the following costs, detailed by *The Guardian* January 6, 1995:

The Chairmen of Britain's 10 privatised water companies have received salary rises of up to 571 per cent and shared in multi-million pound share and pension packages in the four years since the companies left the public sector and water bills began rising sharply. Twenty five senior water company directors became at least £500,000 each better off as a result of privatisation—including five new millionaires—after sharing in executive share option schemes and enhanced pensions totaling £20 million, according to a new analysis by the Labour party . . . The five senior directors, executive chairmen or chief executives, whom Labour calculated to have made at least £1 million more than they would otherwise have done since privatisation are: Southern's William Courtney whose share option, pension and pay package is worth an extra £1,250,000; another Southern director, Francis Midmer, with £1.1 million; the ex-chairman of Welsh Water, John Elfed John, whose total additional package was £1.7 million; North-West's first chairman, Denis Grove, with £1.1 million, and the late Sir Roy Watts, chairman of Thames Water (£1 million), who drowned in the Thames in mysterious circumstances in 1993. (quoted from Shearman et al., forthcoming, 104)

In New Zealand privatization and economic rationalism have led to 70 percent of wage earners earning less than $NZ 27,000 per year. A kilogram of chops in a country that is proud of its sheep farming costs $NZ 9 and cheese $NZ8.50 a kilogram in a land with a highly efficient dairy industry. Thirty percent of children in New Zealand live in families with incomes below the poverty line. Ninety-five thousand people are on hospital waiting lists, which often necessitates a 2–3 year wait for surgery. Many people die waiting. In Germany, Europe's miracle economy, unemployment is at the same level, as of February 1997, as it was when Hitler came to power—12.2 percent (Franchetti and Smith, 1997). Japan still struggles to free its economy from the stagnation that has characterized it throughout the 1990s. An atmosphere of economic gloom and social decay is beginning to grip many major Western cities. James Walter gives the following description of his return to London in 1990:

I found a city transformed. It wasn't just the disappearance of civility from the public domain, the ubiquity of beggars, the tent cities of homeless in Lincolns Inn fields, the rubbish in the gutters, the pot holes in the roads. It was also the chaotic way in which the material aspects of urban life—phones, water, gas, transport—were managed, by private bodies with limited accountability (despite their vaunted "citizen's" charters), and no central coordination. This was a new frontier: a city in which commitment to the public weal had apparently been withdrawn. And it was a city that no longer worked well. (Walter, 1996, 3–4)

A concern that economic globalization has gone too far and is now beginning to have destabilizing effects has been expressed by a number of authorities, from across the political spectrum. It is worthwhile to survey this opinion here. Robert Heilbroner and William Milberg, in their book *The Crisis of Vision in Modern Economic Thought* (Heilbroner and Milberg, 1995), recognize that economic globalization will have destabilizing effects:

This "globalization" of production carries unsettling implications for all the advanced capitalisms, including the lowering of social, environmental, and labor standards through the forces of market competition, and the rise of newly industrialized countries as major rivals for market shares. In a related development, the volume of international financial flows into the United States alone has grown to previously unimaginable levels. On a worldwide scale, this internationalization of finance seriously limits the ability of advanced nations to carry out domestic fiscal and monetary policies that are not compatible with the "will" of a stateless world financial market. On a still longer front, world population growth threatens to bring another billion people into existence within a generation, raising the specter of large immigration pressures for the advanced world, with serious consequences whether the flows are accepted or denied. Ecological problems on a global scale are already on the agenda of world affairs, and seem certain to increase as a result of heat and other emissions. And everywhere the forces of ethnic and national unrest are apparent, together with sporadic terrorism. (Heilbroner and Milberg, 1995, 121)

Robert Harvey, in his book *The Return of the Strong: The Drift to Global Disorder* (Harvey, 1995), also recognizes that "the globalization of capitalism carries with it the seeds of worldwide political instability" (Harvey, 1995, 258). The dust jacket of the book states that:

Economically, global capitalism may be at a stage not far different from national capitalism at the end of the last century: its authoritarian nature, disregard for national and personal sensitivities, enormous power and incompetence could give rise to a perilous reaction. The parallel is with the complacency of the Edwardian era, which foreshadowed four decades of war, revolution and economic turbulence. The major powers at the end of this century, as Cold War memories fade, exude the same self-congratulation as at the end of the last. Unless action is taken we will gaze upon the same horizon of global horrors as our great-grandfathers, this time through a nuclear haze. The world is probably a more dangerous place than it has been in nearly half a century.

The principal cause of this is decline of the nation-state:

The old nation-state has been bypassed, and no longer controls the huge flows of international trade, investment and finance that determine the fate of nations today. Nation-states are increasingly democratic and responsible to the people: the giant interests that manage these flows are not, and are more powerful. A world in which people, far from gaining control over their own destinies through the spread of liberal democracy, are in fact losing it through the globalization of non-responsible economic forces is surely one moving in a dangerous direction. In fact, it is in the very same direction that the communists moved for more than 70 years. (Harvey, 1995, 206–7)

Harvey believes that "Doomsday—global anarchy, the state of nature, where the strong prey on the weak unchecked . . . is a real possibility" (Harvey, 1995, 327). Ethan B. Kapstein has also expressed concern about the social consequences of economic globalization, seeing a new crisis of capitalism emerging, a "failure of today's advanced global capitalism to keep spreading the wealth" (Kapstein, 1996, 16). Moreover:

The global economy is leaving millions of disaffected workers in its train. Inequality, unemployment and endemic poverty have become its handmaidens. Rapid technological change and heightening international competition are fraying the job markets of the major industrialized countries. At the same time systematic pressures are curtailing every government's ability to respond with new spending. Just when working people most need the nation-state as a buffer from the world economy, it is abandoning them. (Kapstein, 1996, 16)

Lester Thurow (1996) observes in his book *The Future of Capitalism* that many successful societies, such as ancient Rome and classical China, have existed with inequalities. None, however, had both inequalities and democracy, which Thurow regards as an incompatible and potentially explosive mixture. Thurow recognizes the possibility of a "new dark age" with the government sector collapsing due to the erosion of the taxation base necessary to maintain the social infrastructure.[4] However, he believes that capitalism will not implode as communism did: "Without a viable competitor to which people can rush if they are disappointed with how capitalism is treating them, capitalism cannot self-destruct" (Thurow, 1996, 325). He completely ignores the possibility of social collapse or anarchy occurring. Nevertheless, even more conventional thinkers recognize the possibility of a global economic meltdown occurring. James Dale Davidson and Sir William Rees-Mogg, in their book *Blood in the Streets*, state that "the world financial system is out of control. It does not have any ultimate standard of value, such as gold provided during the gold standard period. If one assumes that a high proportion of the sovereign debt will never be repaid, then the world banking system is collectively insolvent. If they faced reality in debt provision, the banks would topple over like dominoes" (Davidson and Rees-Mogg, 1989, 12). In their book, *The Great Reckoning*, Davidson and Rees-Mogg also predict that a financial armageddon, a great reckoning, a settling of accounts will occur: "The end, when it comes, will not only reveal the insolvency of many individuals and corporations, it may also bring bankruptcy to the welfare state and widespread breakdown of authority within political economies. . . . More than you may now imagine, you are vulnerable to financial, economic, and political collapse" (Davidson and Rees-Mogg, 1992, 12–13). As with most prophets of doom, Davidson and Rees-Mogg were in error in their prediction of "doom-soon." At the end of the 1990s, we are only beginning to see some of their predictions coming true. The possibility of a new great depression is already beginning to be discussed (Palley, 1996; Levine, 1996; Tough et al., 1996).

Kenichi Ohmae, as we saw at the beginning of this section, is an internationalist who celebrates the increasing economic irrelevance of the nation-state and the rise of regional economies, interconnected in the global market place. In his book, *The End of the Nation State* (Ohmae, 1995), he offers a number of objections to Samuel Huntington's "clash of civilization thesis." He observes correctly, but irrelevantly, the truth of Huntington's thesis, that clashes have and will occur within the same civilization. Ohmae's main objection though is this:

Even more important than such cultural differences within a civilization, and what Huntington's line of thought leaves out, is the issue of historical context. The particular dissolution of bipolar, "great power" discipline that so greatly affects us today is not taking place in the 1790s or the 1890s, but the 1990s. And that means it is taking place in a world whose peoples, no matter how far-flung geographically or disparate culturally, are all linked to much the same sources of global information. The immediacy and completeness of their access may vary, of course, and governments may try to impose restrictions and control. Even if they do, however, the barriers will not last forever, and leakages will occur all along the way. Indeed, the basic fact of linkage to global flows of information is a—perhaps, *the*—central, distinguishing fact of our moment in history. Whatever the civilization to which a particular group of people belongs, they now get to hear about the way other groups of people live, the kinds of products they buy, the changing focus of their tastes and preferences as consumers, and the styles of life they aspire to lead. (Ohmae, 1995, 15)

Ohmae seems to ignore the prospect—unpleasant for his globalism—that the free exchange of information may bring war, instead of peace, and instability, instead of stability, even in a borderless world. Conflict may develop between "regional economies" or even within particular economies. Sir James Goldsmith, in his book *The Trap* (Goldsmith, 1995a), has developed an argument along such lines, which although framed within the conceptual bounds of the nation-state model, is still applicable to Ohmae's borderless world. Goldsmith's argument against global free trade is simple, yet powerful: "When the same technology is available but labor in one country costs [more than forty times more than in another] the sharing of value-added between capital and labor is radically altered. And the consensus that emerged painfully in the West, as a result of strikes, lockouts and political debate, is shattered" (Goldsmith, 1995a, 21). China, for example, has 120 million unemployed people forming a free floating population as large as Japan itself. The borderless world must integrate four billion people at once into the global supermarket, a proposal Goldsmith rightly observes as "blind utopianism" (Goldsmith, 1995b, 40).

George Soros, a billionaire who made his fortune from speculation on the world currency markets, believes "the untrammelled intensification of laissez-faire capitalism and the spread of market values into all areas of life is endangering our open and democratic society. The main enemy of the open society . . . is no longer the communist but the capitalist threat" (Soros, 1997, 26). The problem here lies with orthodox neo-classical economics, which takes supply and demand as independently given. This assumption is false in Soros' opinion, certainly as far as the financial markets are concerned. The shape of supply and demand curves in financial markets cannot be taken as given, as these curves "incorporate expectations about events that are shaped by those expectations" and, rather than tend towards equilibrium, "prices continue to fluctuate relative to the expectations of buyers and sellers" (Soros, 1997, 27). Prices often exist at far-from-equilibrium conditions and if they return to equilibrium at all the equilibrium reached is not the same as that that would have existed counterfactually without the intervening period of time. The empirical irrelevance of the equilibrium concept means, Soros notes, that orthodox economics cannot justify its core presupposition that the free market leads to an optimal allocation of resources. However, it is faulty market values upon which the modern world is increasingly being based:

As the market mechanism has extended its sway, the fiction that people act on the basis of a given set of non-market values has become progressively more difficult to maintain. Unsure of what they stand for, people increasingly rely on money as the criterion of value. What is more expensive is considered better. People deserve respect and admiration because they are rich. What used to be a medium of exchange has usurped the place of fundamental values, reversing the relationship postulated by economic theory. What used to be professions have turned into businesses. The cult of success has replaced a belief in principles. Society has lost its anchor. . . . Our global society lacks the institutions and mechanisms necessary for its preservation, but there is no political will to bring them into existence. I blame the prevailing attitude, which holds that the unhampered pursuit of self-interest will bring about an eventual international equilibrium. I believe this confidence is misplaced. I believe that the concept of the open society, which needs institutions to protect it, may provide a better guide to action. As things stand, it does not take very much imagination to realize that the global open society that prevails at present is likely to prove a temporary phenomenon. (Soros, 1997, 27)

The potential for economic breakdown and the resulting tidal waves of social unrest is intrinsic to the capitalist economic system (Smith et al., forthcoming). Worse, attempting to run an economy based upon a flawed theory such as neo-classical economics (for a review of criticisms see Smith et al., 1997) will inevitably lead to large-scale problems.

Not only does the global capitalism of the borderless world face the problem of integrating the existing population of the world into a harmonious economic system, but it must also deal with the problem of technologically generated unemployment. Jeremy Rifkin has discussed this problem in depth in his book *The End of Work* (Rifkin, 1995). Rifkin begins his book with the problem of global unemployment: over 800 million people are unemployed or underemployed, a figure that is now over one billion people (Smith et al., forthcoming). In this situation a third industrial revolution is occurring by virtue of rapid developments in computers and information technology, in which the twenty-first century will see nearly fully automated production. The service industry is also contributing to this pool of unemployed. Labor-saving technologies and corporate restructuring in the single month of January 1994 resulted in America's largest employers laying off over 108,000 workers, most being in the service sector (Rifkin, 1995, xvi). More than 75 percent of the industrial labor force of most nations performs repetitive tasks that machines will be able to replace. In the United States alone, over 90 million jobs in a workforce of 124 million could, in principle, be replaced (Rifkin, 1995, 5) so that "massive unemployment of a kind never before experienced seems all but inevitable in the coming decades" (Rifkin, 1995, 5). The reason for this is that this third industrial revolution is based on the replacement of the human mind. This may be done by "re-engineering," making organizations computerized and in turn enabling entire structures of management and jobs to be eliminated. In the United States this could lead to the loss of up to 25 million jobs. Rifkin does not discuss in any depth how the World Wide Web and the information superhighway may eliminate jobs. Imagine that you wished to study philosophy, mathematics, or physics at university and you live in a small regional city. Why study at a small regional university in your city when the World Wide Web already offers to some extent a "virtual university" that would improve your employment prospects?

The major challenge to employment stability comes from the new technologies of genetic engineering and artificial intelligence. Genetically engineered vanilla can be produced for less than $US 25 per pound compared to natural vanilla which sells for $US 1,200 a pound. As Rifkin notes: "The export of vanilla beans accounts for more than 10 percent of the total annual export earnings of Madagascar. In Comoros, vanilla represents two thirds of the country's export earnings" (Rifkin, 1995, 124–25). Further technological advances raise the possibility of molecular farms that eliminate orthodox agriculture altogether and replace conventional food by indoor tissue-culture food production based on biomass crops, artificially flavored by genetically engineered flavors. Thinking machines—the duplication of consciousness in a thinking robot—have the potential to replace humans in any job if they can be constructed. In summary:

We are rapidly approaching a historic crossroad in human history. Global corporations are now capable of producing an unprecedented volume of goods and services with an even smaller workforce. The new technologies are bringing us into an era of near worker-less production at the very moment in world history when population is surging to unprecedented levels. The clash between rising population pressures and falling job opportunities will shape the geopolitics of the emerging high-tech global economy well into the next century. (Rifkin, 1995, 207)

Rifkin's own solution to the "end of work" problem lies beyond the market place in the independent or volunteer sector. Presumably, this sector will be financed by the transnational corporations—as governments would no longer have the taxation base to finance this. But why should the very people who have thrown millions upon the scrapheap of history contribute to a living wage? Rifkin totally underestimates the ruthlessness of international capitalism, which sees human life and the natural world as mere resources for exploitation and profits as everything (Smith et al., 1997). As Rifkin's own solution is inadequate (Smith et al., forthcoming) we are left then with his more realistic, pessimistic conclusion:

If massive unemployment of a kind unknown in history were to occur as a result of the sweeping replacement of machines for human labor, then the chances of developing a compassionate and caring society and a world view based on transformation of the human spirit are unlikely. The more likely course would be widespread social upheaval, violence on an unprecedented scale, and open warfare, with the poor lashing out at each other as well as the rich elites who control the global economy. (Rifkin, 1995, 247–48)

As Rifkin notes, in Europe (and perhaps soon in the United States), those who have been made redundant by the global economy and the new technologies have joined criminal gangs or else fascist and neo-Nazi groups, which blame Jews for the rising unemployment. Kapstein observes that fascist and neo-Nazi groups are rising as a counter to globalism (Kapstein, 1996, 37). This is bitterly ironic, as the Australian Jewish social commentator Eva Cox has observed:

The stimulus for the establishment of the modern welfare state was the rise of fascism and communism arising from the depression of the 1930s. Europe, America and Australia had shown signs of social disintegration as veterans from the war joined private armies to protest against unemployment and poverty. The seeds of fascism fell on some fertile ground. While Germany stands out as the worst example of totalitarianism, there were fascist-type militias and parties in many countries. The welfare state, Western governments believed, would prevent 'it' ever happening again. (Cox, 1995, 44–45)

History seems set to repeat itself.

Let us draw together the threads of the argument of this section. In the previous section we examined technological and ecological mechanisms that may lead to a breakdown of established order and the destruction of modernity. Here we have focused on economic forces—primarily the juggernaut of economic globalization—which are allegedly leading to the economic irrelevance of the nation-state and the creation of a borderless world with the free flow of individuals, information, and capital. We do not doubt that the process of globalization as described by Ohmae and others is occurring at a rapid pace. However, we do *not* believe that this process will bring peace, harmony, and economic well-being to the majority of people in both the developed and developing world. On the contrary, economic globalization and the widescale application of economic rationalist doctrines are contributing to increased environmental pollution, higher unemployment, and the breakdown of communities. We illustrated this with a discussion of privatization and its social impact. The present authors are not alone in their concern with the potential instabilities seemingly intrinsic to the global economic system, and in this section a number of authorities were quoted who share our concerns. Economic globalization and the new technologies have built-in "revenge effects." Both forces integrate the world and create expectations of the good affluent life for billions of people. However, if the authorities quoted here are correct, these expectations will not be met. This will create a very dangerous situation with the prospects of race riots, terrorism, the revival of fascism and neo-Nazism, and widespread social breakdown—a global meltdown—as outlined earlier in this chapter. In this section and the previous one, we have outlined the mechanisms of the coming anarchy, the forces that will break down civilized order and lead us to "Doomsday—global anarchy, the state of nature, where the strong prey on the weak unchecked" (Harvey, 1995, 327). We believe that this breakdown will occur because humanity is facing an overload of problems and the Earth itself is facing "planetary overload" (McMichael, 1993). The economic, ecological, and technological problems we face interact in a complex non-linear fashion and in such systems it is only to be expected that in the end, chaos rules (Gleick, 1987).

CONCLUSION: THE STATE OF THE ARGUMENT

This concludes our outline and general defense of the global meltdown thesis, the thesis of the doomsday of civilized order. Obviously, in this book alone we cannot "conclusively" defend such a broad and comprehensive thesis. In our previous book, *Healing a Wounded World* (Smith et al., 1997), we discussed and defended the limits to growth thesis. To attempt to fully justify each of the threads of our argument with a full length empirically supported study would require dozens of volumes. We believe that the works we have summarized here do in fact supply such a justification. Treated each as individual pieces in a picture puzzle, each placed in order produces a completed picture that shows the future to be terrifying—not merely because of the potential rivers of blood, and darkness, death, and destruction—but also due to the seeming inevitability of the remorseless working of things. It is as if the human drama is a cosmic movie viewed by malevolent demigods who have left us with no escape from our own hubris. As Whitehead has observed:

Let me here remind you that the essence of dramatic tragedy is not unhappiness. It resides in the solemnity of the remorseless working of things. This inevitableness of destiny can only be illustrated in terms of human life by incidents which in fact involve unhappiness. For it is only by them that the futility of escape can be made evident in the drama. This remorseless inevitableness is what pervades scientific thought. The laws of physics are the decrees of fate. (Whitehead, 1962, 15–16)

In the following chapter we shall support the central thesis of this work through a consideration of the case study of Australia. Australia is obviously the part of the world that we know best—we live there! Australia is also thought to have, at least by many people not living there, a relatively unpolluted environment. It is allegedly a successful multicultural and multiracial society. Consequently, Australia is an ideal test case for the global meltdown thesis. In *Immigration and the Social Contract* (Tanton, et al., 1996) we advanced this thesis through the case study of the United States. In the case of the United States, there is little disagreement that large scale racial problems exist. The situation seems, at least if we can believe the published papers and books of Australia's academics, to be different in Australia. Although Australia's economy is in poor shape (for a review see Smith et al., 1997), Australian society is allegedly cohesive.

Yet if even Australia faces massive environmental destruction and the prospects of social disintegration and turmoil, then what nation-state is safe from the forces of the global meltdown?

NOTES

1. In *Healing a Wounded World* (Smith et al., 1997), we argued that the human population problem, because of carrying capacity considerations, is much more serious than orthodox demographers and population theorists believe. Even a very cautious theorist such as Joel Cohen grants that "the possibility must be considered serious that the number of people on the Earth has reached, or will reach within half a century, the maximum number the Earth can support in modes of life that we and our children and their children will choose to want" (Cohen, 1995, 367). This is a conclusion that a number of other workers in the field have reached (Abernethy, 1993a, b, 1995a; Burke, 1996; Dailey and Ehrlich, 1992; Daily et al., 1994; Ehrlich et al., 1993; Giampietro et al., 1992; Mazur, 1994; Moffett, 1994; Pimental et al., 1994). Michael Tobias is right, in our opinion, in seeing the population problem as "World War III," like "a terminal cancer that corrodes the body from within" (Tobias, 1994, xix) and that "The world is currently in the throes of a mature disease, brought on by both the best and the worst of humanity" (Tobias, 1994, xix–xx), or that "Morality disintegrates on the battlefield, which is where we are now" (Tobias, 1994, xxiii).

This position is based on conventional demographic theory (Abernethy, 1995b). Hern observes though that from the perspective of chaos theory, things may not be so rosy:

We have not yet recognized or acknowledged any negative feedback loops that seriously endanger our survival as a species even though they loom before us. The result is unregulated growth and potentially lethal population instability that degenerates to figurative, literal, and mathematical chaos.

Chaos theory predicts that undamped oscillations proceed to extinction as a function of increasing rates of growth. . . . Small changes in initial conditions, especially in growth rates, may result in large, deterministic, but unpredictable oscillations in future population cycles. Our experience with other biological species and our own recent history should tell us that we are dangerously close to irretrievable chaos if we have not already long since established the pattern that will lead to that result. It is possible that the increase in the human population growth from 0.001% per year to 0.1% per year at the end of the Paleolithic led us to enter a deterministic chaotic regime that spans thousands of years and which we cannot foresee. Is it likely that we will completely escape the ecological restraints experienced by other species? . . . Is it likely that, for humans, there is no limit to the "carrying capacity" of the earth's ecosystem? If there is a limit, how much longer will it take us to arrive at it? . . . What will happen when we do? (Hern, 1990, 33)

Umpleby (1998, 1990) believes that the idea of a steady world population growth rate of 1.7 percent is too slow (see also Bartlett, 1993, 370). The UN Population division's latest biennial analysis, as of December 1996, puts the average rate of growth of world population from 1990 to 1995 as 1.48 percent per year. The previous predicted growth rate was 1.57 percent (Pearce, 1996a, b). It took 70 years from 1880 to 1950 for world population to increase from 1.25 billion to around 2.5 billion, and 37 years from 1950 to 1987 to double yet again (Umpleby, 1988, 122). According to the von Foerster equation (von Foerster et al., 1960), the next doubling of the world population will take 23 years, not the orthodox prediction of 41 years maintained by most demographers. Demographers claim that since the mid-1960s, world population growth rates have been declining, but as Umpleby and others have noted, population growth rates have been such that they have "exceeded a curve based on an assumption of increasing growth rates" (Abernethy, 1993a, 124). As Abernethy observes, demographers may be underestimating world population growth rates for the following reason:

Mathematicians stick with the estimate of the total world population made *closest* to the date that is being estimated; then a comparison of totals at the two dates shows up all of the numerical increase. . . . [However] . . . *demographers adjust the numbers well after the year being estimated is passed.* Demographers then compute the growth rate using the revised base. If the revision of the base was upward, part of the "growth" being calculated gets excluded from the computation: it got lost in the revision. (Abernethy, 1993a, 122–23)

These arguments contrast strongly with the demographic analysis of the Institute for Applied Systems Analysis in Austria, which maintains that today's world population of 5.8 billion is unlikely to double again. It will allegedly peak toward the year 2000, then decline slowly (Coghlan, 1996a). This report, edited by Wolfgang Lutz, examined changes not only in birthrates, but also deathrates, the impact of migration on fertility and mortality. The Institute for Applied Systems Analysis asked experts in fertility, mortality, and migration to produce a total of 4,000 scenarios. Sixty-seven percent of the scenarios suggest that the world population will not double again. World population will peak at 10.6 billion at around 2080, fall to 10.35 billion by the end of the twenty-first century, and continue to fall after that. One scenario has world population rising to 23 billion by 2100. Another, because of disease and falling birthrates, sees world population reaching four billion. Lutz estimates that the chance of this happening is less than one percent.

Clearly all such models are only as good as the probability data on which they are based. Lutz's scenario offers us a world population of about one billion people less than many conservative estimates. We do not gain much comfort from that: a world of 5.8 billion people is already producing enormous environmental damage. Further, as F. MacIntyre of the University of Amsterdam has observed, "not a single professional demographer in the past three centuries has believed that the population could double. Remember when the US population was going to level off at 180 million?" (MacIntyre, 1996). This statement may be a slight exaggeration, but the central point is correct.

2. The Ecological Foundation, an environmental group in Delhi, and the United Kingdom Food Group, a coalition of development aid groups, released a report by Devinder Sharma entitled *In the Famine Trap* (October, 1996), examining India's food sustainability. A combination of population pressure, the degradation of arable land, and "India's push to become a food exporter are undermining the country's food security" (Patel, 1996b, 10). The report is rejected by the Indian government, which maintains that production has more than tripled since the "green revolution" of the 1960s. Sharma's concern is with the plateau of productivity in growth that has been reached in the northwest grain states, where population growth is likely to outstrip grain production. The states of Punjab and Haryana have experienced substantial land degradation due to poor water management and crop rotation patterns. The World Bank also found extensive land degradation in this region that is reducing harvests of wheat, rice, and nine other crops by four to six percent per year. The Special Secretary in the Indian Agricultural Ministry, B. K. Taimni, while rejecting the report, *In the Famine Trap*, accepts that approximately ten percent of land in the principal grain-growing regions is degraded (Patel, 1996a).

The problem of agricultural sustainability may not be the exclusive concern of the Third World. According to Pearce (1996c), "Empty reservoirs, dried-up rivers and eroded soils that have haunted southern Europe in recent years could signal a permanent shift in climate" (Pearce, 1996c, 12). The first stages of desertification may already be occurring in Spain, Portugal, Greece, and Italy. The United Nations Food and Agriculture Organization said in May 1996 that "the sustainability of Mediterranean agriculture appears questionable unless urgent and drastic measures are taken" (Pearce, 1996c, 12). Southern Europe could warm by 1.8°C by 2030. The winter rainfall may drop by 10 to 20 percent in the driest parts of the Mediterranean, and the summer rainfall may decline by up to 30 percent (Pearce, 1996c, 13). Water will become a major constraint on the development of Mediterranean cities.

3. For further discussion of the debate over internationalism, globalization, regionalism, and federalism see (Giddens, 1985, 1990; Smith, 1986; Palmer, 1991; Camilleri and Falk, 1992; Johnstone, 1992; Lepsius, 1992; McConkey, 1992; Piccone, 1992, 1995; Woods, 1992; Ruggie, 1993, 1994; Barber, 1994; Calleo, 1994; di Zerega, 1994; Dunn, 1994; Fleming, 1994; Harris, 1994; Hawthorn, 1994; Hont, 1994; Hueglin, 1994; Hurrell, 1994; Kaviraj, 1994; Piccone and Ulmen, 1994, 1995; Tully, 1994; Wallace, 1994; Brown, 1995a; Clark and Graham, 1995; Fingleton, 1995; Gerrans, 1995; Gowan, 1995; Inayatullah and Blaney, 1995; Juergensmeyer, 1995; MacLachlan, 1995; Manzo, 1995; McInerney, 1995; Pauly, 1995; Philpott, 1995; Poole, 1995; Taguieff, 1995; Walzer, ed., 1995; Wellhofer, 1995).

4. Thurow's metaphor of a "new dark age" is appropriate. Elliot (1996) argued that the global economy, manifested at the local level, is a type of feudalism (or more accurately techno-feudalism): "the rich and powerful who live in their walled fortresses, protected by retainers, who avoid paying taxes whenever they can, and demand that the government keep the peasants in check with an increasingly draconian criminal justice system" (Elliot, 1996, 14).

3

The Remorseless Working of Things: Population Collides with Environment

We inhabit a paradox. Our age is tragic, and catastrophe does threaten, but though the future is obscure, it does not come to us inexorable and inescapable. Our tragedy lies in the richness of the available alternatives, and in the fact that so few of them are ever seriously explored. It lies in the rigidity of war machines, the legacies of colonialism, the inflexibilities of the industrial tradition, the solaces of consumerism, the cynicism born of long disappointment, the habits of power. No wonder, given all this, that our age seems not merely tragic but tragic in the classical sense, that despite all possibility, we seem trapped in just that "remorseless working of things" that the Greeks saw as the core of tragedy. (Athanasiou, 1996, 306–7)

Australia is heading for extinction. The world's driest habitable continent, already groaning under the weight of its existing population, is exhausting its soils and may well go the way of Easter Island—where civilization descended into anarchy and eventually collapsed. . . . The noted American biologist Jared Diamond, who has visited Australia every year since 1964 . . . told the meeting [the ANZAAS meeting in Canberra], that modern Australians are consuming the meagre resources of their parched continent so fast that they are heading for extinction. . . . "Australia is the continent whose human population faces the most problematic future," he said. (da Silva, 1996, 9)

WELCOME TO OUR NIGHTMARE

In this chapter we will argue that Jared Diamond's assessment of the ecological fate of Australia is largely correct: Australia is heading toward extinction from ecological overshoot. This conclusion should be of interest in itself for the support it lends to the global meltdown thesis. However, there is an epistemological twist we wish to add to Jared Diamond's position. If Australians can be blissfully facing doom (albeit the doom of future Australians), then what good reasons can people of other nations have in complacency about the fate of their nations and societies? Australia is regarded as something of a "last frontier" by many people who do not live there. It has a relatively small population of just over 18 million people; it has vast mineral wealth and a relatively high standard of living. Australia is also thought to have one of the few successful multiracial and multicultural societies. Yet we shall see in this chapter that Australia is faced with ecological collapse and social chaos. If Australians are not safe from the Global Meltdown, then who can be?

THE AUSTRALIAN POPULATION AND ENVIRONMENT DEBATE

In 1994, the House of Representatives Standing Committee for Long Term Strategies, of the Commonwealth of Australia, published a report entitled *Australia's Population 'Carrying Capacity': One Nation—Two Ecologies* (House of Representatives Standing Committee, 1994a). The inquiry that resulted in this report occurred within the context of a significant academic debate about the relationship between population increase and environmental impact and the sustainability of Australia's ecological resources (Smith, ed., 1991; Fincher, 1991; Dovers et al., 1992; Norton et al., 1994; Flannery, 1994). This report is the result of an investigation into what size population Australia can support. The committee adopted its terms of reference in February 1994 and the report was published in December. The committee was chaired by the Labor Party member of the House of Representatives, Barry Jones (hence "the Jones Inquiry," and "the Jones Report"). The terms of reference for the inquiry were:

- the population that can be supported in Australia within and then beyond the next fifty years, taking account of technology options, possible patterns of resource use, and quality of life considerations;
- the range of community views on population size and its political, social, economic, and environmental significance;
- the provision of a comprehensive information base on which future debates about population growth can be carried out without causing division in the Australian community, and including the provision of an accessible inventory of population research; and
- policy options in relation to population, including the need for national, regional, and local perspectives.

Two hundred and seventy-one submissions were received, with over 90 percent advocating population stability or lower population growth.

The Jones Inquiry itself was a welcome development. Consideration of the impact of Australia's rapidly growing population on the natural environment and on urban quality of life has been neglected by Australian politicians. The 1988 Fitzgerald Enquiry into immigration was dismissive of environmental concerns about population growth (Committee to Advise on Australia's Immigration Policies, 1988). The 1991 report of the Population Issues Committee of the National Population Council (the Withers Report) (Population Issues Committee,

1991) was the first major population report to acknowledge the impact of human population on the environment. It recommended that the government adopt a population policy to influence population growth. The Jones Report also called on the government to adopt a population policy that set out options for long-term population change. This report argued that the policy should seek to stabilize population at a level that takes account of the quality of life Australians want and that is precautionary and ecologically sustainable. The Jones Report called on the government to ensure that long-term population trends are not at the mercy of varying yearly immigration targets (House of Representatives Standing Committee, 1994a, 19).

However, given the short-term political considerations that have often dominated the size of Australia's immigration intake since the 1980s, it remains to be seen whether the present Liberal government, or any government, is capable of constraining immigration intakes. Politicians of both major parties have used the immigration program to try to win the approval of humanitarian and church groups and to secure the political support both of minority ethnic lobby groups and those sectors of industry producing for the home market, such as the housing industry, which lobbies for an ever-growing domestic market. The Jones Report hinted at this: "the *status quo* is that Australia's population is currently growing rapidly (doubling every 30 to 40 years) and the short term political pressures for this to continue seem to be stronger than any countervailing pressures" (House of Representatives Standing Committee, 1994a, 117).

The report critically examined the idea of human "carrying capacity" and considered resource constraints on population growth. In considering the various factors that contribute to the environmental impact of Australia's expanding population, the Committee conducting this inquiry favored the formula, proposed by the CSIRO (Commonwealth Scientific and Industrial Research Organization) in its submission, $I = PLOT$, where I is impact, P is population, L is lifestyle, O is organization, and T is technology. This formula is a slight variation on the better known Paul Ehrlich equation $I = PAT$ where P is population, A is affluence or consumption, and T is technology. In opting for the CSIRO's formula, the committee showed its interest in the O (organization) factor. For example, the organization of space in relation to how population growth is handled appealed to it, and the committee discussed the recent government policy of urban consolidation that has arisen in response to urban expansion.

The Committee was uncomfortable with the anti-population growth sentiment of the bulk of submissions. It was troubled, the report said, by "the prevailing fatalism in many submissions which suggest that changing the migration intake is the only variable in determining Australia's future population, resource use, waste disposal and urban form" (House of Representatives Standing Committee, 1994a, 18–19). The committee thought that techniques of water and waste management should have been considered by those people who made submissions. However, this was an inquiry into population and submission-writers could hardly be blamed for concentrating on population. The Committee's complaint about many submissions suggests that debating changing the way

Australians do things may be more acceptable to politicians than debate on changing the politically sensitive immigration program.

The Committee found that "continuing population growth will lead to more local extinctions of plant and animal species, particularly as much population growth is in areas of above-average biodiversity" (House of Representatives Standing Committee, 1994a, 69). Despite the evidence, presented in the CSIRO's submission to the inquiry, on worsening air and water pollution in large urban areas, the Committee found that submissions that argued that urban-dwellers had experienced declining quality of life as population has grown were based on "subjective" experiences.

The Committee regarded land and water degradation, as well as species loss, in rural areas as totally divorced from population pressures in urban areas. The Committee here ignored the external economic pressures on Australia to export its natural resources as burgeoning urban populations push up both imports and foreign debt while scarce capital resources are eaten up by expanding housing and other infrastructure to cater for Australia's ever-growing population. Despite the Committee's skepticism about declining quality of urban life as a result of population growth, it recommended that quality of life indicators should be col-lected and published by the Australian Bureau of Statistics and that regular population reports, including standard of living and quality of life indicators, should be presented to Parliament.

The Committee considered that if population growth confers any short-to medium-term economic benefits, these are small. It found that there was little evidence on the long-term economic effects of population growth. The Commit-tee remained skeptical of the argument that there is no causal relationship be-tween immigration and unemployment. It noted that unemployment rates among recent migrants in the past two recessions had been over 30 percent. On the question of living costs, the Committee concluded that population growth may impose more costs than benefits on the existing population.

The Jones Inquiry recognized that the Department of Immigration and Eth-nic Affairs is seen to have a client relationship with the large migrant community and consequently to lack objectivity about population issues. The report recom-mended that the political and administrative responsibility for population and immigration should be separated. Responsibility for the population policy, the report recommended, should lie with a Cabinet committee on population. It is surprising that the Jones committee failed to consider the well-known pro-immigration bias of the Bureau of Immigration, Multicultural and Population Research. The report has merely recommended that the Bureau be renamed the Bureau of Population Research and transferred to the Department of Prime Min-ister and Cabinet to service the proposed Cabinet committee on population. In 1996 the Bureau was closed down by the new Howard Liberal government.

Like the 1991 Withers Report, the Jones Report shied away from supporting a population target for Australia. In its concluding chapter the report cited an estimate of the 1975 Borrie Report that a population of 50–60 million was pos-sible for Australia. This target is currently supported by Professor John Caldwell, former Head of the Department of Demography at the Australian National University for 20 years and an expert witness for the inquiry. As a lower estimate the Jones Report cited Professor Jonathon Stone, who prefers stabilizing Australia's population around 23 million. The Jones committee appeared more comfortable with the higher figure (House of Representatives Standing Committee, 1994a, 143).

Surprisingly, the Committee found: "There is no numerical population level beyond which the social fabric and environmental quality might be expected to go into precipitous decline" (House of Representatives Standing Committee, 1994a, 143). Not even 100 million? This is plainly incorrect. Most submission writers, and a good number of other Australians, do think that Australia is already experiencing significant social, environmental, and economic decline, due in no small part to the doubling of our population in the past 40 years. In the end, the Committee appeared to back away from endorsing a high population option of 50–100 million. While it pointed out that the population range of 17–23 million had strong community support, the committee remained uncommitted on this option.

To reduce the environmental impact of Australia's population, more effort should be made to cut high rates of resource consumption and to use less environmentally damaging technologies, the report argued. In what appeared to be wishful thinking, the Committee proposed that, "Willingness to accept a higher population than, say 23 million in 2040 would depend on a national willingness to accept some degree of resource constraint, with more environmental sensitivity, control of urban sprawl, less car dependence, giving higher priorities to waste management strategies, and adopting technology to use resources . . . far more efficiently" (House of Representatives Standing Committee, 1994a, 129). But some resource constraints and technological improvements are hard to achieve. Improving waste management strategies is proving difficult. Stopping urban sprawl as the population grows has proved impossible to date. The danger is that Australia will have continued high population growth while being unable to deliver major improvements in technologies and resource consumption. In any case, reining in population growth and improving technologies and resource consumption levels are not alternatives if Australia wishes to safeguard its quality of life. As the CSIRO submission (No. 259) pointed out: "Any rise in population will increase the necessity and urgency to do *what already needs to be done.* Resource and infrastructure issues, especially regarding water and energy use and waste disposal already require more attention. . . . If these issues are not adequately addressed, Australia can expect further degradation of land and water resources . . . and inland river systems . . . *even at current population levels*" (House of Representatives Standing Committee, 1994a, Submissions Document, 1146, emphasis added). Like most documents written by committees, the Jones Report does not make a pleasant read. There is an air of condescension about sentences such as "Although views contained in the submissions come from a variety of perspectives, many contain overt or inherent assumptions about the need to continue or enhance the quality of life which Australians currently enjoy"

(House of Representatives Standing Committee, 1994a, 93). Did the Committee really expect concerned citizens to write in pleading for a lower quality of life? Similarly the report exhibits a worryingly "voluntarist" and overly optimistic attitude to reforming environmental practices. All human behavior is open to change, the Committee assures us (House of Representatives Standing Committee, 1994a, 144). Taken most cynically, this could imply that even citizens concerned about population growth can be brow-beaten into submission. Also, in a fashionably relativist tone, the Jones Report refers several times to "culturally determined" assumptions and values. For example, "Population densities at which congestion of roads and airspace is recognized are culturally determined" (House of Representatives Standing Committee, 1994a, 98). Presumably the next few generations of Australians will not even know what they have lost as the planners and engineers pack us into ever tighter housing lots, more crowded roads, and noisier airports.

The next major important contribution to the intellectual debate about an ecologically sustainable population level for Australia was the 1994 Annual General Meeting of the Australian Academy of Science, which had as the theme of the symposium, the future population of Australia (Australian Academy of Science, 1995). Most of the contributors disagreed with the policy of non-commitment of the Jones Report. A Joint Statement of the Population 2040 Working Party concluded with these words:

Australia's land mass, though large, is less rich than other continents in many biologically important elements. As a consequence, its ecosystems are relatively fragile, and human impact on the environment is particularly severe. This impact has been documented even for the relatively sparse, low-consumption Aboriginal societies. The impact of modern Australian society is much more severe.

If our population reaches the high end of the feasible range (37 million), the quality of life of all Australians will be lowered by the degradation of water, soil, energy and biological resources. Cities such as Sydney and Melbourne will double or triple in size, multiplying their current infrastructure problems and their impact on the surrounding regions of the continent. Alternatively, new cities of their present size and impact will have to be sited, built and serviced. Moreover, this large population would continue to grow for decades after 2040, and the quality of Australian life would continue to fall.

It is therefore essential that the issue of the continent's population becomes part of national debates over our future. From such debates, the Federal Government must develop a policy on population, which should include the issue of population size.

In our view, the quality of all aspects of our children's lives will be maximized if the population of Australia by the mid-21st Century is kept to the low, stable end of the achievable range, i.e. to approximately 23 million. (Australian Academy of Science, 1995, 135–36)

EATING THE FUTURE

In 1994 T. Flannery published a book, *The Future Eaters* (Flannery, 1994). This is a biogeographical history of Australia that documents much of the damage done to its environment. The author argues that Australia should limit its population size by reducing immigration. The book received relatively sympathetic media coverage (Cribb, 1994d; Dusevic, 1994) and it won two South Australian book awards (Brice, 1996).

Flannery points out that the "new" lands of New Holland (as Australia was once called), New Guinea, and New Zealand were not colonized by Europeans until relatively recently. Partly as a result of the late hour of this colonization, the environmental impact of European migrants entering these countries has been disastrous. Much earlier colonists of these lands also wreaked environmental havoc. Flannery writes:

The deception experienced by each wave of human immigrants into the 'new' lands is one of the great constants of human experience in the region. To the earliest Aborigines, it must have seemed as if the herds of diprotodons stretched on forever. To the Maori, the moa must have appeared a limitless resource. European agriculturalists saw what they imagined were endless expanses of agricultural land of the finest quality. Early Chinese immigrants to Australia saw [*xin jin shaan*] (new gold mountain), and now each new immigrant sees an opportunity to prosper in the land of plenty. In short, all have seen a cornucopia, where there is in fact very little. (Flannery, 1994, 144)

The ecological histories of the different colonists of the "new" lands follow a similar path. Initially deluded about the magnitude of natural resources, the colonists experience great optimism. But this soon turns to disillusion as resources are depleted. In the end comes "a long and hard period of conciliation, during which the land increasingly shapes its new inhabitants" (Flannery, 1994, 145).

Originally lying in the Antarctic Circle as part of the great southern land mass Gondwanaland, the Australian continental plate separated some 40 million years ago and began to drift north. Flannery argues that Australia's biota was shaped by continental drift, regional geology, and climate. He believes that long-term climatic stability in Australia was a pre-condition for biological diversity, for it takes millions of years for diversity to evolve. By contrast, Europe and North America have experienced deteriorating climatic conditions, since great ice sheets wiped all life from the northern parts of these continents. Today Australia still retains a rich biological heritage, more diverse than that of Europe. Even during the ice ages, Australia escaped large-scale glaciation. Australia has had a stable geological history and has preserved some of the oldest rocks on Earth. But without volcanic activity or glaciers, soil is not renewed. Consequently Australia has the poorest soils of any continent.

Despite Australia's long-term climatic stability, in the short term its climate is erratic, being dominated by non-annual climatic change. The cycle that drives its climate is the El Niño Southern Oscillation (ENSO). This occurs as a result of variations in the temperature of coastal waters off South America, which ultimately affect rainfall over large parts of eastern Australia, frequently bringing droughts. ENSO also affects parts of New Guinea. The length of the ENSO cycle is variable, ranging from two to eight years. This variability creates major difficulties for living things to cope with. Flannery shows how all of these Australian

features—long isolation, geological stability, poor soils, and variable climate—
have had a profound effect on the evolution of life in Australia.

The first colonization of the "new" lands of Australia and New Guinea happened at least 45,000 and probably 60,000 years ago by the ancestors of the
Australian Aborigines and New Guineans. These people are thought to have
come from South East Asia. The people of New Guinea developed agriculture
over 9,000 years ago. In parts of New Guinea, especially in the highland valleys,
the existence of deep fertile soils, abundant rain, and many plants suited for cultivation encouraged the development of agriculture. Hunting is difficult in the
dense New Guinea rainforests and this too may have encouraged the rise of agriculture. Agriculture in turn fostered growth of human populations in other parts
of New Guinea.

Flannery points out that today there are no people resembling Aborigines or
New Guineans in South East Asia west of the Moluccas and Timor. This is apart
from a few tiny groups of pygmy negrito people in the Philippines and on the
Malay Peninsula. The ancestors of Australia's Aborigines were probably displaced from South East Asia by invading Mongoloid peoples. This displacement
may have occurred fairly recently as it was only about 8,000 years ago that Mongoloid people in China began to build up substantial populations based on rice
cultivation and the keeping of domestic dogs, pigs, chickens, and possibly cattle
and water buffalo. Further south, in South East Asia, the sub-tropical climate
suited rice growing while the fertile swampy and alluvial river floodplains were
suited to rice paddies. Flannery ponders why the Asian agriculturalists did not
pursue their conquest across Wallace's Line and into New Guinea and Australia.
He believes that part of the answer may lie in the unique nature of Australia and
New Guinea, which were joined together during past ice ages to form Meganesia:

Even on the margins of Meganesia, on the Wallacean islands of Halmahera and Seram,
agriculture is a risky business. I have visited a *Transmigrasi* settlement in northern Halmahera. There, in the middle of a vast clearing made in what was once a densely forested
plain, some few hundred transmigrants from Java were attempting to coax a crop of rice
from the infertile soil. It had not rained for some time and the soil, composed of fine,
whitish volcanic ash, blew between the rough wooden houses, coating everything in a
fine siliceous grit. In infertile and ENSO-dominated Australia, Javanese style *padi* is
often not a viable option. (Flannery 1994, 148–49)

Another reason why the invasion stopped at Wallace's Line was that

those few areas of Meganesia which are suitable for agriculture had already been occupied and cultivated for millenia by the time the rice-growers arrived in the region. . . .
They may have found—as Australian would-be plantation owners who arrived in Papua
New Guinea in the 1950s did—that there is simply no room in New Guinea's fertile
regions for any more agriculturally based people. (Flannery 1994, 149)

The most striking and well-documented animal extinction in the "new" lands
was that of New Zealand's moas. Twelve species of moa, weighing between 20
and 250 kilograms, lived in New Zealand until about 600 years ago. Throughout

New Zealand, particularly in the south east of the South Island, hundreds of old Maori cooking sites, packed with moa remains, have been found. The Maoris arrived in New Zealand some 800–1,000 years ago. Within 300–400 years of the arrival of Maoris, all moa became extinct. Over-hunting by Maoris seems to have caused this loss.

In Australia a range of megafauna existed before the arrival of the ancestors of the Aborigines. These included a seven meter long goanna weighing over 200 kilograms, a large land crocodile weighing over 200 kilograms, a very large py-thon-like snake weighing over 100 kilograms, several types of crocodile, large kangaroos, 200 kilogram horned turtles, large flightless birds, giant echidnas, giant wombats, and marsupial tree-dwellers resembling the South American sloth. There is evidence that the megafauna were extinct in southern Australia by 35,000 years ago. But there is no clear evidence about interactions between hu-mans and megafauna. Some researchers believe that climate change wiped out Australia's megafauna. But Flannery argues that it is more likely that humans caused these extinctions. He maintains that when humans arrived in Australia some 40,000 years ago, they were "spectacularly successful predators, for they appear to have killed off all of the Australian land-based creatures which were larger than themselves" (Flannery 1994, 115). To support this claim he argues that the megafauna was a diverse group of species, drawn from all environments. The one thing they all had in common was their large size. The smallest were slow-moving mammals or flightless birds:

The few large marsupials that survive to the present include the very fastest kangaroos and wallabies and the recently extinct thylacine. The only other large survivors are wom-bats, which can burrow for protection, and the koala, which hides in trees. All of this suggests that a predator, rather than change in climate, was responsible for the extinc-tions. Climate change does not select against slow-moving species, nor for the survival of burrowing or tree-dwelling species. But more recent extinction events show that human hunters can rapidly cause the extinction of the largest, slowest and most obvious species in any habitat. (Flannery, 1994, 207)

Furthermore, he argues, the pattern of extinction seen in New Zealand and on other Pacific islands in the past few thousand years provides good models for what probably happened in Australia over 35,000 years ago. The extinction of Australia's megafauna was more extensive than the megafauna extinctions that occurred on any other continent. In terms of the genera of large mammals lost, Australia has lost 94 percent, North America 73 percent, Europe 29 percent, and Africa (south of the Sahara) five percent. While pointing out these differences, Flannery chooses not to speculate on their causes.

He believes that the loss of Australia's megafauna is related to the role of fire in shaping the landscape. Sediment cores taken from various sites show that an abrupt change in Australia's vegetation occurred sometime between 38,000 and 100,000 years ago, with increased charcoal fragments in some sediment cores as well as evidence of more fire-tolerant plants, such as eucalypts, replac-ing fire-sensitive species such as sheoaks and pines. As the ancestors of today's Aborigines arrived in Australia between 40,000 and 60,000 years ago, humans could have affected the types of vegetation. The Aboriginal system of firestick farming evolved over thousands of years. Could this use of fire have rapidly changed the plant communities recorded in the fossil record? Flannery argues that it is too simplistic to maintain, as is often done, that when the Aborigines arrived in Australia, they began to light fires, thereby increasing the frequency of fire and so encouraging the growth of fire-tolerant plants. It is now known that fire occurs widely and frequently in Australia through natural ignitions such as lightning strikes. Under this naturally high fire frequency regime, lighting more fires simply increases the frequency and lowers the intensity of fires, but does not burn more plant material. Flannery says:

How then, can the remarkable change in fire frequency in prehistoric Australia be explained? Because the natural fire frequency is so high, the only way that the consumption of plant matter by fire could be increased is through increasing the standing fuel load. Something must have happened, therefore, that left more combustible plant matter lying around. While an increase in rainfall could accomplish this, it would also mitigate against fire. Furthermore, rainfall has increased and decreased many times in Australia's past without producing such an effect. Further . . . the change seen in the sediment cores does not correlate with a suitable climate change.

There is only one other conceivable way in which the standing fuel load could have been increased. This is through the accumulation of vegetation which would normally have been recycled through the guts of large herbivores. I suspect that it was this change, not increased fire lighting by Aborigines, which holds the answer to the puzzle. (Flannery, 1994, 229)

Human hunting of Australia's megafauna carried off every large herbivore and suppressed the populations of the few remaining medium-sized species. Throughout the landscape, this left large quantities of vegetation that fueled fires.

Flannery believes that fire further impoverished the already poor Australian landscape. By removing fire-sensitive plants, fire simplified plant communities. It promoted the spread of fire-loving plants from Australia's nutrient-poor heathlands, which had adapted to fire over hundreds of thousands of years. As a recycler of nutrients, fire was inferior to the large herbivores, which once performed this task. Fire causes the loss of large quantities of plant nitrogen and sulphur to the air and other nutrients to inorganic compounds in ash, which may be washed into rivers by heavy rain. Flannery notes that the consequences are worse: "the nutrients are not alone in being vulnerable to loss through water transport. For after a fire has bared the soil, wind can strip it away in massive sheet erosion" (Flannery, 1994, 233).

This cycle accelerates the natural selection for fire-loving scleromorph plants that can survive in nutrient-poor soils. A cycle of soil impoverishment, soil drying, and exposure is then begun. Water is lost through run-off before it can be transpired through the leaves of plants. This lowers rainfall. Fire-loving plants also encourage blazes that kill fire-sensitive plants. Flannery writes:

As a result of these changes, I have no doubt that fire has made Australia—originally the most resource-poor land—an even poorer one. Fire saw the fat of the land slowly flushed on to the floodplains and into the estuaries, where today it supports swamp and mangrove. It is no accident that such areas supported the greatest density of Aboriginal population at the time of European settlement. The bones of the land, along the ranges and away from the sea and rivers, in contrast, supported tiny populations. (Flannery, 1994, 233–34)

Once the magafauna became extinct, he argues, there was little the Aborigines could have done to avoid the consequential build-up of plant material and the ensuing greater conflagration of vegetation:

Firestick farming was doubtless the best way to mitigate the effects of fire, for by lighting many small, low-intensity fires, the Aborigines prevented the establishment of the vast fires that stripped soils and nutrients most dramatically. . . . Most importantly . . . firestick farming supported the diverse communities of medium-sized mammals that Aborigines were so dependent on for food. (Flannery, 1994, 236)

In one of several chapters on New Zealand, Flannery paints a hair-raising picture of future eating by the Maoris. With the demise of the moa and other over-hunted species, the Maoris' struggle for survival intensified over time, with the emergence of a war-like and often cannibalistic people by the time European explorers reached New Zealand. In New Guinea, too, warlike tribes evolved in the highlands. Due to the productivity of agriculture in highland valleys, agriculture supports about 1614 people per square kilometer in those areas. This is the highest density of a rural population in the world. Such a population density, however, brings its own problems:

One of the most striking features of many traditional New Guinean highlands societies is the enormous antagonism and xenophobia displayed towards members of other tribal groups. Even today, the highlands are infamous for the tradition of payback which takes quite literally the biblical injunction of an eye for an eye. . . . But in New Guinea the offender himself (and they are almost invariably male) need not be the target of revenge, for any member of the group to which he belongs will suffice. Often, an old woman or a child becomes the victim, for they are most vulnerable.

The payback system involves virtually every group in the highlands in almost continuous conflict with some other group. . . . So universal and frequent is violence in the highlands that injuries inflicted during payback are now a burden upon the Papua New Guinean medical system. . . . It seems likely that the payback system thrives in New Guinea because it is resources, not people, that are at a premium. Every square kilometer of the highland valleys supports enough people to be genetically self-sustaining in the long term, while the more constant climate means that groups do not have to depend upon each other during frequent hard times. In these conditions, evolution selects for individuals who fight hardest for land, women and pigs. (Flannery, 1994, 296–97)

Flannery is at his best when discussing New Guinea, where he has worked as a research zoologist. He provides a fascinating account of tribal people who inhabited the fringes of the densely populated highlands. Often small communities living in marginal environments had poor health, short life spans, and high infant mortality. While poor soils and steep slopes were a disincentive to agriculture in these areas, big game, such as pigs and cassowaries, was relatively abundant as a result of low human populations. Some of these communities practiced cannibalism. Flannery states:

These people of the highlands fringe often live in close proximity to the dense populations of the fertile and healthier highlands valleys. In some areas, they exploited the
dense human populations of the valleys as a resource. Indeed, until the 1960s some of
these groups were the most feared of all New Guinea's cannibals.

I lived among one such group called the Miyanmin, for several months in the 1980s
and was intrigued by their economy. They told me that in traditional times (until the
early 1970s), the drier part of the year was known as the pig-hunting season and the wet
as the human-hunting season. The human-hunting season was particularly important for
them, for it provided children as well as meat. Children were valued because high infant
mortality meant that almost no infants survived to childhood in some villages. Many of
my informants were brought into the village as booty after raids and are now leading
members of society. (Flannery, 1994, 297)

The indigenous people of New Guinea and Australia are genetically similar.
The history of New Guinea shows that people of Australoid stock can be successful in agriculture, given the right conditions. While New Guineans were
among the world's earliest farmers, Australia's Aboriginal people did not practice agriculture. For a long time Europeans took this as evidence of the back-
wardness and laziness of Aborigines. The British saw Australia as a vast unused
and unowned land, because for them "the very essence of ownership constituted
tilling of the soil" (Flannery, 1994, 280). Flannery argues that the Aborigines'
lack of agriculture, far from being a primitive trait, was an intelligent adaptation
to the effects of a highly variable climate on the productivity of the land. He explains:

ENSO brings more variability and unpredictability in weather patterns to the eastern two
thirds of Australia than are experienced almost anywhere. Even with all the benefits of
irrigation, a modern transportation system . . . and extra-ordinary storage technology,
Australian agriculture is at the mercy of ENSO. . . . It is easy to imagine the difficulties
that Aboriginal people may have encountered had they attempted to intensify plant management into agriculture. Were they living in an area with tolerably good soils and if
ENSO was kind, they may have done very well for a couple of years, increasing their
numbers and investing effort in the development of a permanent camp. Then, one year,
no useful rain would fall. Even if they had stored food on the scale that European farmers
use to get through the winter, it would have been insufficient to save them for the critical
difference between ENSO and a European winter is predictability. European farmers
know, with a margin of error of a couple of weeks, how long winter will last. . . . In contrast, an ENSO drought might last for months—or years. It might be followed by useful
rain or devastating floods. Without a tight social and economic network that spans a
continent and the technology necessary to store and transport vast amounts of food, such
obstacles are probably insurmountable difficulties for agriculturalists. It makes an enormous amount of sense to me to see the lack of agriculture by Australian Aborigines as a
fine-tuned adaptation to a unique set of environmental problems, rather than as a sign of
'primitiveness.' (Flannery, 1994, 281–82)

Similarly he views the patterns of Aboriginal settlement and resource use as
heavily influenced by an irregular climate: "Nomadism was clearly an adaptation
to tracking the erratic availability of resources as they are dictated by ENSO"
(Flannery, 1994, 282). One great cost of nomadism is that possessions must be
strictly limited. Likewise, investment in building shelters is constrained for it is

pointless to erect large structures when they could be deserted for long periods of time.

Flannery notes that at the time of white settlement, Aboriginal tribes were generally not as xenophobic and warlike as were the people of New Guinea and New Zealand. He attributes this to environmental pressures that encouraged natural selection for widespread social networks among Aborigines:

An important facet of the cultural life of the Aborigines is that extraordinary social obligations must sometimes be honored. This is because in the most difficult of droughts, people abandon their land temporarily and seek refuge with neighbors. It takes remarkably strong social bonds for people to share their limited resources with guests at such times. Doubtless, warfare and bad relations between neighbors existed in Aboriginal Australia, but they appear to have been common only in those few areas where population density was high or the impact of ENSO lessened. One example comes from densely populated Arnhem Land, where approximately 25 percent of males of reproductive age were killed in inter-tribal skirmishes. (Flannery, 1994, 283)

Overall, he attributes the lack of xenophobia and constant warfare among Aborigines to the development of extensive social networks that were important if people were to survive ENSO. In addition, ENSO and the poverty of Australia's ecosystems kept Aboriginal populations relatively low for long-term genetic survival. This made neighbors who were potential marriage partners valuable.

The European colonizers of Australia came from a continent that was biogeographically very different from Australia. Europe has predictable seasons. It is mountainous and fertile. Much of it is relatively newly emerged from the ice sheets of the last Ice Age, with the last ice vanishing from northern Europe about 8,000 years ago. Of the emergence of northern Europe from ice, Flannery writes:

Life responded extraordinarily to the changing conditions and a vast variety of plant and animal species . . . began a great race polewards to colonise the north. So rapid was the dispersal that by 8,000 years ago the distribution patterns of plants and animals were beginning to resemble those seen in historic times. (Flannery, 1994, 303)

Europe's environment is dominated by weedy plants:

The plant species that we call weeds all have certain characteristics in common that are frighteningly similar to those traits selected for after the Ice Age in Europe. Perhaps the most important is that they are invasive, that is, they can rapidly colonise any bare soil left after a disturbance. They can also travel over vast distances, and can dominate an environment when they arrive. As their history suggests, the plants of Europe arrived after what was in effect a great weeds sweep-stakes.

The animals that survived in the new European environments were also those which were able to reach the north fastest and which were pre-adapted to disturbed environments. Such species are usually generalists with broad ecological niches. They can breed rapidly and disperse widely, are adaptable, and can tolerate close human settlement. Furthermore, because nutrient shortage is not a great constraint, they grow and breed rapidly. . . . These characteristics of its flora and fauna have made Europe a 'weedy' environment. Mobile, fertile and robust, Europe's life forms were purpose-made to inherit new lands. (Flannery, 1994, 304)

The plants and animals of northern Europe did not have much time to form complex ecosystems before humans began to exploit the land for agriculture from about 7,000 years ago. Consequently, Europe is not as rich in plant and animal species as is Australia. The species Europe does have, however, are often found in great abundance. The physiology of European species too is often different to that of Australian species: "The Europeans are profligate energy users, for soil nutrients are abundant in Europe. In Australia, in contrast, soil infertility limits all" (Flannery, 1994, 305). But the starkest contrast between Europe and Australia is their different capacities to support the most energy hungry species of all—humans and other warm-blooded carnivores:

Europe is only slightly larger than Australia, but is home to over 600 million people, compared with Australia's 17 million. Despite its enormous human population it still has the resources needed to support 27 species of mammalian carnivores, including two species of bears, which are the largest land-based carnivores of all. . . . The warm-blooded carnivore assemblage of Australia is pitiful by comparison, the largest of its few species (most now extinct) weighing a mere 60 kilograms. (Flannery, 1994, 305)

Flannery steers clear of discussing the evolving relationship between black and white Australians. This relationship is changing quite rapidly with recent decisions of Australia's High Court having held the British concept of *terra nullius* (empty land) to be invalid. Aboriginal people are now able to claim nonfreehold owned land where they can establish historical links with it. This has created anxiety among many white Australians and contributed to some rising racial tensions between black and white Australians (Windsor, 1996; Ceresa, 1997; Fagan and Carruthers, 1997). With the legitimacy of European Australia being challenged from within, many Australians have also been recently expressing concern about changes foisted on the country from without. In particular, the calls from much of Australia's elite since the 1980s for Australia to become part of Asia, coupled with an unprecedented surge in Asian immigration, have fostered a new sense of unease and cultural uncertainty among many Australians.[1]

Flannery points out that many people outside Australia still view Australia as *terra nullius*:

Each new wave of people, arriving from the resource-rich lands to the north, sees in the unoccupied regions of Australia . . . room for development and space in which to flourish. In part perhaps because of this sheer sense of space, each new wave of settlers can identify some virgin resource—some field untilled, sea unfished, or forest unfelled—with which they can make their future.

Yet these unoccupied spaces and apparent opportunities in fact represent something very different, for they are the necessary accommodation that each group makes to life in a hard land. For the Aborigines, that accommodation meant foregoing agriculture and hence leaving a very different kind of mark on the land. For the Australians of European origin, it meant leaving the center and north largely empty and the creation of vast national parks on what appears to be useable land. . . . These necessary accommodations have created a sense of paranoia in living Australians. Perhaps because of their own recent use of the concept of *terra nullius*, many fear that people from Asia will perceive in Australia, if not an empty land, then an under-utilized one. (Flannery, 1994, 145)

The continuation of Australia's mass immigration program is a loud and clear signal to the people of Asia that Australia's politicians, economists, and businessmen (if not its people) still perceive Australia as an under-developed country ripe for further exploitation.

Many of the early European colonists believed that Australia was rich in resources and would become a prosperous and powerful country, rivalling the United States in terms of its population size and might. This overly optimistic assessment of Australia's natural resources persists in many quarters down to the present day. Flannery believes that this illusion has been a tragedy:

Even today many Australians see their nation as having the potential to be a second North America, with the ability to support hundreds of millions of people. In a sense, it is this great illusion that has been the tragedy of the European Australians. It is the illusion that has pushed them towards limitless growth in population and expenditure. It has encouraged them to be profligate with their few resources and to imagine a grander future than their land would ever have permitted. (Flannery, 1994, 351)[2]

Australia's population stood at seven and a half million in 1947. Fifty years later it has passed 18 million. Flannery notes that while the country could feed a population of some 50 million, this would cancel its food exports to other countries that now rely on them. He argues that as Australia is ENSO-prone and has a fragile environment, it would make good sense for Australians to observe the "golden rule" of population observed by hunter-gatherer societies, that is, that in normal times, the human population of a given area rarely exceeds 20–30 percent of the land's carrying-capacity. Australians might then decide that an optimum long term population lay in the 6–12 million range. With a smaller population, he points out, natural resource conflicts would become less intense. "If Australia's population were smaller, we could afford to do many things differently. The argument over logging of old growth forest, for example, would be less intense, for the housing construction industry, which uses much of the hardwood timber produced, would be scaled down" (Flannery, 1994, 372). Despite its apparent implausibility, Flannery's radical call for a smaller Australian population has provided a useful element in what passes for the current population "debate," positing a conservative counter-balance to the "Australia unlimited" school of politicians, economists, and businessmen who call for a population of 50 million and up. In the meantime it's business as usual for the land developers and speculators, real estate agents, and state governments, ever eager to beat each other in the population-growth sweepstakes as if in a race to see which state can destroy its environment most completely in the shortest time.[3]

PEOPLE, POLICY, AND CHOICES

The next major work on population and the environment was by Doug Cocks, a research scientist in the wildlife division of Australia's CSIRO. The Jones Report on Australia's population carrying capacity was used to good effect by Cocks in his book *People Policy: Australia's Population Choices* (Cocks, 1996). Cocks also argued that Australia should stabilize its population. He urged an immigration intake of less than 50,000 a year that would allow Australia's population to plateau at around 19–23 million within a few decades. Cocks based his argument on environmental and social concerns about population growth. In 1994 he worked for six months for the Jones Inquiry. In developing his case against Australia's current immigration program, Cocks draws extensively on the 271 submissions made to the Jones Inquiry, most of which supported stabilizing Australia's population in the near future.

Cocks presents a wide-ranging environmental and social critique of Australia's continuing population growth. On the environmental front, beaches, wilderness, water-bodies, and snow-fields are amenity capital that can always be better managed, but they cannot be fundamentally increased. A growing population reduces amenity capital per head of population. For example, while on an international comparison, Australia is well endowed with water per head of population, it is poorly endowed with water per hectare. Providing good quality water to urban Australians is already a major political, technical, and economic problem. Cocks argues that while it would be feasible to water twice the present population in fifty years' time, this would come at a high cost to the natural environment, the quality of life of Australians, infrastructure costs, user charges, and in terms of social conflict.

Primary production, such as mining, farming, forestry, and fishing, destroys natural capital (soils, water supplies, landscapes, forests, rangeland, and fish stocks). But, Cocks argues, since most of this production is for export, little of this destruction is due to domestic population growth. Would farm exports (and hence the land degradation farming causes) fall if Australia had a smaller population? Probably not, Cocks suggests. However, the Population Issues Committee of the National Population Council found that population growth may affect the scale of primary production (Population Issues Committee, 1991, 42). It argued that the increased imports that a larger population generates may increase pressure to relax environmental constraints on export-oriented resource industries. Furthermore, this committee found that "even in industries such as forestry, fisheries or tourism, where there is evidently a large export element, there are still very clear and important domestic components" (Population Issues Committee, 1991, 42). While maintaining that past degradation of natural resources has resulted from production for largely export markets, Cocks acknowledges that continued population growth is likely to cause further degradation of agricultural, forestry, and pastoral lands, as Australia tries to increase exports to fund the rising imports necessitated by a growing population in an increasingly deregulated global market.

The environmental impact of each urban dweller extends far beyond the city: "Even if a city's residents never leave town, they are using land indirectly to grow the food they eat, to harvest the water they drink, to grow the forests that provide packaging and timber for their houses, to generate their electricity, to accept their wastes" (Cocks, 1996, 101). While Cocks views the impact of Australia's population on the degradation of natural resources used for production as largely indirect, he identifies the direct impacts of population growth on natural resources used for production as loss of prime agricultural land to urbanization, loss of soil nutrients in sewage, and loss of fish breeding and nursery areas to coastal pollution. In considering the relationship between population growth and environmental impact, Cocks examines the formula, developed by Paul Ehrlich, I = PAT, where I = human impact on the environment, P = population size, A = the activity mix (or affluence level), and T = the technology used, as well as variations thereon such as I = PLOT, where I = human impact on the environment, P = population size, L = lifestyle (particularly consumption), O = organizational style of the society, and T = the technology used (Smith et al., 1997). He suggests that these formulae are not wholly satisfactory as they are not testable theories, or at least not yet (Cocks, 1996, 114). Two of the reasons for the failure of testability are lag times between causes and effects and interactions between the causal variables in the environmental impact formulae. The differing sensitivities of different environments to human activity seems to be another complicating factor. Perhaps, Cocks suggests, we need a theory of environmental quality, rather than environmental impact. Indicators of environmental quality could be measured over time to show whether our environmental quality is improving or declining. He believes that we would need at least two theories of environmental quality, one for individual coastal-city regions and one for individual city hinterlands (which produce the primary products, support the infrastructure, and provide recreational areas for city people).

Most population growth in Australia is occurring in coastal cities. Cocks points out that population growth triggers a process of land use change and intensification. The use of a piece of land normally progresses from a less to a more intensive use. Land use change is a one-way street. For example, it is difficult and expensive to return land covered with home units to a natural forest. The consequence of land use intensification is that the functional capacity of natural resources, especially biodiversity, is reduced (Cocks, 1996, 117). In addition to reducing the capacity of natural resources to function well, land use intensification processes generate local pollution, resulting in "a local build-up in the concentration of unwanted materials which make sites less attractive for various activities" (Cocks, 1996, 120). Within a coastal city region, population growth triggers land use changes that affect the quality of life of present residents. These changes include the spread of urban areas on to farmland, recreational land and natural areas, urban consolidation (which is the policy aiming to house more people in a given already urbanized area), and increasing traffic. Cocks examines people's attachment to landscapes and their frequently experienced sense of loss when land uses are intensified. He does not mention that while Australia's elite now recognizes the deep attachment of many Aboriginal Australians to the land, the bonds between other Australians and their familiar landscapes are not officially recognized. Indeed, in an increasingly globalized economy and in a country whose leaders are committed to upholding the mobility of both capital and labor, such attachments are actively discouraged as they tend to militate against economic "efficiency" and the "flexibility" that the labor force is frequently told it must assume.

Cocks envisages a theory of environmental quality that includes a study of the effects of population change on Australia. Such a theory must recognize that the residents of new suburbs seldom pay the external costs that they impose on the residents of older suburbs:

The external environmental costs of population growth are pervasive and cumulative; i.e. they affect many people and these effects are, at least, proportional to the magnitude of the population growth. In fact, it is reasonable to hypothesize that in many situations (e.g. traffic congestion), impact thresholds . . . and the marginally increasing effects of unit impacts on environmental quality will make the quality effects more than proportional to population growth. (Cocks, 1996, 119)

Urban quality of life is, he argues, the most important issue in the population debate. He cites a 1988 Commission for the Future survey, which found that 79 percent of people believed that pollution and environmental quality had worsened over the past 20 years (Cocks, 1996, 138).

Cocks devotes part of his book to examining social arguments about the increasing size and density of city populations. He argues that it "is widely recognized but not well documented that per capita rates for crime, drug addiction, alienation, sociopathy and other social problems are higher in big cities than in small cities and towns" (Cocks, 1996, 139). Even if crime rates do not rise, he points out, a growing city population will produce more crime overall. People are expressing rising concern about crime and (with the help of the media) people are responding to the total crime figure, not to crime rates. Bigger city size can also produce unfriendliness. The more people work and the longer it takes them to travel to and from work, the less time they have for relationships. There is some 1980s research that suggests that in developed countries, social and economic benefits may increase as city size grows to about 500,000, while after it passes one million people, social conditions deteriorate and after about two million, economic conditions also deteriorate (Bairoch, 1982). Cocks cites submissions to the Jones Inquiry that identify a range of activities that population growth has or will make harder to do as they are increasingly regulated, or disappear, or take longer or more money to accomplish. These include burning autumn leaves, lying on a quiet beach, and living in a detached house on a large block of land. Restrictions on pet ownership also increase with city size, with dogs now banned from some Sydney and Melbourne beaches in summer.

Cocks also has doubts about the concept of ecologically sustainable development (ESD), which was in vogue in the early 1990s in Australia: "In a strict sense it is doubtful if the goal of ecologically sustainable resource use can be met at any population level if this term means that the capacity of those systems to continue to function as at present should remain completely unimpaired" (Cocks, 1996, 88). However, he regards ESD as a positive concept, expressing the hope that land use can be intensified without a negative impact on natural resources. Nevertheless, he believes that sustainability, in this sense, is a chimera due to entropy and the laws of conservation of energy and mass. He argues that low population growth will assist the very general goal of ESD and high population growth will make the ESD goal more difficult to achieve (Cocks, 1996, 237).

In working his way through the arguments both for and against population growth, Cocks considers concerns about recent large increases in temporary migration. Australia now has 26 separate temporary entry visa categories. Temporary skilled, business, and professional migration into Australia is being promoted as the way of the future. Mass tourism is also touted as Australia's savior. Cocks points to evidence that tourism degrades tourist attractions and suggests that tourism may be a form of "slow mining." He believes that with a large projected growth in foreign tourist numbers, a way of converting tourists and visitors to "residential equivalents" needs to be found and factored into an Australian population policy. Likewise, the impacts of other groups such as New Zealanders (who have a right to unregulated entry into Australia), temporary workers, and foreign students should be estimated and incorporated into a population policy.

Further, of direct importance to our "global meltdown" theme, Cocks argues that resource conflicts are likely to worsen as Australia's population continues to grow: "Within the last 15–20 years there has been a massive increase in social conflict over natural resource allocation and management issues—e.g. logging native forests" (Cocks, 1996, 144). Society has failed to develop ways of resolving such conflicts that are largely caused by land use intensification, associated with the demands of larger populations. The possibility of bitter social conflict over land management issues should not be ruled out: "Much social conflict between interest groups in Australia follows land use change and land use intensification, two processes which are strongly associated with population growth in city regions" (Cocks, 1996, 183).

In South Australia, for example, a dispute of the type Cocks identifies recently deeply divided the community. This was a conflict over land usage in the city of Adelaide's hinterlands. Real estate developers proposed a bridge be built from the mainland to an island in the mouth of the River Murray. The scheme provoked a bitter and prolonged dispute between the developers, local opponents of the proposal, city environmentalists, and Aboriginal groups. This dispute mushroomed to national proportions, entangling both State and federal governments and provoking the resignation of a senior Federal Liberal Party member from his then shadow portfolio. It also increased the unpopularity of the federal Labor government, due to its handling of the issue, prior to that government's defeat at the 1996 election (Chandler, 1995; Devine, 1996; Cohen, 1997; Johns, 1997). This provides a classic example of conflict over the process of land use intensification. As Cocks points out, under the "business as usual" scenario of continuous population growth, such disputes are set to increase in Australia.

Significant population growth will markedly and inequitably increase the real per capita cost of providing Australians with many goods and services based on natural resources, such as food, water, biodiversity, residue sinks, and amenity resources, according to Cocks. While many an environmentalist would wring their hands in despair at talk of the per capita cost of providing Australians with biodiversity, Cocks' CSIRO-honed language has obviously evolved to reach politicians who are most comfortable with hip-pocket talk. As examples of population growth increasing the costs of providing people with natural resource based goods and services, Cocks points to the rising real marginal cost of supplying clean domestic water and positional goods such as wilderness having to be rationed. The inequities associated with such price rises, and/or rationing, are between the present rich and poor of Australia and between the current generation and future generations of Australians (Cocks, 1996, 188).

Cocks believes that significant population growth in the order of doubling Australia's population size over the next fifty years will produce a marked deterioration in a range of urban quality of life indicators for most Australians. These include levels of pollution, traffic congestion, a decline in the provision of services and amenities, and social indicators such as rates of personal relationship failure and reduction of freedoms. Referring to what he sees as a lack of hard data to justify the claim that Australia's urban quality of life is in decline, Cocks maintains "the evidence is *prima facie* and unchallenged but, to many, the niceties of formal argument are irrelevant, the matter is self-evident" (Cocks, 1996, 182). Nevertheless, the supporters of lower population growth are always expected to argue their case. Cocks points out that the proponents of population growth have failed to present any significant reasons or arguments as to why population growth might improve any environmental or social aspects of quality of life. In their absence he concludes that the *prima facie* case against population growth, on urban quality of life grounds, is quite strong.

He is critical of the results of the Jones Inquiry into Australia's population carrying capacity, as the Committee avoided making any firm recommendation about what Australia's immigration-population policy should be—and many believed that it was precisely this question that the Jones Report should have addressed (Cocks, 1996, 8). This is only the latest in a long line of failures to come to terms with the population issue in Australia. Cocks points to the unwillingness of the major political parties to address this issue. Instead of being concerned about the long-term welfare of the Australian people, they "conspire to ignore the strong likelihood that the population growth they are generating . . . will continue to have severe adverse consequences for the quality of life of most present and future Australians" (Cocks, 1996, 308). While most of the public support reducing immigration, the Labor government opted for a relatively high immigration intake target of approximately 100,000 in 1995/96. Cocks believes that the population issue is not seriously discussed in this country. His suggestions for why this is so include a lack of media interest (and sometimes active discouragement on the grounds debate could increase ethnic tensions), fear of being called "racist," lack of a forum to question the immigration policies of the major parties, the minor effect cutting immigration would have on the quality of life in the short term, the long term nature of the immigration issue, public ignorance, lack of clear causal links between population growth and different quality of life measures, and the different values people attach to these. The population limitationist movement in Australia is, he points out, small and fragmented, lacks powerful friends or a power base in the bureaucracy, is seen as politically incorrect, and lacks media support. Governments have been largely able to ignore this movement. So there is a vacuum in Australian public debate. The population issue is not addressed. It is business as usual for the immigration industry. Cocks suggests that the winners from continued mass immigration include the housing industry, the multiculturalism industry, immigration agents and lawyers, owners of fixed assets such as land (as prices are bid up by a larger population), and migrants themselves whose establishment costs are subsidized by residents. Losers include entrepreneurs who suffer rising input prices such as land prices and rates, consumers who suffer price rises for goods and services, first home buyers, workers who are shed by industries sidelined by changing patterns of demand, taxpayers who pay the public costs of establishing migrants, and city residents who suffer uncompensated losses to their environmental and social quality of life as a result of population growth. Cocks cites research that finds a greater polarization between rich and poor as city size grows (Murphy et al., 1990).

Why is there a public inability to address the population issue in Australia? Cocks locates the problems in the nature of democracy. While our system of government often ensures stability, it is incapable of pre-empting or even seriously debating problems because of "pluralistic stagnation," where competing interest groups often nullify each other's proposals (Cocks, 1996, 276–77). We will elaborate upon this point in this book. Cocks also believes that our society suffers from "social myopia," the incapacity to respond to long distance problems, while mobilizing enormous energy to deal with immediate threats. We discussed this matter in detail in *Healing a Wounded World* (Smith et al., 1997), and concluded that "social myopia" is part of the human condition. The failure of nations and individuals to respond to the environmental crisis with at least the same urgency as one would respond to a military threat is the Achilles' heel of both democracy and humanity. It justifies our pessimistic prognosis of the human prospect.

AUSTRALIA'S ENVIRONMENTAL CRISIS

Cocks' diagnosis of the environmental plight of Australia can be supported by further argument and evidence. We turn now to that task.

As we have seen, considerable damage has been done to Australia's environment in only 200 years of European settlement. Continuing population growth and the endless search for economic wealth have contributed to this damage. Historically, the links between Australia's population growth and environmental damage have generally been ignored. It has been hard for us to grasp that a wide brown land, seemingly largely empty of people, has been significantly affected by us, mostly city-dwellers as we are. But does the decline of parts of Australia's natural environment pose any checks on our future population growth?

Environmental impacts are influenced by population size, levels of consumption, and the types of technologies people use. The environmental impact of a permanent population is augmented by that of foreign tourists coming to a country. International tourists to Australia "are often attracted to our most precious natural and cultural heritage areas" (State of the Environment Advisory Council [SEAC], 1996, ES–5; Collins, 1994; Kremer, 1994). Such tourists can damage our environment, as can our own citizens through their recreational activities. Six million foreign tourists are expected in the year 2000 (Tourism Forecasting Council, 1996).

But how does Australia's largely urban population affect the environment? Our cities, in which about 70 percent of us live, take up barely one percent of the continent's land mass. However, the environmental impact of urban dwellers extends far beyond the city. While they may never leave the city, land must be provided to grow the food city people eat, to harvest the water they drink and wash in, to grow forests for their packaging and timber for their houses, to generate their electricity, and to accept their wastes. As well, city people occupy land for housing, driving, shopping, and recreational purposes. The total area of land used by a city's residents, both directly within the city and indirectly outside the city, is called an "ecological footprint"[4] (Foran, 1996; Foran and Poldy, 1996; Rees, 1996). Each individual person, too, has an ecological footprint. Urban land is a fairly minor part of the footprint (Foran and Poldy, 1996). Recent research indicates that the average Australian needs three to four hectares of productive soils to maintain the average Australian lifestyle (Foran, 1996).

Environmental constraints on Australia's future population growth may be imposed by some natural resources that are nonrenewable. If we destroy our native forests, bush, and grasslands, degrade our rivers, coasts, and wetlands, stand by as our soils are blown away, or dispatch more of our native plants and animals into extinction, we lose resources which are irreplaceable.[5] Even if we continue to build up our Gross Domestic Product, our quality of life will decline.

Much of Australia, although totally in the Southern hemisphere, lies in the Earth's desert zones, defined as being between 20° and 35° north and south of the equator. It is the world's driest inhabited continent. It is a land of drought, fire, and flood. Australia's highly variable climate exacerbates many human impacts on the environment. Our landscape is flat and eroded. Our soils are old and weathered and generally infertile. Only six percent of Australia's land is suitable for intensive agriculture (cropping and improved pasture), compared with 20 percent in the United States (State of the Environment Advisory Council, 1996, ES–17). Degradation of existing crop and pasture land is a serious threat to the sustainability of our production systems. Problems include excessive loss of native vegetation, soil salinity, soil erosion, and acidification (Gifford et al., 1975; Bonyhady, 1995; Dayton, 1995). For example, 15 percent of Australia's rangelands is so damaged that removal of grazing stock is needed for the land to recover (State of the Environment Advisory Council, 1996, ES–18). If such destocking occurs, it will help the rangelands, but it will result in less production of meat and wool, fewer exports, a worse balance of payments deficit and a lower standard of living in the short term for our existing population. Land salinization is another major problem in Australia (State of the Environment Advisory

Council, 1996, ES–21; Cocks et al., 1995, 5; Da Silva, 1996, 9). As a result of intensive agriculture, Australia is rapidly losing its best soils (State of the Environment Advisory Council, 1996, 6–28).

If the ecological footprint of each Australian is about four hectares, for a population of 20 million, our total ecological footprint starts to equal our stock of reasonably good soils (Da Silva, 1996, 9; Beale, 1996). If we tap more and more into our poorer soils, our costs will rise and our standard of living decline.[6]

The scale of destruction of Australia's native vegetation raises serious questions about the sustainability of our society. Native vegetation performs a range of valuable functions. It stabilizes soil, absorbs rain, produces oxygen, stores and recycles nutrients, helps maintain regional rainfall patterns, provides a sink for greenhouse gases, provides wood, conserves genetic resources, provides a habitat for wildlife, provides a sense of identity and place, and provides places for recreation (Biodiversity Unit, 1995). At the time of European settlement, Australia had fewer natural forests than any other continent except Antarctica. About 40 percent of its total forest area has now been cleared, with another 40 percent having been logged. Nearly 90 percent of temperate woodlands and mallee has been cleared. Almost 70 percent of all native vegetation has been removed or significantly modified by humans since 1788 (State of the Environment Advisory Council, 1996). Most clearance has been for cropping and grazing purposes (State of the Environment Advisory Council, 1996). The wholesale clearance of native vegetation over the past 200 years has underpinned the rise of large agricultural and pastoral industries. The exports of these industries have helped secure a high standard of living for an ever-growing urban population.

In the last two decades, 95 percent of all population growth in Australia has occurred in the coastal zone, and populations of non-metropolitan coastal towns have grown more quickly than have cities (Hamilton and Cocks, 1994). While most native vegetation clearance occurring today continues to be for cropping and grazing, the ongoing clearance of remnant vegetation in south-east Queensland and the coastal fringe of New South Wales is largely due to population growth (Calterall and Kingston, 1993). Remnant vegetation plays an important role in the conservation of biodiversity, and clearance of remnant vegetation is a significant threat to the nation's biodiversity. A high rate of population growth in the coastal zone of New South Wales over the past 20 years has led to only three 10 kilometer long sections of the New South Wales coast being free of human occupants (Biodiversity Unit, 1995). This population increase has caused substantial disturbance to ecosystems and the loss and fragmentation of habitats. In south-east Queensland, all lowland vegetation communities in mainland areas have been acutely affected by human impact, and loss of bushland has occurred as a result of rapid urban expansion, including development of low density "rural residential" style areas (Biodiversity Unit, 1995).

Coastal wetlands continue to be destroyed by urban expansion. As a result of population growth, all of Australia's capital cities continue to expand, with ongoing negative impacts on native bushland and coastal wetlands (Biodiversity Unit, 1995).[7] The continued decline of Australia's biological diversity shows that

Australia is not ecologically sustainable. Biological diversity provides us with sources of food, medicines, and industrial products. Biological diversity provides us with a wide range of ecological services, including the maintenance of hydrological cycles, climate regulation, soil production and fertility, protection from erosion, nutrient storage and cycling, and pollutant breakdown and absorption. These are fundamental to our quality of life. Many people also value biological diversity for aesthetic and ethical reasons.

Due to its size, long isolation, and varied climatic zones, Australia is one of the 12 most biologically diverse countries in the world (State of the Environment Advisory Council, 1996). However, our rate of biodiversity loss has been high, particularly in the last 50 years (Biodiversity Unit, 1995, 1996). We city-dwellers have been reluctant to accept responsibility for the dramatic decline in our country's biological richness. We tend to blame the early settlers, farmers, feral animals—anyone but ourselves (Crome et al., 1994). The recently published *State of the Environment* report on Australia found that

The greatest pressures on biodiversity come from the demands on natural resources by increasing populations of humans, their affluence and technology. Habitat modification—especially the removal of native vegetation for agriculture, urban development . . . and forestry—has been, and remains, the most significant cause of loss of biodiversity. (State of the Environment Advisory Council, 1996, ES13)

But does losing a few more plants and animals present any real limit to Australia's population growth? Does it matter if an extra ten million Australians dispatch a few more insignificant looking plants, a few mammals, and a dozen or so birds into oblivion?[8] Loss of biodiversity poses no immediate limit to our population growth. However, as our population grows and our biodiversity declines, we will gradually lose those valuable ecological services that our biodiversity provides and so our quality of life will decline.[9] While most threats to plant species today come from agriculture and pastoralism (State of the Environment Advisory Council,. 1996, 4–7), our main population growth areas tend to be in regions of high biological diversity (Crome et al., 1994).[10]

Does the quality of life in our cities, in which most Australians live, impose any constraints on our population growth? Air pollution is recognized as a major constraint on Sydney's population growth (Commonwealth Scientific & Industrial Research Organization, 1994; Sweet and Beale, 1996; Beale et al., 1996). The airsheds of Melbourne, Brisbane, and Perth are also incapable of effectively dispersing much greater quantities of photochemical smog than at present (State of the Environment Advisory Council, 1996, 3–44).[11] Motor vehicles are the main source of air pollution in our cities. While there have been improvements in some vehicle emission components in recent years due to stricter emission controls, as a result of population growth, the growing number of vehicles travelling farther distances will probably make city air quality worse in future (Gilchrist, 1996a).

With a bigger population and more vehicles on our roads, increases in traffic congestion may be more than proportionate to population growth due to the marginally increasing effects of unit impacts, combined with impact threshold effects (Cocks, 1996, 119). Without significant changes in the way people travel, this will reduce the quality of life of many people. The recent battle over the third runway at Sydney airport showed that noise is now a major environmental and health issue in Australia. Many people are concerned about noise. In a national survey, 40 percent of respondents claimed that noise interfered with their listening or sleep, with noise from traffic being the main concern (State of the Environment Advisory Council, 1996, 3–45). As our population grows noise levels in Australian cities will increase.

Near our major population centers, the pollution of rivers and coastal waters is a major environmental concern. Disposal of sewage and stormwater are the main problems that require improved technology. Population growth will increase volumes of stormwater and sewage to be handled, thus making improvements in disposal more difficult to achieve.

As we have said, beaches, wilderness, water bodies, and snowfields are amenity capital and cannot be fundamentally increased. Population growth reduces amenity capital per head of population. Access to open spaces such as beaches and nature parks will become more expensive or have to be rationed in other ways, as the Australian population grows (Cocks, 1996). Imposing extra population onto a fixed base of natural resources will raise the marginal costs of providing food and water (Cocks, 1996, 82). Land and infrastructure costs will also grow, resulting in housing becoming more expensive. High housing costs have been a major contributor to the outflow of people from Sydney for years. This outflow has fanned the ecologically unsustainable population boom in coastal towns in Queensland and New South Wales (State of the Environment Advisory Council, 1996, 3–51).

As Australia's cities continue to grow, they are facing an increasing problem in disposing of solid waste. Each Australian produces 681 kilograms of garbage each year. This compares poorly with the average figure for other industrial nations of 513 kilograms (State of the Environment Advisory Council, 1996). New South Wales, the most populous state, is facing an environmental crisis due to a growing mountain of tires being dumped on native bushland and private farming properties. Unscrupulous operators are dumping or burying more than one quarter of the five million tires worn out in New South Wales each year on secluded bush sites or leased private properties (Wainwright, 1996).

This problem pales in comparison to the problem of the enhanced greenhouse effect. Dr. Sherwood Rowland, atmospheric scientist and Nobel laureate for chemistry for his work in showing in 1974 that the synthetic chlorofluorocarbons (CFCs), used in propellants and cooling systems, damage the Earth's ozone layer, has said: "If we don't figure out how to solve the energy problem . . . then I think we've got very very serious problems. Five thousand years from now, at first glance, the planet would probably look much as it does now. There would be greenery. . . . There just wouldn't be humans on it" (Dayton, 1996, 3). Human activities are increasing the atmospheric concentrations of a range of gases including carbon dioxide, methane, ozone, nitrous oxide, and chlorofluorocarbons.

If large reductions in current global greenhouse gas emissions do not occur, the concentration of most greenhouse gases will rise well into the twenty-first century (State of the Environment Advisory Council, 1996). Climate models suggest that these increases may raise the Earth's global surface temperature, relative to 1990, by about 2°C by the year 2100 (State of the Environment Advisory Council, 1996). The most recent United Nations Climate Conference in Geneva in July 1996 concluded that the "continued rise in greenhouse gas concentrations in the atmosphere will lead to dangerous interference with the climate system" and that "the projected changes in climate will result in significant, often adverse, impacts on many ecological systems . . . including food supply and water resources, and on human health" (Bita, 1995a, 1996c).

Despite public skepticism about the enhanced greenhouse effect (Maddox, 1995; Pearce, 1995; Cribb, 1995a, b), a range of unusual weather events in the 1990s seems to indicate that climate changes are occurring (Pearce, 1995; Nuttall, 1995, Ryan, 1995; Bita, 1996b; Bouma et al., 1996). The 1980s was the warmest decade on record and was characterized by an unprecedented number of extreme climate events such as storms and droughts. Furthermore, a change in the growth pattern of trees, plants, and grasses in the northern hemisphere, with spring growth earlier than usual and an extra 20–40 percent growth, has recently been documented, providing further evidence for the enhanced greenhouse effect. This research is based on measurements of atmospheric carbon dioxide over Hawaii and Alaska. There are seasonal variations in atmospheric carbon dioxide levels that fall in spring as vegetation in cooler climate zones blooms and absorbs carbon dioxide by photosynthesis. Compared with the 1960s, the annual dip in carbon dioxide has begun earlier and it has become more pronounced. In the growing season in Alaska, 40 percent more carbon dioxide is being absorbed, while in Hawaii, where the tropical climate makes for less seasonal variation, 20 percent more is being absorbed (Gilchrist, 1996b).

While Australia contributes only between one and two percent of world greenhouse emissions, per head of population, Australia's emissions are among the world's highest (State of the Environment Advisory Council, 1996). This fact is due to the country's large geographical area, combined with a relatively small population, its heavy reliance on fossil fuels for generating energy, coal exports, and energy-intensive manufacturing. Most of Australia's emissions come from the burning of fossil fuel, land clearance, and agriculture (State of the Environment Advisory Council, 1996). Australia has committed itself to the voluntary target of cutting its carbon dioxide emissions by 20 percent below their 1990 levels by the year 2005, but it has been unwilling to pursue this target actively (McLean, 1995; Woodford, 1996a; Bita, 1996b, c). Australia's emissions of greenhouse gases have increased by seven percent since 1990 (Bita, 1996a) and grew much more than those of other OECD countries, overall and per capita (for 1990–1994), according to the Australian Academy of Science and the Australian Academy of Technological Sciences and Engineering. The main reason for this is that some OECD countries have cut their fossil fuel consumption per unit of output at a faster rate than has Australia (Cribb, 1995a). The continuing growth in Australia's greenhouse emissions has been strongly criticized by both Greenpeace (Gilchrist, 1996a) and the Worldwatch Institute (Woodford, 1996a; Simonion, 1995). At the July 1996 United Nations conference on climate change in Geneva, Australia, along with New Zealand, Canada and the OPEC oil producing nations, disassociated itself from a United Nations declaration calling for legally binding targets for industrialized countries to reduce greenhouses gasses. Dr. Sherwood Rowland expressed dismay at Australia's stance. He said he was surprised that Australia seemed unwilling to take steps to protect itself from the serious impacts of greenhouse-induced climate change, especially as Australia was the first country to experience another serious atmospheric change, the Antarctic ozone hole, which in 1987 covered Melbourne and Sydney (Dayton, 1996).

Successive Australian governments since 1992 have been unwilling to tackle seriously the task of reducing greenhouse gas emissions because they fear it would reduce economic growth. Australia's continued population growth, which is one of the highest of any developed country, also mitigates against cuts in its emissions of greenhouse gases. As the population grows the required per capita cuts in carbon dioxide emissions grow disproportionately. The 20 percent voluntary cut required by the 1992 UN Convention on Climate Change was a per capita cut of 20 percent. But if Australia's population were to double, the required reduction per head of population would be 60 percent (Cocks, 1996). According to a federal Treasury paper, Australia's strong population growth places it at a disadvantage in trying to meet international commitments on greenhouse gas reductions (Dwyer, 1995; Sturgiss, 1995). Australia, with a projected population growth of at least 10 percent from 1990 to 2000, would need to reduce per capita emissions by at least 10 percent relative to 1990 merely to stabilize greenhouse gas emissions at 1990 levels (Sturgiss, 1995). But the Department of Foreign Affairs and Trade has estimated that by the turn of the century, Australia's output of greenhouse gases will be almost 25 percent higher than its 1990 output. By comparison the United States' output would be 10 percent higher, New Zealand's 15 percent higher, while Japan's and Europe's would be 6 percent higher (Bita, 1996b).

Ironically, even if the industrialized nations significantly reduced their greenhouse gas emissions, developing countries in the Asia-Pacific region will nearly double their energy use by 2010 to produce over half of the world's greenhouse gas emissions within 50 years (Bureau of Industry Economics, 1996). An Australian Bureau of Agriculture and Resource Economics study has found that the actions of developed countries will do little to reduce the growth of atmospheric greenhouse gases due to the rapid growth of developing economies (Denholm, 1996).

A 1995 report by the Australian Bureau of Agriculture and Resource Economics also found that even if developed countries stabilized their emissions of carbon dioxide, this would make little difference to the growth in global carbon dioxide emissions, which would still rise 75 percent by 2020 (Cribb, 1995). This study found that meeting the 1992 international agreement to cut greenhouse gas emissions would cost developed countries $US 80 billion a year by 2020 (Cribb, 1995). These findings were based on the first major use of the Australia Bureau of Agriculture and Resource Economics' MEGABARE computer model, which *The Sydney Morning Herald* found had been partly funded by the Coal Association, the Business Council of Australia and coal producers BHP and CRA (Stott, 1995).

We turn now from Australia's problems with controlling greenhouse gas emissions to a consideration of some other environmental problems associated with population increase. Eighty-six percent of Australia's population lives in the coastal zone. Most population growth now occurs there. Most tourist and recreational activities, as well as much industrial activity, also occur in this zone. Population growth in the coastal zone has increased pressure on coastal resources, especially with respect to housing, leisure, and recreation (Resource Assessment Commission (RAC), 1993). The Chairman of the Resource Assessment Commission, Donald Stewart, has said of Australia's urban sprawl: "The future is bleak. If we do not have constraint, we will soon have a ribbon of urban sprawl on every beach and headland from the bottom of Victoria to the top of Queensland" (McNicoll, 1993).

The coast is an ecologically sensitive area. The concentration of population growth and new developments on the coastline has placed it under great pressure. Over-development is destroying and degrading coastal habitats and the situation is deteriorating (State of the Environment Advisory Council, Executive Summary, 1996). Coastal development "hot spots" face the greatest threats. These include Cairns to Townsville, Brisbane to the Gold Coast, Coffs Harbour to Port Macquarie, Newcastle to Sydney to Wollongong, far south New South Wales, and Perth to Bunbury (Cribb, 1992; Resource Assessment Commission, 1993, 15–16). These are all experiencing rapid population growth. In its inquiry into the coastal zone, the Resource Assessment Commission found that:

The coastal zone is suffering the environmental and social stresses of continuing urbanization which is occurring both on the fringe of metropolitan areas and in an increasing number of coastal regions outside capital cities. If no action is taken to change the way in which coastal resources are used, there is a very considerable risk that ecosystems will be destroyed, the recreational amenity of the coast will be degraded, and economic growth and employment opportunities will be lost; in short, the collective benefits provided by the coastal zone will cease to be available to Australians. (Resource Assessment Commission, 1993, 357–58)

The Commission was critical of settlement patterns, but reluctant to attribute the damage caused to the coastal zone by urban development to population growth. It said, "It has not been established to date that an increase in Australia's population is in itself, the cause of degradation of the environmental amenity of the coastal zone" (Resource Assessment Commission, 1993, 44).

If only more Australians would live in high rise units, the Commission seems to be hinting, then the problem of urban sprawl along the coast would not occur. To date governments in Australia have had limited success in persuading Australians to abandon their back yards. With continuing rapid population growth along the coast, continuing coastal development seems likely. According to Dr. Miles Furnas of the Australian Institute of Marine Science, "The Californication of the Queensland coast is inevitable. The whole axis of development is clearly up the coast" (Cribb, 1993a). Governments at all levels in Australia have been reluctant to control coastal development. As Cribb has noted: "The most difficult issue is coastal development. Marine managers find they can influence matters as far as the high tide mark and no further. If local government wants untrammelled industrial, commercial, agricultural or marina development, little can be done to stop it" (Cribb, 1993a, 31).

For example, a recent study of remnant bushland in south-east Queensland found that there will shortly be virtually no native bush left on the Gold Coast (Catterall and Kingston, 1993). An inappropriately close relationship between the local Council and Gold Coast developers has been pointed to as one reason why the interests of developers dominate South-East Queensland (ABC TV, *7:30 Report*, August 12, 1996).

The State of the Environment Advisory Committee has pointed out that where Australia's marine and estuarine habitats are relatively untouched by humans, they are, on the whole, in good condition: "We have many different marine and estuarine environments. Most are far away from major population centers and are little affected by human activities. Large stretches of our coastline are among the least-polluted places on earth" (State of the Environment Advisory Council, 1996, ES-38).

The relatively pristine state of much of Australia's coastal environments is due to the relatively modest size of its population compared with the Australian continent's land mass, the population's concentration on the southern temperate coast and east coast, and the elapse of only 200 years since Western culture started to make inroads into the continent's coastal resources. Good weather, good soils, good water supplies, and a larger population spread around more of its coasts would paint a different picture, as would the lapse of another 200 years.

While the State of the Environment Advisory Council regards our marine and estuarine environments as being in good condition on the whole, the committee points out that such environments "in areas of high population density or intense human activity, however, . . . are often degraded as a result of urban, agricultural and industrial development and tourist and recreational activities" (State of the Environment Advisory Council, 1996, ES-38). Furthermore, despite the extensive coastal zone management reforms recommended by the Resource Assessment Commission in 1993, "Increasing development on and near the coast is removing or degrading marine and estuarine habitats, and reducing water quality and there is a 'continuing deterioration' in regard to this" (State of the Environment Advisory Council, 1996, ES-41). Onshore population growth and development have destroyed and continue to destroy coastal native vegetation and important land forms such as coastal dune systems. Wetlands have been and continue to be drained. Coastal mangroves are still being removed. Offshore seagrass beds are damaged, especially near major population centers (State of the Environment Advisory Council, 1996, ES-40).

Mangroves, until recently, were despised as mosquito-ridden wastelands, but are now recognized as providing an important habitat and food source for crustacea and many fish. Mangroves also produce food for fish that live outside mangroves. Australia has the third largest area of mangroves in the world, but the area of mangrove habitat is shrinking, especially in the tropics (State of the Environment Advisory Council, 1996). Coastal development is the main threat to mangroves. According to Dr Peter Saenger, a coastal management researcher at Southern Cross University in Queensland, governments have often been the main destroyers of mangroves. He says:

The biggest losses of mangroves have occurred because of very controversial, very public programs, often run by governments . . . with the stamp of government approval on it. In Darwin now, they [the government] are looking at reclaiming the foreshore for expanding the port, that's about 1000 hectares. . . . that's what happens, they say we need it for the airport or we need it for the port or we need it for this or we need it for that. (Scott, 1994,10)

Private developers have also destroyed mangroves, especially in the 1980s boom, when waterfront developments such as canal estates sprang up. There is a fairly strong link between the destruction of mangroves and population growth. Large-scale coastal tourist developments are also linked with mangrove destruction. Saltmarshes, which are a primary link in the marine food chain, have been severely reduced and degraded by canal estate developments, reclamation, drainage, weeds, and the dumping of rubbish (Cribb, 1995d). There is a moderately strong relationship between the destruction of saltmarshes/wetlands and both population growth and tourist development. Drainage of wetlands has also occurred to serve agriculture and pastoralism.

Australia has the largest area of coral reefs in the world. These reefs are, however, now exposed to significant deterioration, especially those close to major population centers (State of the Environment Advisory Council, 1996, ES-40). The Great Barrier Reef is the largest system of coral reefs in the world. Extending over 2500 kilometers, it consists of 2900 separate reefs and 940 islands. The Reef harbors a high diversity of species, including 400 corals, 4000 molluscs, 1500 fish, six turtles, 35 seabirds, and 23 sea mammals (State of the Environment Advisory Council, 1996, ES-40). The Reef was placed on the World Heritage List in 1981. It is the largest protected marine area in the world. It is managed by the Great Barrier Reef Marine Park Authority. The Reef is Australia's most popular tourist attraction. About two million people visit it each year and this number is growing by 10 percent a year (State of the Environment Advisory Council, 1996, ES-40). There are several pressures on the Great Barrier Reef. These include fishing, tourism, ballast water from shipping, the threat of oil and chemical spills, the destruction of coral due to outbreaks of crown-of-thorns starfish and the degradation of water quality in inland areas due to increased sediments and nutrients (State of the Environment Advisory Council, 1996, ES-40). Coastal development is also a significant threat to the Reef.

According to the State of the Environment Advisory Committee, pollution of the marine environment is the most serious coastal environmental problem in Australia today (State of the Environment Advisory Council, 1996). Close to population centers, coastal marine water quality is declining due to rising levels of nutrients and sediments (State of the Environment Advisory Council, 1996, ES-39). All of Australia's coastal cities discharge stormwater heavily laden with sediments, nutrients, bacteria, heavy metals, and organic chemicals into the sea. Near developed areas, estuaries and coastal lakes are affected by serious nutrient pollution from stormwater runoff, sewage, and industrial and shipping discharges. Increased sediment run-off is also a problem, with scientists estimating that in Queensland the amount of sediment entering the sea each year has increased some three- to fivefold since European settlement (State of the Environment Advisory Council, 1996, ES-39).

Australia's marine waters contain the greatest diversity of seagrasses and some of the largest seagrass beds in the world (State of the Environment Advisory Council, 1996). Seagrass meadows are a major nursery for fish and crustacea. There has been widespread and serious dieback of the nation's seagrass meadows (Zann and Sutton, 1995). Coastal pollution and siltation have destroyed seagrasses in several localities along the southern and east coast of Australia (State of the Environment Advisory Council, 1996, 8–25), most of these being near major population centers.

By world standards Australia's seas, including a 200 nautical-mile Exclusive Economic Zone that covers part of the Pacific, Indian, and Southern Oceans, are not very productive. This is due to lack of an upwelling of nutrient-rich cold waters and a lack of runoff from much of the land (State of the Environment Advisory Council, 1996, ES-11). As a result of increased fishing, the limits of many of Australia's fisheries have now been reached. According to the State of the Environment Advisory Council, "Fishing, both commercial and recreational, imposes heavy pressure on marine species and their habitats. Most major Australian seafood species are now fully exploited. Some, such as the southern bluefin tuna and eastern gemfish, have been over-exploited" (State of the Environment Advisory Council, 1996, ES-39).

As Australia's population continues to grow, and as tourism increases, recreational and commercial fishing pressures increase. The rising prices that Australian seafood attracts on Asian markets are related to the world's human population explosion and over-exploitation of the world's fisheries. Worldwide, many fisheries are in a parlous state. According to the director-general of the International Center for Living Aquatic Resources, Dr. Meryl Williams, the global fish catch is falling and fish stocks may never recover (Cribb, 1996a). Declining catches are due to over-fishing, pollution, and marine habitat destruction. The poor state of many fish stocks threatens more than one billion people who rely mainly on fish for protein, in addition to 150 million people employed in the fishing industry worldwide (Cribb, 1996a).

Despite warnings on low fish stocks, the Australian Fisheries Management Authority, the statutory body charged with ensuring the ecologically sustainable use of Commonwealth fisheries, has allowed unsustainable fish catch levels. According to the Australian National Audit Office, eighteen fisheries under Commonwealth government control are at risk due to mismanagement (Australian National Audit Office, 1996). This audit report states that no environmental impact assessment had been made for any of the Authority's fishing decisions. The Authority's jurisdiction extends from the three nautical mile limit to the 200 mile nautical limit. Industry sources say that the Authority is a captive of the fishing industry. So high are its quotas that they effectively allow unlimited fishing of species of which the status of ocean stocks is unknown. The fishing industry provides over 50 percent of the Authority's funding, and commercial and recreational fishing representatives have majority control of the Authority's nine management advisory committees (Hoy, 1996).

Foreign fishing vessels have been illegally entering Australian territorial waters in growing numbers in recent years. In 1988 Coastwatch apprehended 32 foreign fishing vessels in Australian waters. In 1994 arrests were 126 boats, 82 of which were from Indonesia. Increasingly these incursions are made by modern well-equipped fishing vessels (Cribb, 1995c). These incursions are expected to go on increasing as fish stocks in the east Asian region dwindle, according to Dr. Russ Reichelt, director of the Australian Institute of Marine Science. He believes this invasion is a threat to Australia's marine resources. Most of these incursions occur in the rich fisheries of the north, from the Kimberleys to Cape York. This is the last part of Australia's waters where fish stocks are not yet fully exploited (Cribb, 1995c).

There are also reports of live fish boats that clean-out individual reefs of juvenile snapper and coral trout in order to serve them live in the high-priced Asian markets. These boats have invaded several areas of the Pacific and have been recently seen in Australian waters. Sometimes cyanide is used in small doses to stun the fish. This is a very destructive practice as it destroys other marine life and whole coral reef systems (Cribb, 1995c, e). An investigation by Tasmanian coral ecologist Dr. Bob Johannes has revealed the scale of destruction of Asia's reefs by cyanide fishermen seeking live fish for eating. He found that the lucrative live fish trade, which is centered in Hong Kong, was pumping hundreds of tonnes of sodium cyanide into coral reefs every year, killing thousands of marine creatures for every live fish captured and destroying the living coral habitat. The industry had largely destroyed the coral reefs and fish stocks of the Philippines and would do the same in Indonesia within a few years (Cribb, 1995e). Hong Kong's Marine Conservation Society has claimed that Asian fishermen, using cyanide, had reached the northern part of Australia's Great Barrier Reef (Cater, 1995).

State governments control the catch from fisheries within the three mile nautical limit. These fisheries consist mainly of coastal crustacea, including the high-value prawn, rock lobster, and abalone fisheries (Hoy, 1996). According to Dr. Joe Baker, the chairman of the Australian Academy of Science's national environment committee, there is in Australia a developing ethnic culture in which people collect limpets, sea urchins and "anything with flesh to eat" from hundreds of inter-tidal areas that had been left alone by "established" (i.e., largely Anglo-Celtic) Australians (Woodley, 1990). Illegal fishing in State-controlled waters is a multi-million dollar industry. Rising prices for seafood, especially on Asian markets, has stimulated this development. For example, dried abalone fetches $A400–$800 a kilogram on the black market in Asia where it is highly valued for its supposedly aphrodisiac qualities (Foreshew, 1996; Morgan and Papps, 1996). In New South Wales, abalone poaching by crime gangs has reached epidemic proportions, with poachers estimated to steal at least the same amount as the legal yearly catch of 330 tonnes (Foreshew, 1996). Vietnamese crime groups involved in heroin dealing and money-laundering are believed to be involved in poaching abalone from South Australia's west coast and selling it to Asian restaurants in Adelaide and Melbourne at prices far below the retail price (Papps, 1996). Following ongoing surveillance of an Asian gang that was illegally netting bream and selling them to Asian shops, two South Australian Fisheries Department officers pursued members of the gang in a four kilometer car chase north of Adelaide one night in August 1995. During the chase gang members forced the car of a Fisheries Compliance Unit Officer off the road (Haran, 1995), signaling a rising level of violence and danger associated with attempts to control illegal fishing. Asian crime groups are believed to steal South Australian abalone to fund heroin deals. The shellfish is poached from the coastline, transported to interstate docks, and illegally shipped to the so-called Golden Quadrangle—Laos, Burma, Thailand, and Vietnam. Returns from the sale of the abalone are used to purchase heroin from the Golden Quadrangle to be shipped to Australia. Stolen South Australian abalone is also sold to interstate restaurants, supermarkets, and Asian tourist shops. According to the head of the South Australian fisheries compliance unit, Rod Coombes, Asian tourists were a prime target for stolen abalone. He said:

Just before they are due to leave Australia, they are given their abalone and they are out of the country and are serving the abalone within hours. The abalone sold to the tourists have all the signs of coming from a legal source and the tour guides who sell the abalone get a cut. It happens mainly in Queensland where the abalone is not recognized as a fish and is not covered by any Act. (Morgan and Papps, 1996, 1)

In recent years aquaculture has developed into a $250 million a year export industry in Australia. In Boston Bay at Port Lincoln on South Australia's west coast, bluefin tuna are being reared in huge cages submerged in the sea for export to Japan. In the rush to secure lucrative export markets, successive State governments have shown little interest in controlling this new industry. In April 1996 a storm hit Boston Bay, stirring up nutrient-rich sediment (a mixture of undigested fish food, excreta, and silt) and resulting in the deaths of 75,000 tuna worth $60 million (Kerin, 1996; James and Weir, 1996). According to Mike Elliott, leader of the Australian Democrats in South Australia and Member of the Legislative Council, successive State governments have failed to heed warnings from senior government scientists about aquaculture. He said that a 1993 tuna industry management plan had been criticized on the grounds of lack of an independent audit, concerns about whether Boston Bay was suitable for tuna farming, inadequate recognition of problems such as algal blooms, lack of environmental impact monitoring, and lack of any long-term investigations into the impact of tuna farming (Kerin, 1996).

From March 1995 the mass deaths of billions of pilchards began to be reported along the southern coast of Australia. First reported off Adelaide's coast in March, by May a 30 kilometer slick of dead pilchards was seen off Sydney's beaches. The mass deaths were spread along more than 3000 kilometers of southern coastline and northern Tasmania (Anonymous. b, 1995). At first thought to be due to algal blooms, it is believed that a tropical or foreign disease, possibly from a foreign ship's ballast, might be responsible. According to New South Wales Fisheries principal habitat manager, Mr. David Pollard: "Everybody has been talking about algal blooms. . . . Algal blooms don't travel at 100km a day over a 3000km stretch. It is more likely it is a disease, virus or protozoan" (Anonymous b, 1995, 8).

The final environmental variable we will consider here, in this discussion of Australia's declining environment, is water. Australia is the driest inhabited continent in the world. Compared to other continents, Australia has the least river water, lowest water run-off, and least area of permanent wetlands. In one third of Australia there is almost no water run-off while two thirds of the average annual water run-off occurs in the north of the continent (State of the Environment Advisory Council, 1996, ES-34). Australia's rainfall and stream flows are the most variable in the world. Droughts and floods are relatively frequent occurrences. Due to its dry and variable climate, Australia stores more water for each person than does any other country. For example, Sydney stores 932 kilolitres of drinking water per person compared to New York's 250 and London's 18.2 (State of the Environment Advisory Council, 1996, ES-34). This suggests that each human in Sydney has a bigger environmental impact on rivers and freshwater ecosystems than does each human in London or New York.[12] Because of Australia's need to store large quantities of freshwater per person, it has tried to insure against drought by building dams, which has in turn dramatically altered the seasonal flow regimes of rivers in most areas and the lack of water as a flushing mechanism, leading to greater incidence of toxic algal blooms (State of the Environment Advisory Council, 1996, ES-37).

Irrigation uses 70 percent of all developed water resources (State of the Environment Advisory Council, 1996, ES-35) and has itself led to environmental problems such as waterlogging and salinization of soils and nutrient and pesticide pollution (State of the Environment Advisory Council, 1996, ES-37). After irrigation the major cities consume most water. This is mostly for domestic use (State of the Environment Advisory Council, 1996, ES-35). As a result of growing population and rising per capita consumption, total household water use has increased. To curb domestic water use, prices are rising. One estimate is that 1994 water prices will double by 2000 and continue to rise thereafter, according to Professor Peter Cullen, director of the Cooperative Research Center for Freshwater Ecology (Cribb, 1994b). The over-allocation of water to consumption is severe in the south-east of Australia and this situation is deteriorating (State of the Environment Advisory Council, 1996, ES-37).

The Great Artesian Basin, lying under one fifth of the continent at depths of one to two kilometers, is crucial for much of the eastern part of inland Australia. The basin is recharged mainly along the western slopes of the Great Dividing Range in New South Wales and Queensland. The recharging of underground aquifers is a slow process. For example, after flooding rains surface water can travel from the Great Dividing Range in Queensland to central Australia in weeks, whereas the ground water of the Great Artesian Basin takes about one million years to travel the same distance (State of the Environment Advisory Council, 1996, ES-35). Underground water is invisible and poorly understood. It is therefore often abused through over-extraction and pollution (State of the Environment Advisory Council,1996, ES-35). If pollution of groundwater occurs, it is almost impossible to remove it, due to the time it takes for groundwater to be replenished.

Due to the dependence of much of inland Australia on groundwater, in 60 percent of Australia, people are totally dependent on groundwater. In a further 20 percent of the country, people use more groundwater than surface water (State of the Environment Advisory Council, 1996, ES-35). So throughout 80 percent of Australia, people are totally or largely dependent on groundwater. In the United States the use of groundwater has doubled since 1950 (State of the Environment Advisory Council,1996, ES-35). Pollution has degraded the quality of much underground water in the United States. In Australia there are similar trends in use and quality of groundwater (State of the Environment Advisory Council, 1996, ES-35). As early as 1991 the Bureau of Mineral Resources warned that inland underground water was being rapidly depleted. This threatened both rural industries and tourism (Cribb, 1991). Much of the water being used in the center of Australia is "fossil water" accumulated during a wetter climate period 10,000 to 25,000 years ago. A Bureau hydro-geologist, Robert Abell said:

Since rainfall is now much reduced because of aridity, no adequate recharge mechanism exists to replenish these ancient stocks of ground water. Their exploitation is tantamount to mining a valuable natural resource. Over the last 30 years extraction has lowered the water table, so that groundwater availability has become not only more expensive but exploitation is fast depleting it. (Cribb, 1991)

This situation remains unchanged. In 1996 the State of the Environment Advisory Committee reported that: "Australia is effectively mining its groundwater with reserves being used much faster than they are replenished. Groundwater is often very old, with some bores tapping water that entered the ground 1–2 million years ago" (State of the Environment Advisory Council, 1996, ES-35).

According to Dr. Bob Wasson, assistant chief of the CSIRO Division of Water Resources and chairman of the 1996 *State of the Environment* report's section on inland waters, the level of damage to rivers is so severe that population curbs may be needed to control it (Beale and Woodford, 1995). Dr. Wasson considers that with the exception of parts of northern Australia where water is plentiful, Australia has reached the limits of its water resources (Woodford,

1995c). Further growth in water usage will lead to increased ecological decline of large and small river systems, rising levels of chemical contamination, and increasing outbreaks of blue-green algae (Woodford, 1995c). As the country's water managers have come to appreciate the disastrous impact over-extraction of water has had on many of Australia's rivers and inland waters, there have been increasing calls for water usage to be cut (Cribb, 1995c, g; Woodford, 1995 b; Este and Stapleton, 1996). In 1994 Federal, State, and Territory governments agreed to cut water consumption by 15 percent nationally through restrictions, user-pays pricing, and public education (Bita, 1995b). During the 1995 National Water Week, the then Prime Minister Paul Keating pointed out that population growth and modern lifestyles were putting great demands on the country's water resources. According to Keating, Australians had to cut water usage to protect valuable waterways to ensure the quality of this limited resource was maintained. He said, "I urge every Australian to use water more wisely, to save water, save money and save the environment" (Anonymous a, 1995, 6). Even if Australians cut their water consumption, this will do little to save the environment while Australia's population continues to increase rapidly.

Australia's water resources are continuing to decline in quality. The orthodox opinion is that the quality of drinking water in Australia's large cities is satisfactory to good (Aquatech Pty. Ltd., 1994). However, at a conference held by the Australian Medical Association in Canberra in October 1995, the then Senator John Coulter of the Australian Democrats warned that Australia's water quality was declining, due to rising levels of salt, chlorine, natural toxins, and dangerous microbes. Coulter said, "It is therefore alarming to see the corporatisation and privatisation ideology leading governments to divest themselves of this responsibility."[13] He believed that Australia would have great difficulty in ensuring water quality to protect public health (Cribb, 1995f).

According to the director of the National Centre for Epidemiology and Population, Professor Bob Douglas, Australia's drinking water is a long way from meeting national health and safety guidelines (Cribb, 1995h). Outbreaks of blue-green algae in recent years have endangered the water supplies of some small towns and outback areas. If swallowed, toxins in algal blooms can cause serious illness. In February 1994 toxic blue-green algal blooms in Lake Alexandrina, into which the River Murray flows in South Australia, caused the closure of the main water pump supplying the township of Strathalbyn with the lake's water. The small town of Clayton on the edge of Lake Alexandrina was also badly affected as its normal water supply came from the lake (Morgan, 1994). An algal bloom in the Darling River killed thousands of sheep and cattle in 1990 and residents on north Queensland's Palm Island suffered severe poisoning in 1979 (Hailstone, 1996). Blue-green algae is suspected of causing stomach and bowel tumors. There is evidence of this from Brazil, where liver damage was seen in kidney patients who had undergone dialysis in which algae-contaminated water was used. From China there is some evidence that algal contamination causes liver damage (Hailstone, 1996). According to the director of gastroenterology at Royal Melbourne Hospital, Dr James St. John, bowel cancer is a major problem in Australia. Over 9,000 new cases were reported in 1996 and 4,500 people died of it (Hailstone, 1996).

Australia's largest river system is the Murray-Darling Basin, which drains about one seventh of the continent (State of the Environment Advisory Council, 1996, ES-34). In terms of river length and catchment area, the basin is one of the world's largest, but it carries a much smaller quantity of water than comparable river systems. For example, in less than one day, the Amazon River in South America carries the River Murray's annual flow (State of the Environment Advisory Council, 1996, ES-34). The Murray-Darling Basin is known as the breadbasket of Australia (Woodford, 1996b), with an annual value of agricultural produce from the basin exceeding $10 billion. The basin provides half of Australia's crop land, producing wheat, cotton, rice, oil seed, fruit, and vegetables, and supports a quarter of Australia's cattle and dairy herds and half of its sheep (Murray-Darling Basin commission, 1995; Turner, 1995).

About 80 percent of the divertible or accessible water in the Murray-Darling Basin is extracted for human use (State of the Environment Advisory Council, 1996, ES-34). The natural flow in the basin is over 11,000 gigalitres in a normal year, but over-extraction has cut this by almost 80 percent to less than 2,500 gigalitres. In a dry year up to 99 percent of some rivers is taken for human use (Cribb, 1994c). So much water has been allocated from the Darling River that in dry years the river almost dries up and toxic blue-green algae, bloom (Cribb, 1994b). Unlike the River Murray, the Darling River is not a permanent river. In 1994, for the tenth time this century, it stopped flowing. With more irrigation water extracted over the past 20 years, the river's flow has dropped on average 40 percent below natural levels. While big floods still occur, medium floods have almost stopped. Without these, billabongs are not being recharged and trees are dying (ABC TV *Landline*, September 22, 1994).

More than 95 percent of the water taken from the basin is used by irrigators and more than half of the extracted water is used by New South Wales farmers (Woodford, 1995a). In the years 1988 to 1994, the quantity of water being extracted from the Murray-Darling Basin increased by 8 percent (Chamberlin, 1995; Woodford, 1995a). Irrigators are set to drain an extra 100 billion litres of water from the Murray-Darling system each year (at 1 percent growth rate per year), draining wetlands and contributing to blue-green algal blooms (Bita, 1996d). In the past 20 years, rapid development of rice and cotton industries, which are concentrated in New South Wales, have placed additional stresses on the basin (Stapleton, 1995; Chamberlain, 1995). Cotton production now exceeds $1 billion annually, being Australia's fourth largest agricultural export (ABC TV *Landline*, September 25, 1994). Of the Darling river, D. Nicholas writes:

Australians should weep at what is happening in this river basin. Land which blind Freddie knew long ago could not sustain broad-hectare cropping, with evaporation rates far too high for even medium-term water storage, is now studded with capital-intensive, water-ravenous cottonfields interspersed with shallow tanks so large that you can hardly see across them for the heat haze. (Nicholas, 1996)

Continuing expansion of the irrigation industry comes at a big cost (Woodford, 1995a). For example, the Gwydir wetlands in the Darling Basin, West of Moree in northern New South Wales, once covered 270,000 hectares and included freshwater meadows, scrub country, and coolibah woodlands. But due to excessive irrigation over the last 15 years, mainly for the expanding cotton industry, the wetlands have shrunk to less than 5,000 hectares and what remains is badly degraded (Meade, 1995).[14] The seasonal flooding that once made Gwydir Valley cattle properties rich grazing land no longer occurs. Howard Blackburn, Gwydir property owner and grazier, has said, "You should have seen this paddock 13 years ago, when I first came here. There was water as far as you could see and waterbirds everywhere you looked. We had huge amounts of ibises, ducks and pelicans" (Meade, 1995). Mr. Blackburn's wetlands have gone and his property was ravaged by drought in 1995. The birds too have long gone. By the end of February 1994, dead and dying Murray Cod lay in stinking heaps along the dry margins of two of the largest inland lakes in New South Wales, Lakes Menindee and Cawndilla on the lower Darling river system. A combination of drought, upstream irrigation, and local water consumption had left the lakes, which provide the main water supply for Broken Hill and the surrounding area, depleted (Cribb, 1994b). Local residents were concerned about shortages of water for domestic use and livestock and an upsurge in mosquito-borne diseases such as Ross River fever. The residents were also distressed and angered by the sight of huge 50-year-old Murray Cod left to die and rot on the shores of the emptying lakes (Cribb, 1994a).

Human demand for Murray-Darling Basin water has not only reduced river flows, it has significantly changed natural flow patterns. Over-extraction of water for human use has removed seasonal flooding along much of the basin, depriving floodplain wetlands of water. Seasonal flooding provides the breeding trigger for waterbird and native fish populations. When flooding does not occur, the natural ecology of the river system and the life cycles of organisms dependent upon it are disrupted.

The salinity of rivers in the Murray-Darling Basin is rising. Increasing river salinity is a result of both saline groundwater inflows and reduced river outflows. Saline groundwater inflows are exacerbated by land clearance, irrigation, and drainage management. Salinity in some basin rivers in northern New South Wales is growing by one to four percent a year (Woodford, 1995a). Salinity in the River Murray is now so bad that hot water systems in Adelaide (which draws a significant part of its water supply from the River Murray) have an average life span of only nine years, compared with 15 years in Melbourne (Turner, 1995; Woodford, 1995a). Salinity costs Australia $65 million a year. In 1994 the chief executive officer of the Murray-Darling Basin Commission, Don Blackmore, warned that the saltiness of River Murray water would rise by nearly one third by the mid twenty-first century unless action were taken immediately to prevent it (Cribb, 1994c).

According to Murray-Darling Basin Commission estimates, 1.3 million hectares of prime irrigation farmland will be salinized or waterlogged by 2040.

The area of dryland salinity will expand by 1–2 million hectares, a 400–500 percent increase, over the same period (Cribb, 1994c). Noel Fitzpatrick, who retired in 1994 as chairman of the Murray-Darling Basin Commission, has said: "Dryland salinity was not seen as a problem in the basin till the mid-80s. Now we estimate it will be four or five times as bad within 20–30 years. If we stuff it up, it's for good. We don't get a second chance" (Cribb, 1994c).

Groundwater levels in the basin are rising. This is occurring as a result of widespread vegetation clearance, which significantly increases the rate of recharge to the water table. In the vicinity of efficient irrigation practices, as well, groundwater levels are rising because even efficient irrigation creates some drainage water. This drainage water adds to the local groundwater and builds a groundwater mound below the irrigation area.

According to the Murray-Darling Basin Commission's 1995 report, *An Audit of Water Use in the Murray-Darling Basin*, the biodiversity of the basin is collapsing due to the continuing extraction of water from the basin for human use. Many species of birds, fish, amphibians, insects, and plants have been seriously reduced in number or driven to local extinction. The decline of wetlands, as a result of upstream water extraction, has had a dramatic effect on biodiversity. For example, the basin once supported flocks of Magpie Geese in large numbers similar to those found in parts of the Northern Territory's Arnhem Land today. But these flocks of geese have long gone from the basin (McLean, 1994).

In the lower River Murray, the elimination of natural rises and falls in the river is implicated in huge declines in the biological productivity of the river, according to Dr. Terry Hillman, director of the Murray-Darling Freshwater Research Centre in Albury (Cribb, 1994c). Due to river regulation commercial catches of native fish in South Australia have dropped 20 percent since the 1950s. The billabongs on the river's floodplain once harbored a rich biodiversity—River Redgum forests, rich plant life, birds, and fish. Periodic floods linked the billabongs with the main river channel. Murray Cod, when young and at a certain stage in their development, rely on microscopic creatures in water. Only in the billabongs can the young cod find enough micro-organisms to survive. The exclusion of Murray Cod from the billabongs is one reason for their decline along most inland waterways. The same pattern is repeated for many other species (Cribb, 1993b).

Blue-green algal blooms are a natural phenomenon, but they are occurring more often lately along the basin's waterways. In recent years in summer, blooms of toxic blue-green algae stretch for hundreds of kilometers along inland rivers. The algae feed on nutrients from sewage and agricultural fertilizers.

In mid-1995 a moratorium was placed on issuing new licenses for taking further irrigation water from the basin (Chamberlin, 1995; Harris, 1995; Woodford, 1995a). The moratorium was imposed by the Murray-Darling Basin Ministerial Council, which includes the relevant federal government ministers and the State water ministers of the basin States—New South Wales, Queensland, Victoria, and South Australia. In June 1996 the Council voted to extend for twelve months the ban on new irrigation licences. The federal Minister for Primary Industries, John Anderson, said the ban would extend to June 1997 when a permanent cap would be placed on further water diversion (Bita, 1996d).

In September 1995, in an effort to increase the water flow to the imperilled Gwydir wetlands and Macquarie Marshes in northern New South Wales, the State government announced new measures to curb the amount of water available for irrigation, including water price increases and tighter restrictions on its use (Meade, 1995). New South Wales irrigators attacked the new measures, claiming they could damage rural industries and lead to job losses (Stapleton, 1995). The director of natural resources and water with the Australian Cotton Foundation, Graham Pearcey, said, "The fact that there is less water in the rivers is not because of cotton. It's because of drought" (Meade, 1995). Banks warned the State government that large numbers of cotton producers in the Gwydir Valley carried extreme debt after four years of drought and they faced financial ruin as a result of the government's water price rises and water restrictions (Passey, 1995). The New South Wales Irrigators' Council warned that the banks' stand on finance in the Gwydir Valley foreshadowed an impending crisis for farmers in other irrigation valleys in the State (Passey, 1995).[15] Macquarie Valley irrigators claimed that the water price rises and water restrictions would result in farmers losing 25 percent of their water, with a proportional cut in production. Spokesman Tony Wass said: "We are talking well over $100 million in lost revenue to the valley, and ultimately to the nation. The immediate loss of 750 jobs will have a devastating effect on the region" (Stapleton, 1995).

Pressure on water resources in eastern Australia has encouraged developers to look further afield for water. Recently a syndicate of four cotton farmers from the Macquarie Valley in New South Wales has proposed to extract water from the Cooper basin, which straddles remote south-west Queensland and north-east South Australia, for cotton growing (Woodford, 1995c). These investors have bought a grazing property, Currareva, in southern Queensland to enable them to extract 42 billion litres of water from Cooper's Creek yearly to irrigate cotton (Cribb, 1996c). According to Dr. John Kalish, a biologist at the Australian National University, the same mistakes that have ruined the Murray and Darling rivers are about to wreck one of Australia's last wild rivers and historic icon, Cooper's Creek (Cribb, 1996c). He said that extraction of the large quantities of water proposed would severely damage the river's fish and wildlife. While the 42 billion litres of water the syndicate wants to extract from the Cooper each year represents only two percent of its mean monthly flow, it ignores the fact that the monthly flow figures were distorted by one huge flood in 1973. According to Dr. Kalish: "Flows in the Cooper are extremely variable. The cotton farmers are proposing to take an average of 3.2 gigalitres per month—but in 46 percent of months, the flow is less than 4 gigalitres" (Cribb, 1996c).

This extraction of water would virtually eliminate the small floods that are vital for the survival of fish and other wildlife. As the region is very flat, the reduced flooding would mean that large areas that normally receive a few centimeters of flood water every few years would no longer receive any river water and their vegetation would die (Cribb, 1996c). Dr. Kalish said that although the cotton project was proposed in Queensland, its worst impact would be felt along Cooper's Creek. This echoed the damage done to the Darling River in New South Wales by cross-border development in Queensland (Cribb, 1996c). According to Dr Bob Wasson, chairman of the section on inland waters of the 1996 *State of the Environment Report* and assistant chief of the CSIRO Division of Water Resources, "The cotton proposal for south-west Queensland has got to be stopped. It is so wrong. We have seen what cotton farming has done to the Murray-Darling. It is extraordinarily dumb" (Woodford, 1995c). Professor Peter Cullen, Director of the Centre for Freshwater Ecology in Canberra, has said, "To see exactly the same kind of development that has caused such a mess in the Murray-Darling Basin starting up in the Cooper basin—which is almost as large and even more fragile—is crazy" (Cribb, 1996b). As a result of widespread scientific concern about the proposal and lobbying against it by pastoralists and environmentalists, the Queensland government has withheld its approval of the project.

We turn now to a consideration of the degradation of Australia's inland waters. Australia's inland streams are naturally turbid and saline. There are few permanent freshwater lakes. Lakes are usually shallow salt lakes that are frequently dry (State of the Environment Advisory Council, 1996, ES-34). Many coastal and inland Australian salt lakes have suffered significant damage as a result of water diversions, changes to catchment or drainage basins, and pollution (Williams, 1993). For example, Lake Corangamite in Victoria is a large permanent salt lake that has been damaged by water diversion. By 1993 this lake was rapidly shrinking as its salinity grew due to its major inflow, the Woody Yaloak Creek being diverted into the Barwon River by the Rural Water Commission of Victoria. Lake Corangamite, Australia's largest permanent salt lake, is a RAMSAR site, supports a number of birds, and has significant wildlife, recreational, and aesthetic values. But to reduce the possibility of the lake flooding surrounding agricultural land, the diversion scheme operated from 1959. Consequently, from 1959 to 1990, the level of the lake salinity rose from 35 to 60 g/litre. Islands that were refuges for waterbirds have now disappeared. The increased salinity killed the major aquatic food supplies for birds. This is akin to an "Aral Sea crisis" on Australia's doorstep (Williams, 1993). It is only one of a number of such crises. Professor Peter Cullen, Director of the Australian Cooperative Research Centre for Freshwater Ecology, believes that the environmental health of the Hawkesbury Nepean River serving Sydney, is a symbol of the declining state of many of Australia's rivers:

Today more than half of the water in the lower Hawkesbury is treated flow from sewage works. The river has suffered enormously from removal of water for city use, from sand-mining, from nutrient inflows, catchment erosion and urban run-off. It lies in an area of Australia where population is increasing by almost 400 people a week and extraction of water continues to grow at five percent a year to meet that demand. (Cribb, 1994c)

Nineteenth-century paintings depicted the Hawkesbury as a shallow, sandy-bottomed, clear-flowing river supporting an abundance of native vegetation and waterlife. Today it is deep, still and eutrophic. The sand that filtered it has been mined away, and ultraviolet sunlight no longer penetrates its murky waters to clean them (Cribb, 1994c).

The fate of the Hawkesbury-Nepean will be shared by rivers around Australia unless major management changes are implemented and population controlled, according to Dr. Bob Wasson of the CSIRO Division of Water Resources (Woodford, 1995c). The perilous state of Australia's water resources and the impact that population increases are having on their degradation has been well summarized by Williams (1993):

In the absence of better management and a significant rearrangement of how water is presently used, a larger Australian population will bring about increasingly greater impacts upon the aquatic environment. Further growth of our population will be accompanied by further degradation of the aquatic environment. Inevitably, for example, a larger population will mean that the painfully evolving balance now being struck between non-environmental and environmental allocations for water usage will be subject to less benign and more intense pressure than is presently the case. A key point here is that for each small incremental increase in population, there will be a large incremental effect on the environment because much of what is left is marginal and sensitive to disturbance. As such, it often occurs in less well-watered areas and is therefore more precious to its biota, more vulnerable to exploitation, much slower to recover from disturbance and the impacts are more likely to be irreversible due to the loss of naturally occurring biota in these marginal areas. Small rises in population will have a much more severe impact than in the past! (Williams, 1993, 4)

CONCLUSION

The lack of sustainability of agricultural and pastoral activities bodes poorly for future population increase in Australia. The long-term decline of significant parts of Australian agricultural and pastoral land is clear evidence that the standard of living of our present population has been partly achieved by the destruction of our natural resource base. We are fast approaching the limits of that destruction. Population growth will increase pressures to export primary products in order to generate wealth and city jobs. Pressures to maximize output may well work against the need to restore sustainability to our farming and pastoral industries.

As Australia's population increases, growth in water usage will lead to the further ecological decline of many river systems and inland lakes, more water shortages for city populations during drought, and higher water costs for all. Population growth will make more urgent the need for Australians to reduce their water consumption. Population increase is a major threat to natural ecosystems and biological diversity in the coastal zone. Australians will have to decide to what extent they wish to trade off their irreplaceable ecological heritage for population growth—if they still have the freedom to make such decisions.

Australia is suffering from serious environmental problems and many of these are getting worse, not better. This is in spite of greater scientific understanding of what needs to be done to rectify the problems. Whereas the early

European settlers of Australia tried to introduce into an alien environment European farming methods, which turned out to be unsuitable for Australia's soils, climate, and biogeography, this early ignorance about the Australian environment can no longer serve as an excuse for our current actions and inactions. The present environmental crisis in Australia is rooted in the "develop or die" philosophy of the political and economic elite of this country and in their faith in material progress, via continuous population growth, unending economic growth, and technological optimism.

As the economist Steve Dowrick puts it:

The biggest single reason for economic growth in Australia is the rapid rise in population. Australia has had the fastest growing population of all the advanced industrial economies in the postwar period. Population growth has been fuelled by the substantial program of immigration, but it is also due in part to a sustained baby boom. Population has grown by an average of 1.7 percent per year over the last four decades, although this rate of growth has slowed considerably in recent years as the natural rate of increase has slowed and, particularly, as immigration was cut in the wake of the recession of the early 1990s. . . . A fast-growing population will, other things being equal, lead to a rapidly growing labor force which will generate economic growth by expanding employment and its associated output. (Dowrick, 1995, 19–20)

The acceptance of such simple linear correlations is a striking feature of the pro-growth argument in the Australian debate (Clark, 1995; Oaten, 1996; Switzer, 1996). There is little concern about the direction of the causal arrow or whether a genuine causal relationship exists at all. Japan has not had a substantial immigration program over the same period and its economic growth rates in the post–World War II period are envied by Australia's pro-growth lobby. Technological innovation and the increased efficiency of a workforce—quality rather than quantity considerations—are obviously important variables. Further, even if Dowrick were right, it does not follow that economic limits to immigration and population increase do not exist (Corden, 1955), and in fact they must as a consequence of the neoclassical economic law of diminishing returns (Smith et al., 1997). The logic of the Australian pro-growth lobby is the logic of greed, short–term gain, and the satisfaction of sectional interests over the common good of the entire Australian society. The powerful ethnic lobby groups battle for increased immigration so that more of *their* own racial and ethnic groups can come to Australia, while ethnic leaders and other new class elites smear critics of immigration with the debate-stopping label: "RACIST!". Big business lobby groups such as the housing lobby also have a vested interest in keeping Australia's immigration intake at high levels to keep housing prices high (Wood, 1997). These forces are so powerful that they have created a culture—nay, a religion of immigration—among Australia's ruling elite. Immigration may be varied in the short term to deal with politically unacceptable levels of unemployment, but in the longer term immigration must continue. It is the ultimate Australian sacred cow.

This has created a situation of inevitable social conflict, relevant to our global meltdown theme. Even if social, ethnic, and racial conflict does not develop to a destabilizing level in Australia, there remains an ultimate limit to the grand experiment being conducted in Australia. If it is the case that Australia's present population of 18.3 million people is unsustainable, as Flannery (1994) and others believe (Coulter, 1997), then Australia is on the path to its destruction.[16] Not only must this nation deal with the problems of ecological scarcity documented in chapter 1 of this book, but it faces an alarming array of environmental problems. We have only been able to address a small number of these problems here, giving only surface detail. Therefore, we conjecture that Australia will be one of the most devastated of all Western nations by the forces of the global meltdown.

NOTES

1. Some of this unease was documented by the social researcher Hugh MacKay (MacKay, 1993). In 1996 there was a surge of public support for independent member of Parliament Pauline Hanson who said in her maiden speech in Parliament on September 10 that Australians were "in danger of being swamped by Asians" (Hanson, 1997, 7). A poll conducted by the newspaper *The Australian* in October 1996 showed that 53 percent of respondents believed that the proportion of Asian migrants allowed into Australia should be reduced (Short, 1996).

2. Flannery points out that one of the most astute early observers of Australia's natural capacity was the biologist Charles Darwin, who visited Australia in 1836. Of Australia, Darwin wrote:

The rapid prosperity and future prospects of this colony are to me, not understanding these subjects, very puzzling. The two main exports are wool and whale oil, and to both of these productions there is a limit. . . . Pasture everywhere is so thin that settlers have already pushed far into the interior; moreover the country further inland becomes extremely poor. Agriculture, on account of the droughts, can never succeed on an extended scale: therefore, so far as I can see, Australia must ultimately depend upon being the centre of commerce for the southern hemisphere, and perhaps on her future manufactories. Possessing coal, she always has the moving power at hand. From the habitable country extending along the coast, and from her former English extraction, she is sure to be a maritime nation. I formerly imagined that Australia would rise to be as grand and powerful a country as North America, but now it appears to me that such future grandeur is rather problematical. (C. Darwin, *The Voyage of the Beagle.* Republished Edito-Service, S.A., Geneva, cited in Flannery, 1994, 350)

3. The one notable exception to this myopia of State politicians is Premier Bob Carr of New South Wales, who shocked the Australian elite (including his own political party, the Labor Party) in 1995 when he said that Sydney, Australia's largest city, was "bursting at the seams" and called for a lowering of immigration levels (Dusevic, 1995). His comments were condemned by Peter Hollingworth, the Archbishop of Brisbane, as "a pity" and "pre-emptive," as "very emotional" by Ian Spicer, chief executive of the Australian Chamber of Commerce and Industry, as giving "ammunition to the rednecks and radicals" by Lawrence Lau, the president of the Australian Chinese Community Association, and as risking Sydney's status as a regional headquarters for multinational companies in the Asia-Pacific by Senator Nick Bolkus, the Minister for Immigration (Armitage, 1995a, b). Following Carr's call for migrants to be diverted away from Sydney, he was accused, in the New South Wales Legislative Council, of social engineering, racial vilification, and of promoting race-based hatred. A Liberal member of the Legislative Council, Helen

Sham-Ho, said Mr. Carr's views that migrants should be diverted away from sprawling Sydney smacked of the old White Australia policy (Middleton and Pegler, 1995).

4. It should be noted that the most contentious aspect of the ecological footprint concept is that calculations of the size of a footprint may include land needed for forest to absorb carbon dioxide or greenhouse gas emissions or to produce energy from biomass-derived ethanol. (See State of the Environment Advisory Council, 1996, 3–5.)

5. We cannot find adequate alternatives for these resources. Once lost, they are largely gone for good. Soils may be built up again, of course, but this is usually a slow geological process. Wetlands, too, may be created artificially, but they may lack the complexity and biodiversity of natural wetlands. The degradation of rivers may be reversed, but this is usually a slow and expensive process. The end result is unlikely to be as good as what existed prior to the degradation.

6. The production of food does not appear to pose an absolute limit on Australia's population growth over the next 50 years. As well as feeding our population of 18.3 million, Australia now produces enough food to support another 55 million people at Australian levels of consumption (State of the Environment Advisory Council, 1996, 2–24). Most of this "extra" food is exported. While food production may pose no immediate limit on Australia's population growth, the long-term sustainability of our farming and pastoral industries is doubtful. As Australia's population grows, higher domestic consumption may result in lower food exports. This could exacerbate Australia's balance of payments deficits and so contribute to a lower standard of living for Australians.

7. In western Sydney bushland remnants are threatened by the expansion of suburbs. In Adelaide, one of the slower population growth cities, bushland continues to be cleared from the Mt. Lofty Ranges for housing. This is occurring even though the Ranges are an important water catchment area for Adelaide's water supply.

8. Even if we stopped Australia's population growth tomorrow (a clear impossibility), our biological diversity would continue to decline for many years, because most of our past actions, which severely affected Australia's environment, have long lead times. For example, our past excessive clearance of native vegetation has consigned some 50 bird species to extinction in the future, as their populations are now so low as to be unviable (Possingham, 1996).

9. For example, the removal of native vegetation from the banks of many of our urban rivers and creeks to facilitate urban development has not only reduced the biological diversity of these water-ways but also increased the amount of pollution they carry.

10. In 1993 the Resource Assessment Commission estimated that over the next ten years, additional dwellings would require about 35,000 hectares of land in non-metropolitan areas of the coastal zone, (assuming coastal zone population growth in that decade would roughly equal that from 1981 to 1991). This scale of vegetation clearance could reduce and destroy many rare and endangered species and unique ecological complexes, according to the Biodiversity Unit. And this is only for a ten year period! (Resource Assessment Commission, 1993).

11. Photochemical smog is produced by the reaction of nitrogen oxides with volatile organic compounds in the presence of sunlight. As a city grows in size, air quality tends to deteriorate, because the efficiency of dispersal of air pollutants falls (Cocks, 1992). For example, unless growth in motor vehicles is curtailed, photochemical smog will increase in Australia's cities (State of the Environment Advisory Council, 1996, 3–44). Air pollution already contributes to the death of almost 400 people a year in Sydney (Pitt and Dayton, 1996).

12. This is before we consider the per capita water consumption of Australians, which is high compared to consumption in most countries.

13. Concern about downsizing and the restructuring of Australia's water industry, as State governments rush to privatize water authorities, has also been expressed by Professor Peter Cullen, director of the Centre for Freshwater Ecology in Canberra. He believes that downsizing and restructuring has led to a large loss of technical staff and their replacement by managers who do not understand the problems and who are obsessed with finding quick solutions (Cribb, 1996b).

14. The Gwydir Valley now produces about one third of Australia's cotton, worth $330 million in peak years (Passey, 1995).

15. Not all farmers in the Gwydir Valley opposed the government's actions. The Chairman of the Gingham Watercourse Association, Shane Murphy, said cattle stocking rates on wetland farms had dropped by between 50 and 100 percent since cotton farming had boomed in the valley as wetlands dried up (Passey, 1995).

16. Another force contributing to Australia's inevitable decline is the cosmopolitan ideology of political correctness. For example, Tim Flannery, Senior Research Scientist Mammal Section, Australian Museum Sydney, says he has refused to speak to groups such as Australians Against Further Immigration because he believes immigration can be beneficial (Flannery, 1995). He also claims that those who remain silent on the issue of a national population policy give unwitting support to the "racists." With a national population policy, the ground would be cut from under them "by demonstrating that family reunion and refuge intakes can be in the interest of the nation, and occur within the broader context of environmental sustainability." Australia could, if necessary, take in large numbers of refugees without compromising our planning and ecologically sustainable development. He asserts that "While a population policy would regulate (and possibly lower the overall immigration intake, it would also enhance its humanitarian objectives by planning over decade-long periods rather than over a year. Thus Australia could take in large numbers of refugees if a crisis occurred without compromising our strategic planning" (Flannery, 1995, 12). Flannery, we recall, believes that Australia has already overshot its carrying capacity and that an ecologically sustainable population for Australia lies between 6–12 million people (ironically what Australia's population would now be if the undemocratic post–World War II immigration program had not occurred). Clearly, Flannery's politics conflict with his ecology.

As another example of the force of political correctness from the green camp in Australia, consider this review of Joseph Wayne Smith's *The Remorseless Working of Things* by David Munn in *Urban Ecology Annotated Bibliography*:

Smith, Joseph Wayne, The Remorseless Working of Things: Aids and the Global Crisis: An Ecological Critique of Internationalism, Canberra: Kalgoorlie Press, 1992:
Today, the Australian dream of owning the 1/4 acre block is fast evaporating, under the onslaught of a massive immigration program designed to turn Australia into an "Asian nation". There is no doubt that the importation of people who will not object to living in the sardine-like conditions imposed by fashionable intellectual creations such as 'urban consolidation', is the real motive behind much of the guilt-ridden, kowtowing rhetoric exuded by Australian intellectuals who espouse multiculturalism and immigrationism and ride on the gravy trains of internationalism. *Smith uses his undeniable intelligence to desperately defend the unrelenting pessimism that he clings to with almost religious faith. A sad glimpse into the mind of an alienated intellectual whose legitimate concerns about the "triumph of technocracy" and our ecologically unsustainable society all too often sink into a vortex of racism and paranoia.* (Downton and Munn, 1996, 113)

Smith's book was expanded and published by Avebury, Aldershot (Lyons et al., 1995) and has been favorably reviewed in *Population and Environment* (McConnell, 1996). Professor McConnell did not see a "vortex of racism and paranoia" in Smith's work: "This is a definitive work: factual, balanced and generally accurate" (McConnell,

1996, 82). In fact, the real concern of the urban ecologists, judged by the comments above, is not any alleged "racism" but Smith's critique of urban consolidation, the attempt to fit more people in a given area by urban design. Urban ecology, and the so-called *ecopolis*, attempts to do this by the use of environmental technologies, so one lives in a "green" sardine-can rather than a grey one. This movement would seem to capitalize on the dollars of a green new age business class who do not want to feel guilty when consuming their wealth, and in our opinion this is a betrayal of ecology, not an enrichment (Smith et al., 1997).

4

Global Meltdown: A Tapestry of Turmoil at the End of the Modern Age

> We live amidst the ruins of the great, five-hundred-year epoch of Humanism. Around us is that 'colossal wreck'. Our culture is a flat expanse of rubble. It hardly offers shelter from a mild cosmic breeze, never mind one of those icy gales that regularly return to rip men out of the cosy intimacy of their daily lives and confront them with oblivion. Is it surprising that we are run down? We are desperate, yet we don't care much any more. We are timid, yet we cannot be shocked. We are inert underneath our busyness. We are destitute in our plenty. We are homeless in our own homes.
>
> What should be there to hold our hands, is not. Our culture is gone. It has left us terribly alone. In its devastation it cannot even mock us any more, sneer at the lost child whimpering for its mother. That stage too is over. Our culture is past cruelty. It is wrecked. It is dead. (Carroll, 1993, 1)

> There are catastrophes from which there is recovery, especially small catastrophes. What worries me is the irrevocable catastrophe. That is why I am worried about the globalization of the world. If you have only one system, then if anything goes wrong, everything goes wrong. (Boulding quoted from Abernethy, 1993, 113)

A WORLD SPINNING OUT OF CONTROL

In the previous three chapters, an outline and defense of the global meltdown thesis—that modern civilization is hurtling towards its doom—was given. This book, with its own space and resource limits, is by no means a fully detailed attempt to support this thesis. Rather we have attempted, especially by means of extensive referencing, to show the initial plausibility of this thesis as well as to lay down a challenge: *show that we are wrong*. Show us how an entire system of mutually interrelated problems can be dealt with. Show us how all of the environmental problems discussed in our previous book, *Healing a Wounded World*

(Smith et al., 1997), can be dealt with in a world where the nation-state's power is not only waning—its power flowing to multinational business—but where the nation-state itself seems destined to be destroyed by the dual forces of ethno-racial fragmentation and economic globalization. We have yet to see any satis-factory response to these problems, precisely because there cannot be. In a world fast approaching, or overshooting, ecological limits, a world where the global elites have decreed that the world shall be a cosmopolitan supermarket, catastro-phe is irrevocable. If Toynbee is right in analyzing the rise and fall of civiliza-tions in terms of their capacity to respond to challenges, then the evidence pre-sented by the authorities discussed here and in *Healing a Wounded World* indi-cates that the end is indeed nigh (Lyons et al., 1995). As Benedict Anderson (1992) has observed, the world is not heading toward any "new world order," but rather toward disorder, a "new world disorder" produced by the "subversive force" of the global market. We do not follow Leslie (1996) in arguing for the annihilation or inevitable extinction of the human species as such, although we believe his logic is sound. Our interest in this work is with the sustainability of civilized order, the survival of the modern world, and this creature, we believe, has extinction stamped on its rump. In this context we will explore in this final chapter some of the philosophical consequences of the global meltdown thesis. If we are right in our claim that modernity ultimately destroys itself, then this is a decisive *reductio ad absurdum* of modernism and doctrines such as globalism. Although our arguments can do nothing to prevent the remorseless working of things, it is still of intellectual interest to follow the global meltdown argument through to its logical conclusion.

Before outlining the philosophical significance of the global meltdown the-sis, we will discuss the relationship between this thesis and some other major work in our field. Consider first an important article by G. J. Ikenberry published in the May/June 1996 edition of *Foreign Affairs* (Ikenberry, 1996). Ikenberry gives the opposing view to the position of this book, namely that post–Cold War chaos is a myth. The democratic new world order of Western liberalism "is ro-bust, and its principles and policies remain the core of world order" (Ikenberry, 1996, 89). We shall challenge this ahead. However, Ikenberry admits that eco-nomic globalization "is producing much greater inequality between the winners and the losers, the wealthy and the poor. How the subsequent dislocations, dashed expectations, and political grievances are dealt with . . . will affect the stability of the liberal world order more than regional conflict, however tragic, in places like the Balkans" (Ikenberry, 1996, 91). Many authorities believe, with good reason, that the dislocations produced by globalization are being dealt with extremely poorly. Whether the Western liberal democratic world is robust at the present time is of no great significance; what is of interest is the *sustainability* of the system itself subjected to the tapestry of turmoil that we are to experience.

Alvin and Heidi Toffler are technological optimists, but cautious ones (Toffler and Toffler, 1970, 1980, 1983, 1990). Instead of the cornucopianism of Julian Simon, the Tofflers state that "we appear, instead, to be plunging into a new dark age of tribal hate, planetary desolation, and wars multiplied by wars"

(Toffler and Toffler, 1993, 1). The Tofflers see human history as being shaped by three "waves": the first wave, agriculture; the second wave, industry; and the third wave, postindustrial information technology. Human (civilized) history is divided into civilizations corresponding to these three waves: one by the hoe, one by the assembly line, and one by the computer. The Tofflers distinguish their view of civilization from that of Samuel P. Huntington, whose work we will discuss shortly. Civilizations are broad and ontologically mixed entities encompassing technology, ideology, and culture. The Tofflers see a master conflict emerging that subsumes Huntington's proposed clash of civilizations, this clash being of super-civilizations ("civilization" being defined here in Huntington's sense), corresponding to each of the three waves. Third wave civilizations will become less dependent upon first wave civilizations and even second wave civilizations, which will lead to economic stress and social decay in these latter civilizations. Third wave civilizations, according to the Tofflers, cannot stop pollution, disease, and immigrants from penetrating their borders. Hence, a collision course is now being set between the various civilizations of the world. For example, nationalism is a product of second wave economies but third wave economies require globalization. This conflict in itself "could provoke some of the worst bloodshed in the years to come" (Toffler and Toffler, 1993, 27). The civilization conflict problem will also have its impact on the global financial system, a system that could face a "meltdown" in the future, leading to global economic collapse: "Dividing the Pacific into trade blocs, drawing what is in effect an ethno-racial line down its middle, could hack the most dangerous cleavage of all—racial, religious, and economic—into a global system already in danger of multiple fracture" (Toffler and Toffler, 1993, 268).

Tom Athanasiou, in his book *Divided Planet* (Athanasiou, 1996), reaches similar conclusions to the Tofflers, although he divides the civilizations of the world into rich and poor, the major planetary divide on the Earth being between the developed world and the developing world. In Athanasiou's opinion the threats to the planet cannot be halted by the "feel-good environmentalism" of the industrialized world. Only radical social and ecological changes can avert disaster. "Faith in solar democracy, easy reform, deep ecology and simple utopias of all kinds has faded year by year", he tells us. As well: "Asian capitalism is booming, and its boom is an ecological catastrophe" (Athanasiou, 1996, 3). Today's "terrifying new economy" has a highly effective anti-environmental movement, indicating that the "old environmentalism has hit its limits" (Athanasiou, 1996, 7). Quoting Norman Rush (1994) Athanasiou rejects the idea that capitalism will bring about a sustainable new world order: "Capitalism and socialism both have their contradictions, and it may turn out that socialism's contradictions just happened to be fatal first" (Rush, 1994, 92, quoted from Athanasiou, 1996, 28).

Athanasiou is an internationalist and cosmopolitan. He objects to Western critics of mass migration; such people are "neofascist" (Athanasiou, 1996, 35) and "right-wing" (Athanasiou, 1996, 36). He quotes with approval Jacques Attali, socialist, and founding president of the European Bank for Reconstruction and Development, who says in his book *Millennium*:

In restless despair, the hopeless masses of the periphery will witness the spectacle of another hemisphere's wealth. Particularly in those regions of the South that are geographically contiguous and culturally linked to the North—places such as Mexico, Central America, or North Africa—millions of people will be tempted and enraged by the constant stimulation of wants that can't be satisfied. And they will know that the prosperity that is not theirs partly comes at the cost of their well-being and at the price of their environment's degradation. With no future of their own in an age of air travel and telecommunications, the terminally impoverished will look for one in the North as economic refugees and migrants on an unprecedented scale. (Attali, 1991, 14)

We have encountered this "Camp of the Saints" scenario before in this book. Immigration is the last green issue according to Athanasiou. He attacks Edward Abbey for his criticisms of Latino immigrants and regards the view that overpopulation is the root cause of the environmental crisis as "simpleminded" (Athanasiou, 1996, 37). In particular, he is critical of Garrett Hardin's claim that we should "seal the borders" (of Western nations) and let "the wretched nations" of the Earth "go up in flames" (Athanasiou, 1996, 37). As hard as these words are, they are precisely what a people must do if they wish to survive the coming "deluge," and, in fact, Athanasiou's own book ultimately supports such a lifeboat ethics. He has no coherent answer to the environmental crisis and the dominance of global capitalism and his hope for economic democracy on a global scale is a hope without substance.

Athanasiou observes that many greens and environmentalists, such as Anita Gordon, David Suzuki, Mostafa K. Tolba, and Jacques Costeau, all saw the 1990s as crucial if there were to be a turnaround of the environmental crisis. He does not agree with this, favoring a slow death scenario, "slow biophysical cataclysm." Early apocalyptics such as Paul Ehrlich and the authors of *The Limits to Growth* (Meadows et al., 1972), although wrong in a number of points, were correct in the general thrust of their argument. In many aspects *The Limits to Growth* was too optimistic, underestimating crucial biophysical parameters such as soil erosion: since its publication *six* times as much soil as it predicted has been lost (Athanasiou, 1996, 63). However, Athanasiou rejects the Malthusian aspects of environmentalism: "It is a crippling slant, for it implies, above all, the willingness to blame victims and overlook injustice" (Athanasiou, 1996, 77). Malthusianism in Athanasiou's opinion is often "vile nativism" (Athanasiou, 1996, 77). In our opinion there are no "victims": we are all guilty of the original environmental "sin" of simply existing. Further, the proposal of Athanasiou and also Ted Trainer (1995) of a planetary redistribution of resources on a massive scale simply won't occur. It won't happen because lesser changes are not occurring. No advanced nation, Athanasiou admits, has approached the 60–80 percent reduction in carbon dioxide production recommended by the United Nations scientific expert panel on climate change (Athanasiou, 1996, 7). Hence none of Athanasiou's even more radical social and environmental policies will be implemented (recall his own statement about the fading of faith in simple ecological utopias) and we consequently face "ecological catastrophe," an apocalypse that would surely destroy Third World civilizations at a minimum and possibly advanced civilizations as well.

Martin Van Creveld described this emerging world of turmoil in these terms:

We are entering an era, not of peaceful economic cooperation between trading blocs, but of warfare between ethnic and religious groups. Even as familiar forms of armed conflict are sinking into the dustbin of the past, radically new ones are raising their heads ready to take their place. Already today the military power fielded by the principal developed societies in both "West" and "East" is hardly relevant to the task at hand; in other words, it is more illusion than substance. Unless the societies in question are willing to adjust both thought and action to the rapidly changing new realities, they are likely to reach the point where they will no longer be capable of employing organized violence at all. Once this situation comes about, their continued survival as cohesive political entities will also be put in doubt. (Van Creveld, 1991, ix)

Van Creveld's thesis is that the Clausewitzian view of war—that war is a continuation of politics waged by states engaging in unrestricted violence—is fundamentally flawed. Conventional warfare may be dying only to be replaced by unconventional warfare. Full-scale nuclear war has been made redundant, in Van Creveld's opinion, because nobody has worked out a way of actually fighting such a war and winning (Van Creveld, 1991, 5), let alone dealing with the problems of ecological disruption and nuclear winter. This has made it virtually impossible for the superpowers to directly engage in conventional war in a nuclear age (Van Creveld, 1991, 12). The Gulf War was only possible because Iraq did not have nuclear missiles capable of reaching the United States. Technologically superior forces have failed to overcome technologically inferior people in low intensity conflicts as well, an example being the Israelis versus the *intifada*, the rebellion in occupied territories being organized by stone-throwing Arab youth. Israeli tanks are certainly "high tech," but they did not succeed in controlling the urbanized areas of Lebanon in 1982 (Van Creveld, 1991, 75): "So expensive, fast, indiscriminate, big, unmaneuverable and powerful have modern weapons become that they are steadily pushing contemporary war under the carpet, as it were; that is, into environments where those weapons do not work, and where men can therefore fight to their heart's contents" (Van Creveld, 1991, 32). It is one of the "revenge effects" of modern military technology that the expense of conventional warfare has increased to such a degree that "when low-intensity conflict does break out and the opportunity to use the hardware presents itself, it seems wasteful to employ such expensive systems against persons who are often an illiterate rabble" (Van Creveld, 1991, 209). However, the rise of terrorism, unconventional warfare, and low-intensity conflict has the potential to disrupt social, economic, and political order to such a degree that in the long run "the place of the state will be taken by warmaking organizations of a different type" (Van Creveld, 1991, 192), including terrorists, guerrillas, gangs, and Mafia-like bodies. Multiracial America, with its history of violence, may experience massive social disruption if drug-related crime and violence is not stopped and America's economic decline not halted: "One day the crime that is rampant in the streets of New York and Washington D.C. may develop into low-intensity conflict by coalescing along racial, religious, social and political lines, and run completely out of control" (Van Creveld, 1991, 196). Van Creveld's work, obviously enough, also strongly supports the global meltdown thesis.

Another work that, arguably, supports the global meltdown thesis is Samuel P. Huntington's *The Clash of Civilizations and the Remaking of World Order* (Huntington, 1996). Huntington is in the tradition of Spengler, Sorokin, Quigley, and Toynbee. He sees nation-states as having a dominant culture that unites them into broader civilizations, civilizations in turn arising from cultural differences. The world is facing a global identity crisis, with the source of political conflict arising from cultural differences, both within and between nations. In the various "civilizations"—Huntington distinguishes between the Sinic (Chinese), Japanese, Hindu, Islamic, Western, Orthodox, Latin American, and African civilizations— political alliances are being formed between nation-states, resulting in cultural federations. Huntington notes: "The dangerous clashes of the future are likely to arise from the interaction of Western arrogance, Islamic intolerance, and Sinic assertiveness" (Huntington, 1996, 183). Huntington's view is supported by a leading Muslim political scientist Bassam Tibi, who believes that in an era of declining Western political, economic, and ideological power a "war of civilizations" will occur (Walters, 1995). A major philosophical difference exists between the West and "the rest," regarding democracy and human rights. Tibi notes, "In non-Western civilisations there is no cultural underpinning for human rights and if you present to them the Western concept, arguing that they are universally valid they get extremely touchy" (Walters, 1995, 16). Further, "Political Islam and other varieties of fundamentalism stand in the way of cross-religious values and also impede a cross-cultural foundation of human rights" (Walters, 1995, 16). Tibi believes that the universality of human rights can be embraced without viewing Islam as a footnote to European history: "The embracing of secular human rights facilitates placing Muslims in their proper place: humanity" (Walters, 1995, 16). Huntington has, we believe, a more realistic view than Tibi on this issue. He rejects the idea that democratic liberalism is universally valid because it has allegedly triumphed globally: "What is universalism to the West is imperialism to the rest" (Huntington, 1996, 184). The West promotes universalism, but it does so with a double standard: "Nonproliferation is preached for Iran and Iraq but not for Israel. . . . aggression against oil-owning Kuwaitis is massively repulsed but not against non-oil-owning Bosnians" (Huntington, 1996, 184). We will return to this question of universalism versus particularism ahead.

Huntington's "clash of civilizations" thesis has been subjected to considerable criticism since he published his origin paper that he later developed into his book. Ajami (1993) rightly noted that the concept of a *civilization* is vaguely defined. The concept of the *West* is unexamined by Huntington (although *The Clash of Civilizations and the Remaking of World Order*, we believe, answers this objection of Ajami): "No fissures run through it. No multiculturalists are heard from. It is orderly within its ramparts" (Ajami, 1993, 2). Mahbubani (1993) believes that Huntington has underestimated the degree of decadence and decay in the West: "[A] fatal flaw . . . has recently developed in the Western mind: an inability to conceive that the West may have developed structural weaknesses in its core value systems and institutions" (Mahbubani, 1993, 14). The weaknesses of the West include "fiscal follies," the erosion of the work ethic, and a lack of international competitiveness. More importantly, the United States promotes the idea of individual freedom without recognizing the dangers of this:

The United States has undertaken a massive social experiment, tearing down social institution after social institution that restrained the individual. The results have been disastrous. Since 1960 the U.S. population has increased 41 percent while violent crime has risen by 560 percent, single-mother births by 419 percent, divorce rates by 300 percent and the percentage of children living in single-parent homes by 300 percent. This is massive social decay. Many a society shudders at the prospects of this happening on its shores. (Mahbubani, 1993, 14)

Robert Bartley (1993), although allegedly expressing the case for optimism, asks Huntington whether the potential for conflict lies between civilizations rather than within them. Observing China he asks, "Despite the economic miracle of China's Guangdong province, are we really confident that the Confucians have mastered the trick of governing a billion people in one political entity?" (Bartley, 1993, 16) Liu Binyan answers Bartley's question in the negative, maintaining that "spiritual deterioration and moral degradation are eroding China's cultural foundation" (Binyan, 1993, 21). Kirkpatrick also believes that Huntington has underestimated the degree of internal conflict existing within the West, citing immigration as one of the causes of such conflict: "Immigration brings exotic practices into schools, neighborhoods and other institutions of daily life and challenges the cosmopolitanism of Western societies. Religious tolerance in the abstract is one thing; veiled girls in French schoolrooms are quite another. Such challenges are not welcome anywhere" (Kirkpatrick, 1993, 24). Weeks, on the other hand, sees the Huntington debate as "symptomatic of the failure of globalism—specifically the idea of establishing a "new order order"—to take root and the failure to make sense of contradictory trends and events" (Weeks, 1993, 24–25). Harries goes further and sees the West itself as a socio-political construction rather than a natural entity—and a "highly artificial" one at that: "It took the presence of a life-threatening, overly hostile "East" to bring it into existence and to maintain its unity. It is extremely doubtful whether it can now survive the disappearance of that enemy" (Harries, 1993, 42). Consequently, a collapse of "the West" is most likely. The views just summarized are either consistent with or directly support the global meltdown thesis.

Huntington criticizes the chaos/anarchy view for being "too close to reality" (Huntington, 1996, 35); a view of "universal and undifferentiated anarchy" . . . "does not give us an effective tool for predicting anarchy" (Huntington, 1996, 35). The global meltdown thesis does not propose that the coming anarchy is undifferentiated; on the contrary, it is highly differentiated and comes from a number of sources in fields that Huntington does not consider in his book. Huntington gives no consideration at all in *The Clash of Civilizations and The*

Remaking of World Order to the environmental crisis and how it may increase tribal and nationalism conflicts. Huntington, on the last page of his book, however, recognizes the merits of the "coming anarchy"/global meltdown thesis:

Much evidence exists in the 1990s for the relevance of the "sheer chaos" paradigm of world affairs: a global breakdown of law and order, failed states and increasing anarchy in many parts of the world, a global crime wave, transnational mafias and drug cartels, increasing drug addiction in many societies, a general weakening of the family, a decline in trust and social solidarity in many countries, ethnic, religious, and civilizational violence and rule by the gun prevalent in much of the world. In city after city—Moscow, Rio de Janeiro, Bangkok, Shanghai, London, Rome, Warsaw, Tokyo, Johannesburg, Delhi, Karachi, Cairo, Bogota, Washington—crime seems to be soaring and basic elements of Civilization fading away. People speak of a global crisis in governance. The rise of transnational corporations producing economic goods is increasingly matched by the rise of transnational criminal mafias, drug cartels, and terrorist gangs violently assaulting Civilization. Law and order is the first prerequisite of Civilization and in much of the world—Africa, Latin America, the former Soviet Union, South Asia, the Middle East—it appears to be evaporating, while also under serious assault in China, Japan, and the West. On a worldwide basis Civilization seems in many respects to be yielding to barbarism, generating the image of an unprecedented phenomenon, a global Dark Ages, possibly descending on humanity. (Huntington, 1996, 321)

The great clash, Huntington notes, is between Civilization and barbarism, and in this the great civilizations of the world will either hang together or hang separately. The evidence indicates, we believe, that they will hang separately, dying not by a swift snap of the neck, but by strangulation.

This completes our review of recent literature that we believe supports the global meltdown thesis. We turn now to the task of outlining the philosophical significance of this thesis. Much can be said here, but we shall restrict our discussion to issues associated with what Weeks has called "the failure of globalism" (Weeks, 1993, 24–25). As we have said earlier, the global meltdown thesis is a decisive *reductio ad absurdum* of modernism and of doctrines such as globalism and cosmopolitanism. In stating this we are not relying upon a deduction of an evaluative conclusion from purely factual premises, committing a "naturalistic fallacy." Rather, in the conceptual domain there is an analogue to the chaos and anarchy that we have already seen engulfing the world. All is not well in Plato's heaven.

GLOBALISM AND NIHILISM: THE EPISTEMOLOGICAL AND MORAL CRISES

The context of this problem was outlined in our book *Healing a Wounded World* (Smith et al., 1997). Very briefly, even though spectacular technological developments have occurred in the philosophy of science and epistemology, a major crisis of method exists. The problem is multidimensional and involves the issues of rationally justifying basic metascientific principles and methods and establishing the progressiveness of science as a cognitive enterprise, as well as defeating epistemological relativism, anarchism, and the alleged nihilism of postmodernism, deconstructionism, and the sociology of knowledge (Taylor, 1971; Feyerabend, 1978; Rorty, 1979; Newton-Smith, 1981; Zemach, 1986; Goldman, 1991; Wright, 1992; Horgan, 1996). The standard view of science ("Legend") derived from logical positivism and Popperianism is widely regarded to be problematic. Kitcher believes that despite the work of philosophers such as Shapere (1984), "little headway has been made in finding a successor for Legend. If anything, recent work in the history of science and in the sociology of science has offered even more sweeping versions of the original critiques" (Kitcher, 1993, 8).

The situation is much worse in ethics or moral philosophy (Kleinberg, 1991; Poole, 1991). Modernization involves a movement from particularism to universalism (globalism/cosmopolitanism/internationalism) (Parsons, 1970; Berger et al., 1977; Kearney, 1987). Modern moral philosophy and ethics reflect this universalism and cosmopolitanism: the universal point of view must triumph over all other points of view. Anything short of this constitutes prejudice and discrimination based upon the consideration of morally irrelevant properties and relations (Harman, 1989; Browne, 1990; Thompson, 1992; Richter, 1995). As Browne puts it, "From the universal point of view, the local concerns of the self stand in need of moral justification; they are suspect, unless they can be endorsed morally" (Browne, 1990, 408). This universalism can be clarified by contrasting it with various forms of *particularism*. One form of particularism is represented by sociobiology's "group morality" which sees intergroup hostility as an important factor in human evolution:

Humans evolved in small groups and . . . intergroup hostility was a factor in the evolution of such behaviors as group loyalty and violence toward enemies. A behavioral characteristic of almost any group is to treat its members one way and nonmembers another way. The rightness of this is loudly proclaimed by the group in question and furnishes a "group morality". Correspondingly, it supports intergroup immorality or amorality, in a way that often contradicts the standard morality of its members—for example, it contradicts the "absolute" prohibition against killing. (Maxwell, 1990, 5)

Derek Browne, in criticizing the universalism of conventional morality, articulates an interesting form of particularism derived from the ancient ethics of the Greeks:

One might suppose, with the Greeks, that it is unquestionably healthy for me to have a substantial care and concern for my own well-being. One might suppose, with the Greeks, that it is not only healthy but plainly good to have a substantial, special care for my own family and friends. Whatever else was true of human goodness, the Greeks were quite sure that it was a healthy state in which to be. Local loves and commitments are an integral part of such a healthy condition of human life: only those corrupted by morality could ever doubt that. Yet from the universal point of view, local concerns stand in need of moral justification. It might happen, by great good fortune, that the interests of all are in fact best promoted by allowing a due measure of local concern to each. . . . But the very idea that these local concerns are in need of the special sanction of universalist morality is bizarre. According to utilitarianism—a theory which very clearly expresses the universalist thrust of moral thinking—it could happen that local concerns turn out to be morally indefensible. If that were so, then we ought—morally ought—to give them up.

This conclusion is repugnant because it contradicts the way we are. A morality which lacks any plausible grounding in human psychology surrenders its claim to the allegiance of human beings. Universalist morality threatens constantly to break the connection which ethics has with the goodness of a human life—human goodness, not moral goodness. Yet any plausible account of human goodness will be grounded in the facts of real human motivation. (Browne, 1990, 408–9)

Nietzsche and Thrasymachus in Plato's *Republic* both hold that the good life overrides the moral life: if the moral life is not a good life for an individual (and collective as well), then it would be a mistake to lead it. Utilitarianism is a position where the moral life overrides the good life. This is so because what is morally required for each individual is defined with respect to what is optimal for a population of individuals. Nagel notes that utilitarianism has the consequence that "Any coincidence between this [utilitarian moral rightness] and what is best for him in particular will be a matter of luck, or political and social arrangement" (Nagel, 1986, 196). Further, "If he is in a position to benefit others sufficiently at some cost to himself, he will have to sacrifice his income, his personal relations, his health, his happiness, and even his life if that will have more utility than anything else he can do" (Nagel, 1986, 196; Kagan, 1989).

Morality is generally recognized to impose two different kinds of limits upon subjects: (1) limits on our actions making certain actions impermissible even if the greater good could be realized by doing the acts in question (limits imposed *by* morality), and (2) limits imposed on morality and moral requirements. We are not morally obligated to make the greatest possible contribution to the general good. Shelly Kagan has argued on the basis of the doctrine of consequentialism—the view that agents are morally obliged to perform those acts that lead to the best results overall—that morality has no limits in either sense (Kagan, 1989).

There are no limits of the first kind, because any act may be permissible in the right circumstances for the consequentialist, providing it leads to the best results overall. There are no limits of the second kind because there are no limits to the sacrifices individuals are required to make, according to the consequentialist, to achieve the best results overall.

What does such a view of morality entail? It entails that most of our acts are *immoral* because we seldom have optimal, or even efficient, use of our time and resources. Kagan uses the example of a trip to the movies. Instead of doing this, we could donate the money to famine relief. If morality requires that one produces the best consequences overall, then going to the movies is *morally forbidden*. This is the extremist view that Kagan argues is true and that we are committed to in ordinary life. We cannot show where the cut-off point is, limiting our contribution to the general good. However, as this position leads to the impossibility of normal social life, we should strongly suspect that something is wrong with the foundations of morality (Flynn, 1974; Williams, 1985; Wolf, 1982; Brandt, 1989). One philosopher has even claimed that we should share all the food on a global scale, even if everybody starves as a result and the human race becomes extinct (Watson, 1977; Fletcher, 1991). Let him be the first to share.

Ross Poole, in his book *Morality and Modernity* (Poole, 1991), argues that the modern world brings into existence a certain (universalist) conception of morality, but at the same time also destroys the grounds of legitimacy of morality; modernity requires morality but paradoxically renders it impossible:

The paradox of morality in the modern world is that it lays claim to an objective status which is no longer available to it. Whatever is objective is *for that reason* not a value. It may be that we have no option but to accept this position and reject the enterprise of morality, much as an earlier generation rejected religion. This was more or less Nietzsche's position. Morality makes a claim to truth which it can no longer sustain. Insofar as morality itself posits truth as a value, it requires us to reject morality for its own mendacity—and with it, of course, we must reject the moral value of truthfulness. (Poole, 1991, 69–70)

The causes of this crisis of justification are two-fold. First, sociologically, multiculturalism and cultural plurality have taken their toll on the objectivity of morality; as Stauth and Turner put it " a coherent system of values as the basis of criticism presupposes a relatively coherent community as the underlying social fabric of moral systems and ethical arguments" (Stauth and Turner, 1988, 509). Second, as something of a flow-on from arguments in epistemology and the philosophy of science, if there are no theory-neutral scientific observations, there are also no theory-neutral moral observations. Moral intuitions, often taken by analytic philosophers to be the test of moral theories (e.g., "theory X cannot be correct, it has counter-intuitive consequences"), typically have the stamp of some moral theory upon them (Singleton, 1981).[1] Universalist moral philosophy is thus based on a *petitio principii*, a fallacy of begging-the-question. The Enlightenment project of rationally justifying morality is thus a failure, as Alasdair MacIntyre observes in his book *Three Rival Versions of Moral Inquiry: Encyclopaedia, Genealogy and Tradition*:

Whereas it was a tenet of Enlightenment cultures that every point of view, whatever its source, could be brought into rational debate with every other, this tenet had as its counterpart a belief that such rational debate could always, if adequately conducted, have a conclusive outcome. The point and purpose of rational debate was to establish truths and only those methods were acceptable which led to the conclusive refutation of error and vindication of truth. The contrast with contemporary academic practice could not be sharper. For with rare exceptions the outcomes of rational debate on fundamental issues are systematically inconclusive. . . . We can thus contrast the various Enlightenment's strong conceptions of rationality with this weak conception. . . . What would be required, on this contemporary view, for a conclusive termination of rational debate would be an appeal to a standard or set of standards such that no adequately rational person could fail to acknowledge its authority. But such a standard or standards, since it would have to provide criteria for the rational acceptability or otherwise of any theoretical or conceptual scheme, would itself have to be formulable and defensible independently of any such scheme. But—and it is here that contemporary academic practice breaks radically with its Enlightenment predecessors—there can be no such standard; any standard adequate to discharge such functions will itself be embedded in, supported by, and articulated in terms of some set of theoretical and conceptual schemes. Thus since, so far as large-scale theoretical and conceptual structures are concerned, each rival theoretical standpoint provides from within itself and in its own terms the standards by which, so its adherents claim, it should be evaluated, rivalry between such contending standpoints includes rivalry over standards. (MacIntyre, 1990, 172–73)

MacIntyre's position is that the goals of internationalistic, universalistic, post-Enlightenment liberalism, and cosmopolitan modernity are bankrupt (MacIntyre, 1981; Watson, 1989; Horton and Mendus, 1994). In particular, MacIntyre has rejected the view that liberalism can adequately evaluate moral traditions from a standpoint independent of all traditions: "Liberalism can provide no compelling arguments in favor of its conception of the human good except by appeal to premises which collectively already presuppose that theory. The starting points of liberal theorizing are never neutral as between conceptions of the human good; they are always liberal starting points" (MacIntyre, 1988, 345). MacIntyre's position is that moral rationality is tradition-relative. However, traditions can face "epistemological crises" that may lead to the abandonment of the tradition and adoption of a new one. The historicist and allegedly relativist implications of MacIntyre's arguments have generated a vast critical literature (Downing and Thigpen, 1994; Carson, 1985; Gutmann, 1985; Tilley, 1988; Annas, 1989; Barry, 1989; George, 1989; Hittinger, 1989; Larmore, 1989; Nino, 1989; Almond, 1990; Baumrin, 1990; Rasmussen, 1990; Walzer, 1990; Wong, 1990).

The universalism and cosmopolitanism of modern morality is challenged by the "Why Should I be Moral?" problem. If universalism is correct the imperatives of morality must be binding upon every "rational" being, regardless of whether he cares about morality (Mish'alani, 1982; Foot, 1978; Goldrick and Potter, 1982). Can non-moral reasons be given so as to give overriding weight to moral considerations when they conflict with other matters? This is an open problem. Kai Nielsen concludes his own study of this problem with these words: "We have not been able to show that reason requires the moral point of view or that all really rational persons, unhoodwinked by myth or ideology not be individual egoists or classist amoralists" (Nielsen, 1984, 90; 1989). Universalism and cosmopolitanism thus are question-begging against individual egoism or amoralism. Worse, universalism has had great difficulties dealing with the *argumentum ad Nazium*: doctrines such as Nazism, universal genocidism (e.g., humans are cancers that require cleansing by a nuclear knife [Leslie, 1996]), anti-Semitism, and other horrors, have proved remarkably difficult to refute (Donagan, 1965; Hocutt, 1986, 1994; Sullivan, 1994), indicating that there is a problem with orthodox morality and ethics.[2]

John Gray, in his most recent work *Enlightenment's Wake: Politics and Culture at the Close of the Modern Age* (Gray, 1995), follows MacIntyre's arguments through to their logical conclusion. The Enlightenment project of universal emancipation and the creation of a universal civilization, has destroyed local traditions and cultures, but has not produced a new civilization, leaving instead *nihilism*. Gray argues at length that all the schools of political thought, including conservatism, are variants of the Enlightenment project and "that project, though irreversible in its cultural effects, was self-undermining and is now exhausted" (Gray, 1995, viii). This signifies the close of the modern age, and the rise of particularisms such as nationalisms, supports Gray's opinion. The self-undermining of the Enlightenment project "encompasses the dissolution of elements of the Western tradition—such as the humanism of the Christian tradition and the logocentrism of Greek philosophy—which are foundational and primordial in that tradition" (Gray, 1995, 146). In Gray's opinion there is no way back from the Enlightenment, and, after Nietzsche, any return to pre-modern schemes of thought, because the Enlightenment tradition "was itself an authentic development of a central Western tradition going back to Socrates, and indeed beyond, to the pre-Socratics" (Gray, 1995, p. 152). Elaborating upon the consequences of the eclipse of the Enlightenment Gray says: "The most fundamental Western commitment, the *humanist* conception of humankind as a privileged site of truth, which is expressed in Socratic inquiry and in Christian revelation, and which re-emerges in secular and naturalistic form in the Enlightenment project of human self-emancipation through the growth of knowledge, must be given up" (Gray, 1995, 155).

The epistemological and postmodernist collapse of traditional ethics must be distinguished from the collapse of traditional ethics, which Peter Singer believes has occurred (Singer, 1994). Singer is interested in refuting the sanctity of human life doctrine and exploring the bioethical consequences. He is also interested in rejecting speciesism, a doctrine that gives moral significance to "being human," in particular:

Why isn't species a legitimate reason? For essentially the same reason as we now exclude race or sex. The racist, sexist and speciesist are all saying: the boundary of my group also marks a difference of value. If you are a member of my group, you are more valuable than if you are not—no matter what other characteristics you may lack. Each of these positions is a form of group protectiveness, or group selfishness. (Singer, 1994, 203–4)

Well—so what? Singer's argument explicitly assumes that the universalist moral position is correct. A consistent racist, sexist, and speciesist would reject this metaethical doctrine. What is "wrong" with group protectiveness and group selfishness? Surely only that it conflicts with Singer's own universalist utilitarianism. But why should we accept that position? Once more we are back on the epistemological wheel.

In this section we have outlined in a broad sweep the epistemological crisis of modern moral theory. We turn now to a more specific issue of the epistemological crisis of liberalism, the ruling ideology of the West. The follies and failings of liberalism will serve as a convenient foil for the advancement of our own ecologically based form of particularism and defense of group protectiveness and group self-interestedness (Maxwell, 1990, 5).

THE SUICIDE OF THE WEST, REVISITED

In an important but neglected work, *Suicide of the West* (Burnham, 1965), James Burnham begins his discussion of the survival of the West with an examination of the changing colors of the maps of an atlas. Although this book was published by 1965, Burnham discerned even then a "rapid decline, recession, or ebb within the world power structure of the West" (Burnham, 1965, 16), including the ending of Western domination over non-Western societies, as well as the ending of Western domination over societies and regions that have been a part of Western civilization. The changing colors of the maps of an atlas show "that over the past two generations Western civilization has undergone a rapid and major contraction—it still continues—in the quantitative terms of the relative amount of area and population it dominates" (Burnham, 1965, 18). In 1965 Burnham did not anticipate the impact that future "non-discriminatory" mass immigration would have on the United States, Canada, and Australia. Nevertheless, he concluded that this contraction was merely a symptom of a deeper disease and that it was probable that the West was also dying (Burnham, 1965, 20). The contraction was not due to any lack of physical resources, power, or material deficiency. The suicide of the West—the process of contraction and loss of power—arose from internal causes. Although the cause of the contraction is not explicitly dealt with by Burnham, *liberalism* is the "ideology of Western suicide" (Burnham, 1965, 26), meaning "that liberalism has come to be the typical verbal systematization of the process of Western contraction and withdrawal; that liberalism motivates and justifies the contraction, and reconciles us to it" (Burnham, 1965, 26). *Liberalism* is defined very broadly by Burnham to include much of the "left" and "progressive" thought. He gives a diagnostic test of 39 sentences such as: "(1) all forms of racial segregation and discrimination are wrong; . . . (10) we have a duty to all mankind; . . . (30) there are no significant differences in the intellectual, moral and civilizing capacity of the different races" (Burnham, 1965, 40–41). Liberals would tend to believe most of these sentences, reactionaries, few if any. Liberalism, as conceived by Burnham, corresponds to modernism or Enlightenmentism, the intellectual heir of post-Renaissance thought (see also Harries, 1995). The position can be summarized as follows:

1. Liberalism has a philosophical anthropology of human nature, seeing human nature as not being fixed, but changeable. There is the potential for positive, progressive social change. Original sin/evil does not soil human nature. Nothing in human nature prevents the "good society" from being created—peace, justice, freedom from racism are achievable (Burnham, 1965, 50–51).
2. Liberalism is a form of rationalism: "Liberalism is confident that reason and rational science, without appeal to revelation, faith, custom or intuition, can both comprehend the world and solve its problems" (Burnham, 1965, 53).
3. As human nature does not prevent the achievement of the good society, obstacles must be external—primarily ignorance and bad social institutions that require change (Burnham, 1965, 54).

4. Liberalism involves the acceptance of historical optimism, the belief in progress; hence there are solutions to social problems, especially *the* social problems of constructing the good society (Burnham, 1965, 56).
5. Anti-traditionalism is accepted—there is no reason to accept ideas merely because our ancestors accepted them.
6. The need for universal education to eliminate ignorance is also advocated.
7. The need for social reform to eliminate bad social institutions is an essential ingredient of liberalism.
8. The elimination of evils by education and reforming the institutions is another key feature.
9. This education process must be a universal dialogue, a conversation of humanity.
10. Politics as well are part of this universal dialogue.
11. Freedom of speech is required because of epistemological relativism: objective truth is unattainable and we cannot be sure when we are approaching it. Liberalism's commitment to the truth becomes a commitment to the "method of inquiry" of truth, which is the "universal dialogue," the scientific method and the democratic method.
12. Hence, liberalism holds to a democratic theory of government.
13. Further, there is no reason why this should stop at the level of a single state:

> Modern liberal doctrine tends naturally toward internationalist conceptions and the ideal of a democratic world order based through one mode or another on the majority will of all mankind. The logic of liberal principles unites with the normal bias of liberal temperament to incline modern liberals favorably toward ideas, movements, and organizations that can be thought of as steps toward world cooperation, federalism, unification and government: world courts, world league of nations; worldwide cultural exchanges; world congresses and parliaments; world conventions and committees. To the liberal it has become self-evident that "national sovereignty is an outworn concept" that must be drastically modified if not altogether abandoned. (Burnham, 1965, 79)

Liberalism is thus committed to internationalism and cosmopolitanism. It is, of course possible to argue for liberal nationalism on an independent basis, but internationalism is a position that naturally follows from liberalism. If we are right in our argument in this book and *Healing a Wounded World* (Smith et al., 1997) that internationalism is an untenable doctrine, then liberalism itself inherits this problem. Burnham concludes in his work *Suicide of the West* on the point that "Liberalism is not equipped to meet and overcome the actual challenges confronting Western civilization in our time" (Burnham, 1965, 278). We agree.

Allan Bloom's book *The Closing of the American Mind* (Bloom, 1987), although advanced as a critique of higher education in America and how it has failed democracy, confirms many of the points made by Burnham. This is, of course, not Bloom's intention—which is ultimately to criticize relativism and anti-Enlightenment thought which he sees as destructive of the Western canon. We believe though, that it is an arguable interpretation of Bloom's material. The university in Bloom's book can be seen as a symbol, whether Bloom intends this to be so or not, of the logical workings of the liberal world view. Let us now examine, albeit briefly, this argument.

The Western university requires that all views be examined in free debate, but by playing a participatory role in society the university itself has become a problem, "society's conceptual warehouse of often harmful influences" as Saul Bellow puts it (Bloom, 1987, 18). The philosophy of American students is one of cultural relativism and equality; absolutism implies intolerance for them, relativism implies openness. The desire for truth and rightness led to wars in the past, and hence we must abandon these values, many students believe. Bloom notes that this tendency toward indiscriminate freedom was present in the early beginnings of liberal thought such as the work of Locke, although religious beliefs were assigned to the sphere of opinion, not knowledge. Twentieth-century relativism breaks down this distinction.

Indeed, the liberalism of John Stuart Mill and John Dewey, liberalism without natural rights and fundamental principles of moral virtue, neglected civic culture in Bloom's opinion and prepared us for the cultural relativism of the twentieth-century. The main motivation for this culture of openness was the presence in the United States of a pluralism of cultures and races with these minorities being perceived, by themselves and white liberals, to be badly treated because of their race, ethnicity, and culture. The goal of the social sciences became one of overcoming prejudice and the sense of superiority of the dominant American majority—WASPs (White Anglo Saxon Protestants). As Bloom notes, "Much of the intellectual machinery of twentieth-century American political thought and social science was constructed for the purposes of making an assault on that majority" (Bloom, 1987, 31). The Founding Fathers of America viewed minorities as generally bad things: they wished to have a homogeneous cohesive society and saw minorities as generally selfish with no concern for the common good. Twentieth-century social science, however, rejects this negative view of minorities, as well as the concept of the common good. For these social scientists in the Boas tradition, there is no majority as such; there are only minorities and groups each pursuing their own interests, which are defended by the social scientific intelligentsia through a critique of the concept of *prejudice*. Bloom says:

History and social science are used in a variety of ways to overcome prejudice. We should not be ethnocentric, a term drawn from anthropology, which tells us more about the meaning of openness. We should not think our way is better than others. The intention is not so much to teach the students about other times and places as to make them aware of the fact that their preferences are only that—accidents of their time and place. Their beliefs do not entitle them as individuals, or collectively as a nation, to think they are superior to anyone else. John Rawls is almost a parody of this tendency, writing hundreds of pages to persuade men, and proposing a scheme of government that would force them, not to despise anyone. In *A Theory of Justice*, he writes that the physicist or the poet should not look down on the man who spends his life counting blades of grass or performing any other frivolous or corrupt activity. Indeed, he should be esteemed, since esteem from others, as opposed to self-esteem, is a basic need of all men. So indiscriminateness is a moral imperative because its opposite is discrimination. This folly means that men are not permitted to seek for the natural human good and admire it when found, for such discovery is coeval with the discovery of the bad and contempt for it. Instinct and intellect must be suppressed by education. The natural soul is to be replaced with an artificial one. (Bloom, 1987, 30)

Bloom cites a number of examples to support his thesis, the most instinctive being that of the civil rights movement. All significant leaders in the early days of the movement relied on the Constitution and the Declaration of Independence in their demands for equality, and worked through Congress, the presidency, and the judiciary. By contrast the Black Power movement was concerned with black identity, not universal rights, and viewed the status quo as racist and corrupt. Its concern was with power, not rights, and it demanded *respect* for blacks. As Bloom notes, the Constitution does not promise respect for any group be they blacks or Jews—only the protection of human rights. Respect, we should add, is not a right but a privilege—something that has to be earned. But for the advocates of the new curriculum, cultural diversity is a weapon to produce acceptance of different ways of life (Bloom, 1987, 35).

This leaves us with nothing more than a sweet and empty feeling that we should all get along. But as part of our multicultural experience, when studying non-Western cultures, it is found that closedness and ethno-centrism are the orders of the day. Indeed, the study of non-Western cultures confirms the view that one's own race, culture, and ethnic group/tribe is naturally superior to others, and Bloom notes that the multicultural supporters of openness and diversity should therefore, on pain of inconsistency, respect the ethnocentrism found in most cultures apart from the West (Bloom, 1987, 36–37). Further, there are very good reasons for non-Western closeness and ethnocentrism, because people must love and discriminate in favor of their own kind for group preservation (Bloom, 1987, 37). This is said as part of Bloom's *reductio ad absurdum* of his opponent's view as he seeks to show that multicultural relativism comes to see science itself as a threat to culture. Using a view of the good, not of one's own to judge one's own, tends to weaken people's attachment to their own view of the good, Bloom says (Bloom, 1987, 37). People are then more likely to strive for universality, even though this attempt will weaken their peoples. But what is the point of this if in the end it will destroy "the good" anyway? Bloom's answer is that men cannot remain content with what is given to them by their culture if they are to be fully human—citing Plato's image of the cave in the *Republic*. But Plato never implied that culture (being itself ultimately of abstract essence, a form) was to be understood by the cave metaphor, as this was explicitly linked to his own view of knowledge of the Forms. Plato's *Republic* is an unfortunate work for Bloom to choose as a defense, since Plato attacked Athenian democracy in that work for its craven weakness, degeneracy, decadence, and built-in suicidal tendencies. The same case could be made today (Grant, 1916; Oliver, 1981; North, 1992). As North notes, to take but one example, democracies are not "tough-minded enough, to inflict pain on otherwise law-abiding, disadvantaged persons, in order to manage international migration effectively" (North, 1992, 154).[3]

We have examined to date ethical and epistemological arguments that call into question the philosophical, methodological, and epistemological legitimacy of liberalism, universalism, and the Enlightenment project. However, the main challenge to Enlightenment comes from the position of *ecological limitationism* (Smith et al., 1997), that it is biophysically impossible for all the people presently on the Earth to achieve the high consumption lifestyles of the United States, Western Europe, and Japan. Ophuls and Boyan have noted that "liberal democracy as we know it . . . is doomed by ecological scarcity. . . . Moreover it appears that the basic principles of modern industrial civilization are also incompatible with ecological scarcity and that the whole ideology of modernity growing out of the Enlightenment, especially such central tenets as individualism, may no longer be viable" (Ophuls and Boyan, 1992, 3). These consequences are not followed through by Ophuls and Boyan, the implications to be discussed in a work which has not yet appeared.

Garrett Hardin (1993, 1995) has, however, fearlessly pursued this anti-Enlightenment argument through to its logical conclusion, on the basis of biological science and common sense. His work has only been discussed by moral philosophers with the aim of refuting him. However, in the context of both the epistemological problems that we have seen confronts received ethics and morality, a fresh affirmation of the correctness (as far as any doctrine can be "correct") can be given.

Hunger, poverty, war, disease, and injustice were not regarded by premodernists as "problems"; they were misfortunes, primarily because there was little that anyone could have done about them. Describing these tragic aspects of the life of men and nations as "problems" implies that there is a solution, at least in principle. Hardin rejects the idea that there is a technical solution to every "problem." This is so because of what we described earlier as the "revenge effects" of technology ("that ingrained responses . . . thwart solutions to certain sorts of problem" [Hardin, 1986, 140]), and also because not all problems are technical problems. The population "problem" and (world) "hunger" are examples. They can't be solved by technology because they are not technical problems at all. In the case of hunger, Hardin maintains, attempts to eliminate it merely by increasing the supply of food fail for the reason that mankind has known for thousands of years: "When goods are increased, they are increased that eat them" (*Ecclesiastes* 5:11). Tertullian (A.D.?160–?220), one of the Fathers of the Christian faith in the third century A.D. also observed: "As our demands grow greater, our complaints against nature's inadequacy are heard by all. The scourges of pestilence, famine, wars and earthquakes have come to be regarded as a blessing to overcrowded nations, since they serve to prune away the luxuriant growth of the human race" (Hardin, 1986, 142).[4] But the modernist rebels against such premodern wisdom. Our religion is scientific and technological rationality; our God is *Progress*. Every trial and tribulation can be converted into a technical problem and solved by technology. Hardin argues against this idea in his famous "tragedy of the commons" argument (Hardin, 1995), and we have also attempted to refute the idea that "progress is God" here and in other works (Smith, et al., 1997). It is this Enlightenment metaphysics that underlies today's dominant ideology of globalism and the oxymoron that the world is a "global village." It is this Enlightenment metaphysics that has led the West, and now it seems much of the rest of the world, into acceptance of universalism, globalism, and cosmopolitanism. The Marxist, and increasingly globalist principle "From each according to his ability, to each according to his needs," ultimately leads to ecological tragedy and the misery of all by treating the world as a global commons. This principle may be satisfactory when applied to a family group, but it generates disaster when applied to larger groups (Hardin, 1986, 143). Modern moral philosophy ignores the problem of scale; indeed, as a universalistic doctrine it must claim that scale factors are morally irrelevant factors.

We cannot offer a full exposition and defense of Hardin's "lifeboat ethics" here, but we can make our concluding points without it, as Hardin's work is well known. Hardin's "lifeboat ethics" has been rejected for two reasons. First, critics have felt that ecological scarcity and the environmental crisis are not as severe as Hardin supposes. We have argued that on this question Hardin is almost optimistic. Second, critics have attempted to undermine Hardin's ethical system from the perspective of universalistic arguments generated by the machinery of modern moral philosophy. But we have seen that all such arguments will fail, for they will ultimately be circular, question-begging, or incapable of rational justification. Lifeboat ethics require no justification as it is understood at the level of the genitals and gut. It is a natural position to adopt in situations of crisis. It increasingly will become a natural position to adopt in the future. This earthy philosophy of commonsense wisdom, as we have seen, is embodied in many of the great religious and philosophical works of the past. It does not presuppose a great technical knowledge of biology or ecology. It involves the recognition that if you want to put meat on the table, then you (or somebody on your behalf) has to get blood on his or her hands.

It is perhaps just as well. It is an implication of the global meltdown thesis, that science as we understand it will come to an end as the pillars of civilized order crumble. David Price has described this:

Those people [i.e., the survivors] might get by, for a while by picking through the wreckage of civilization, but soon they would have to lead simpler lives, like the hunters and subsistence farmers of the past. They would not have the resources to build great public works or carry forward scientific inquiry. They could not let individuals remain unproductive as they wrote novels or composed symphonies. After a few generations, they might come to believe that the rubble amid which they live is the remains of cities built by gods.

Or it may prove impossible for even a few survivors to subsist on the meager resources left in civilization's wake. The children of the highly technological society into which more and more of the world's peoples are being drawn will not know how to support themselves by hunting and gathering or by simple agriculture. In addition, the wealth of wild animals that once sustained hunting societies will be gone, and topsoil that has been spoiled by tractors will yield poorly to the hoe. A species that has come to depend on complex technologies to mediate its relationship with the environment may not long survive their loss. (Price, 1995, 316)

Having reached the end of this work, we do not have the space for detailed speculation about the ideology that the survivors in civilization's wake will adopt, but we will make a few points in passing. If the messiah does not return, religions such as Christianity and Judaism will completely lose their point. Liberal versions of Christianity and Judaism will fall, we predict, when liberalism itself falls with the collapse of the modern era. With economic collapse and the breakdown of nations and society, people will turn increasingly to "other worldly" solutions that fundamentalist religions uniquely supply. But unless they fulfill their promises and deliver a savior, they are unlikely to continue as they have in the past. If God is like Godot and we must wait for Him until the end of time, or at least until the end of the Earth, then why wait at all? If God is to "come again in glory to judge the living and the dead" and if His Kingdom is to have "no end," then first He must come. One may argue that the game could always be continued, that the wait for Godot could always continue, that faith could be sustained as a matter of social conditioning. Indeed it could if there were social mechanisms for sustaining these belief systems. Even during the "dark ages" in Europe, there was an established order to ensure the continuity of the faith. The global meltdown thesis shows that no such mechanism will be available in the future. The concerns of what remains of humanity will be primarily for survival.

An extraterrestrial biologist will see the Earth of the future, an Earth that the human species by its hubris is making inevitable, as a world where the beetle is the dominant and supreme life form. This is a bitter medicine to swallow. Yet mankind has lived with this possibility before. Norse mythology accepts that good cannot triumph over evil in the universe, but that rather than passively accept a whimpering defeat, heroic resistance should be made against evil while accepting inevitable defeat and destruction. As Hamilton notes:

The world of Norse mythology is a strange world. Asgard, the home of the gods, is unlike any other heaven men have dreamed of. No radiancy of joy is in it, no assurance of bliss. It is a grave and solemn place, over which hangs the threat of an inevitable doom. The gods know that a day will come when they will be destroyed. Sometime they will meet their enemies and go down beneath them to defeat and death. Asgard will fall in ruins. The cause the forces of good are fighting to defend against the forces of evil is hopeless. Nevertheless, the gods will fight for it to the end.

Necessarily the same is true of humanity. If the gods are finally helpless before evil, men and women must be more so. The heroes and heroines of the early stories face disaster. They know that they cannot save themselves, not by any courage or endurance or great deed. Even so, they do not yield. They die resisting. A brave death entitles them—at least the heroes—to a seat in Valhalla, one of the halls in Asgard, but there too they must look forward to final defeat and destruction. In the last battle between good and evil they will fight on the side of the gods and die with them. (Hamilton, 1959, 300)

Perhaps one can do no more.

NOTES

1. Charles Taylor observes that "hermeneutical sciences," such as ethics, inevitably commit us to what rationalists and positivists would call a type of "dogmatism":

In other words, in a hermeneutical science, a certain measure of insight is indispensable, and this insight cannot be communicated by the gathering of brute data, or initiation in modes of formal reasoning or some combination of these. It is unformalizable. But this is a scandalous result according to the authoritative conception of science in our tradition, which is shared even by many of those who are highly critical of the approach of mainstream psychology, or sociology, or political science. For it means that this is not a study in which anyone can engage, regardless of their level of insight; that some claims of the form: "if you don't understand, then your intuitions are at fault, are blind or inadequate," some claims of this form will be justified; that some differences will be non-arbitrable by further evidence, but that each side can only make appeal to deeper insight on the part of the other. The superiority of one position over another will thus consist in this, that from the more adequate position one can understand one's own stand and that of one's opponent, but not the other way around. It goes without saying that this argument can only have weight for those in the superior position. (Taylor, 1971, 46–47).

The epistemology appealed to here is anti-democratic, anti-egalitarian, and in a sense, aristocratic, but is as plausible as any doctrines in the field of epistemology.

2. The problem of the epistemological crisis of orthodox ethics, moral and political theory is well illustrated by the array of problems confronting democratic theory (Nelson, 1980; Levine, 1981). First are philosophical paradoxes, an important paradox being observed by Wollheim (1969). Wollheim believed that his paradox went to the heart of democratic theory. He postulated a "democratic machine," that "at fixed intervals [given] the choices of the individual citizens . . . aggregates them according to the pre-established rule or method, and so comes up with what may be called a 'choice' of its own" (Wollheim, 1969, 76). However, if a voter expresses a choice for A and the democratic machine yields not-A, then the voter as a consistent democrat is committed to the belief that A ought to be the case (by independent arguments, we suppose) and also that not-A ought to be the case (by democracy). This is paradoxical. As is the norm in philosophy, there have been numerous attempts to dissolve, solve, or avoid this paradox, attempts that have been met by restatements or defenses of the veracity of the paradox (Nathan, 1971, 1989; McMullen, 1972; Barry, 1973; Goldstick, 1973; Weiss, 1973; Honderich, 1974; Pennock, 1974; Graham, 1975–76; Haksar, 1976; Estlund, 1989; Hansson, 1993; Wolff, 1994).

Robert Paul Wolff (1970) has argued that an essential component of democracy, majority rule, "is fatally flawed by an internal inconsistency which ought to disqualify it from consideration in any political community whatsoever" (Wolff, 1970, 59). Wolff bases his argument on the "voter's paradox." Again, this proposition has its critics and defenders (Sober, 1972; Steinberg, 1973; Mates, 1973; Davis, 1974; Allen, 1977). The "voter's paradox," however, is only one of a series of paradoxes in the broad field of social choice (Gibbard, 1973; Ferejohn and Fiorina, 1974; Fishburn, 1974; Satterthwaite, 1975; Kelly, 1989; Campbell, 1992b; Schwartz, 1995). For example, the *Ostrogorski paradox* in majority rule occurs when there are two or more parties with contrasting positions on a series of issues—a candidate can win even when he holds a minority position on every single issue (Anscombe, 1976; Rae and Daudt, 1976; Leahy, 1977; Gorman, 1978; Wagner, 1983; Kelly, b, 1989; Nermuth, 1992).

One of the major challenges to democratic theory is *Arrow's theorem* (Arrow, 1951) which has been taken by many theorists to undermine the basic foundation of social choice theory (Friedland and Cumbala, 1973; Routley, 1979; MacKay, 1980; Barbera, 1983; Craven, 1992; Davis, 1992) and to show that "there is an inherent contradiction within democratic theory" (DeLong, 1991, 6). In fact, Arrow's argument is embarrassing because Arrow's inconsistency "infects virtually every method of social choice which can lay a reasonable claim to being called 'democratic'" (Wolff, 1970, 63), the result establishing in effect that a very reasonable set of social choice assumptions can only be satisfied by *dictatorship* (Craven, 1992, 36). Although it is not normally stated as such, Arrow's theorem can be taken as a proof of the principle of dictatorship from liberal premises. Obviously then there have been many attempts to escape Arrow's theorem (DeLong, 1991), but other theorists have generalized the theorem producing more universal impossibility results (Schwartz, 1970; Routley, 1980; May, 1952; Wilson, 1972; Harsanyi, 1975; Kelly, 1976a; Kemp and Ng, 1976, 1977, 1982, Osborne, 1976; Parks, 1976; Kalai and Schmeidler, 1977; Pollak, 1979; Roberts, 1980; Ng, 1981; Malawski and Zhou, 1994). Both individual and collective choice are philosophically problematic (Kavka, 1991; Sugden, 1991), as Sen's paradox of the Paretian liberal also shows (Sen, 1970, 1983; Levine, 1978).

These abstract considerations are some distance from historical reality. The delegates to the Constitutional convention, charged with drawing up the Constitution of the United States of America, such as Alexander Hamilton and James Madison, were aware of the dangers of unlimited majority rule without the checks and balances supplied by law. Democracies in this sense ultimately degenerated into the rule of the mob, leading to despotism and national suicide, the oppression of the people, by the people, for the people. The Founding Fathers of the Constitution offered instead a *republic*: a government of laws, not of men, with both the people and the rulers being subject to the law. Twentieth-century contributions to social choice theory and the mathematical theory of politics, show that this was a wise move.

3. Population growth itself also makes democracy impossible. Garrett Hardin explains:

Easy communication is the *sine qua non* for an enduring democracy. All communication functions are inherently afflicted with *dis*economies of scale, since (for every well defined communication network) the burden created by the communication of *n* people increases as the *square of n*. This burden expresses itself in information-overload, which leads to misunderstandings, social pathologies, and (ultimately) the acceptance of a totalitarian regime as the least of the evils available to an overpopulated political unit. In the face of unlimited population growth the *word* "democracy" can be retained, *but not the fact.* (Hardin, 1985, 473)

4. Modern Christianity, which is essentially the servant of multiculturalism, internationalism, and the new morality of political correctness, differs from premodern Christianity, illustrated by the thought of Tertullian. Why does God allow evil in the world—such as pestilence, famine, wars, earthquakes, and death itself? The early Christians accounted for these evils by the "Fall," but they did not view death with the existential dread that modernists do. People who die from these evil causes are at least free of this veil of tears and if they have been baptized and are forgiven of their sins, will enjoy an eternity of bliss with God. So what then, a modern Tertullian would argue, if the starving billions of the world perish, as long as their souls are saved—and that requires words not food. After all, we are all living in the shadow of death. Premodern Christians (and, we believe, many "ordinary" street-active Christians today) accepted their faith not because of any rational argument or moral considerations but because of Pascalian utilitarian considerations: acceptance means heaven, rejection means hell. Consequently, the premodern Christian promise is one of personal survival and utilitarian satisfaction. One is to believe, not merely because the doctrine is good and true as some piece of abstract philosophy might be, but because belief is a way of maximizing bliss and eliminating pain. This whole world view is inconsistent with the universalism of modern morality, and arguably constitutes a form of cosmological "racism" with the chosen receiving heaven and the rejected receiving hell. Damnation is produced merely by lack of belief and commitment, a prejudice surely much worse from a rationalist perspective than the racist's own rejection of an out-group based on physical characteristics. The damned could have their doubts about Christianity because of scientific and philosophical arguments they find intellectually compelling. The damned may also be morally good people. But premodernist Christianity must discriminate against them, on pain of having its entire system of belief rendered impotent. If God is free to allow into heaven the virtuous non-Christian and if as well there is no hell, then there are no compelling theological (by contrast to social) reasons for becoming a Christian. Modernist Christianity, then, dissolves

into a theological form of multiculturalism, an "ecclesial multiculturalism" (Charlesworth, 1993, 167). But if this is so, the theological problem remains: why accept Christianity at all? Multiculturalism seems to render such premodern belief systems, based upon a metaphysics of monism rather than pluralism, redundant.

Bibliography

ABC TV (1994). *Landline*: September 22.

ABC TV (1994). *Landline.* September 25.

ABC TV (1996). *The 7:30 Report.* August 12.

Abernethy, V. (1993). *Population Politics: The Choices That Shape Our Future.* New York and London: Insight Books, Plenum Press.

Abernethy, V. (1993a). *Population Politics: The Choices That Shape Our Future.* New York: Plenum Publishing.

Abernethy, V. (1993b). The Demographic Transition Revisited: Lessons for Foreign Aid and U.S. Immigration Policy. *Ecological Economics* 8: 235–52.

Abernethy, V. (1994). Optimism and Overpopulation. *The Atlantic Monthly* December: 84–91.

Abernethy, V. (1995a). Review of M. J. Esman, *Ethnic Politics. International Migration Review* 29: 835–36.

Abernethy, V. (1995b). The Demographic Transition Model: A Ghost Story. *Population and Environment* 17: 3–6.

Ajami, F. (1993). The Summoning. *Foreign Affairs* 72, September/October: 2–9.

Allen, G. O. (1977). Beyond the Voter's Paradox. *Ethics* 88: 50–61.

Almond, B. (1990). Alasdair MacIntyre: The Virtue of Tradition. *Journal of Applied Philosophy* 7: 99–103.

Anderson, B. (1991). *Imagined Communities: Reflections on the Origin and Spread of Nationalism.* (Revised edition). London and New York: Verso.

Anderson, B. (1992). The New World Disorder. *24 Hours Supplement* (Radio National, Australia) February: 40–46.

Anderson, I. (1996). African Nations Sow Seeds of Hope. *New Scientist* October 12: 11.

Annas, J. (1989). MacIntyre on Traditions. *Philosophy and Public Affairs* 18: 388–404.

Anonymous a. (1995). Keating Warns on Water Use. *The Advertiser* (Adelaide) October 16: 6.

Anonymous b. (1995). New Masses of Dead Pilchards. *The Advertiser* (Adelaide) May 16: 8.

Anonymous a. (1996). Genocide Warning as Burundi Leader Flees. *The Australian* July 26: 9.

Anonymous b. (1997). CIA Warns of North Korean War Threat. *The Australian* February 7: 7.

Anonymous c. (1997). Muslims Kill 10 Han Chinese in Ethnic Riots. *The Australian* February 11: 9.

Anonymous d. (1997). 100 Muslims Executed as China Acts Over Ethnic Riots. *The Australian* February 13: 9.

Anonymous e. (1997) Dalai Lama Can No longer Guarantee Non-Violence. *The Australian* March 11: 9.

Anonymous f. (1996). Northern Italians Raise the Stakes for Secession. *The Australian* May 14: 13.

Anonymous g. (1996). Greenshirt Guards Raise Italian Civil War Fears. *The Australian* September 9: 14.

Anonymous h. (1995). CIA Chief Predicts Terrorism Will Soar. *The Advertiser* (Adelaide) December 21: 13.

Anonymous i. (1996). Extremist Threat Hits New Peak. *The Advertiser* (Adelaide) March 29: 12.

Anonymous j. (1997). Unrest May Signal 'End of Indonesia'. *The Advertiser* (Adelaide) February 24: 8.

Anscombe, G.F.M. (1976). On the Frustration of The Majority by Fulfillment of the Majority's Will. *Analysis* 36:161–68.

Aquatech Pty. Ltd. (1994). *Water Quality Monitoring in Australia*. Canberra: Report prepared for Environment Protection Authority by Aquatech Pty. Ltd.

Armitage, C. (1995a). Carr's Immigrant Call Risks City's Standing: Bolkus. *The Australian* May 23: 6.

Armitage, C. (1995b). Divisive Immigration Debate Flares Up Over Carr's Claim. *The Australian* May 24: 1.

Arrow, K. (1951). *Social Choice and Individual Values*. New York: John Wiley.

Athanasiou, T. (1996). *Divided Planet: The Ecology of Rich and Poor*. Boston: Little, Brown and Company.

Attali, J. H. (1991). *Millennium: Winners and Losers in the Coming World Order*. New York: Random House.

Auger, J., Kunstmann, J. M., Czyglik, F., and Jouannet, P. (1995). Decline in Semen Quality Among Fertile Men in Paris During the Past 20 Years. *New England Journal of Medicine* 332: 281–85.

Australian Academy of Science (1995). *Population 2040: Australia's Choice. Proceedings of the Symposium of the 1994 Annual General Meeting of the Australian Academy of Science*. Canberra: Australian Academy of Science.

Australian National Audit Office (1996). *Commonwealth Fisheries Management: Australian Fisheries Management Authority*. The Auditor-General Performance Audit, Audit Report No. 32 1995–96, Vols. 1 and 2. Canberra: Australian Government Publishing Service.

Bairoch, P. (1982). Employment and Large Cities: Problems and Outlook. *International Labour Review* 121: 519–33.

Ball, P. (1996). Through the Nanotube. *New Scientist* July 6: 28–31.

Barber, J. (1994). Russia: A Crisis of Post-Imperial Viability *Political Studies* 42: 34–51.

Barbera, S. (1983). Pivotal Voters: A Simple Proof of Arrow's Theorem. In: Pattanaik, P.K. and Salles, M., eds. *Social Choice and Welfare*. Amsterdam: North-Holland: 31–35.

Barry, B. (1973). Wollheim's Paradox: Comment. *Political Theory* 1: 317–22.

Barry, B. (1989). The Light that Failed. *Ethics* 100: 160–68.

Colinvaux, P. (1980). *The Fate of Nations: A Biological Theory of History.* Harmondsworth: Penguin Books.

Collins, C. (1994). Loved to Death. *The Australian* September 28: 20.

Committee to Advise on Australia's Immigration Policies (1988). *Immigration: A Commitment to Australia.* Canberra: Australian Government Publishing Service.

Commonwealth Scientific and Industrial Research Organisation (CSIRO) (1994). *Submission to the House of Representatives Standing Committee for Long Term Strategies, Inquiry into Australia's Population Carrying Capacity.* Canberra: CSIRO.

Connelly, M. and Kennedy, P. (1994). Must it be the Rest Against the West? *The Atlantic Monthly* December: 61–84.

Connor, W. (1994). *Ethnonationalism: The Quest for Understanding.* Princeton, New Jersey: Princeton University Press.

Conway, G. R. (1985). Agroecosystem Analysis. *Agricultural Administration* 20: 31–55.

Corden, W. M. (1955). The Economic Limits to Population Increase. *The Economic Record* 31: 242–60.

Coulter, J. (1997). Population Principles. *The Australian* January 15: 10.

Cowen, E. (1995). *A Truly Civil Society: 1995 Boyer Lectures.* Sydney: Australian Broadcasting Corporation.

Craven, J. (1992). *Social Choice: A Framework for Collective Decisions and Individual Judgements.* Cambridge: Cambridge University Press.

Cribb, J. (1991). Inland Water Drying Up. *The Australian* April 1: 3.

Cribb, J. (1992). The Toxic Cocktail That Threatens Our Coast. *The Australian* July 1: 3.

Cribb, J. (1993a). Oceans in Peril. *The Weekend Australian* June 5–6: 31, 46.

Cribb, J. (1993b). Life and Death of the Billabong. *The Weekend Australian Review* March 6–7: 8.

Cribb, J. (1994). Science Leader Warns of Disaster. *The Australian* February 18: 2.

Cribb, J. (1994a). Residents Blame Bureaucracy for Death of the Darling. *The Weekend Australian* March 5–6: 8.

Cribb, J. (1994b). Death of a Lifeline. *The Weekend Australian Review* May 21–22: 3.

Cribb, J. (1994c). Governments Slammed Over Inaction on Murray-Darling. *The Australian* December 7: 4.

Cribb, J. (1994d). How Humans Became the Future Eaters. *The Weekend Australian* October 29–30: 47.

Cribb, J. (1995). Greenhouse Gas Control to Cost $107 bn a Year. *The Weekend Australian* December 2–3: 6.

Cribb, J. (1995a). Greenhouse Theory 'Still Uncertain'. *The Weekend Australian* March 25–26: 10.

Cribb, J. (1995b). Greenhouse Efforts May be Needless. *The Australian* October 18: 3.

Cribb, J. (1995c). Invaders Threaten Dwindling Fish Stocks. *The Australian* February 2: ?.

Cribb, J. (1995d). Pollution, Poor Policy Threatens Coastline. *The Australian* February 3: 3.

Cribb, J. (1995e). Imports Support Cyanide Fishing. *The Weekend Australian* December 30–31: 3.

Cribb, J. (1995f). Environmental Damage Hurting Health: AMA. *The Weekend Australian* October 21–22: 10.

Cribb, J. (1995g). Call to Slash Water Usage. *The Australian* April 3: 5.

Bartlett, A. A. (1993). The Arithmetic of Growth: Methods of Calculation. *Population and Environment* 14: 359–87.

Bartley, R. L. (1993). The Case for Optimism: The West Should Believe in Itself. *Foreign Affairs* 72, September/October: 15–18.

Batra, R. (1993) *The Myth of Free Trade: A Plan for America's Economic Revival.* New York: Charles Scribner's Sons.

Baumrin, B. (1990). Post Cosmopolitanism. *Nous* 24: 774–82.

Beale, B. (1996). CSIRO Calls for Agriculture Revolution. *The Sydney Morning Herald* July 30: 5.

Beale, B. and Woodford, J. (1995). Blots on the Landscape: Australia's Green Image Exposed. *The Sydney Morning Herald* November 13: 1, 6.

Beale, B., Morris, L., and Woodford, J. (1996). Sydney Choking on Its 10-Cigarette-A-Day Air. *The Sydney Morning Herald* May 28: 3.

Behrakis, Y. (1997). Rebels Try 'Traitors' as Albania Stumbles Closer to Civil War. *The Independent* March 7: 12.

Bellos, A. (1997). 2000 and None. *The Guardian Weekly* March 8: 27–8.

Berger, P. L., Berger, B., and Kellner, H. (1977). *The Homeless Mind: Modernization and Consciousness.* Harmondsworth: Penguin Books.

Berry, A. (1995). *The Next 500 Years: Life in the Coming Millennium.* London: Headline.

Binyan, L. (1993). Civilization Grafting: No Culture is an Island. *Foreign Affairs* 72, September/October: 19–21.

Biodiversity Unit (1995). *Native Vegetation Clearance, Habit Loss and Biodiversity Decline.* Canberra: Biodiversity Series Paper No. 6, Department of the Environment, Sport and Territories.

Biodiversity Unit (1996). *National Strategy for the Conservation of Australia's Biological Diversity.* Canberra: Commonwealth Department of the Environment, Sport and Territories.

Bita, N. (1995a). Global Storming. *The Australian.* November 20: 10.

Bita, N. (1995b). Water Users Warned: Cut Down or Pay Up. *The Australian* March 14: 10.

Bita, N. (1995c). Farmers Face Irrigation Limit. *The Australian* June 28: 7.

Bita, N. (1996a). Greenhouse Gases Increase Despite World Pact. *The Australian* July 8: 3.

Bita, N. (1996b). Changing Climate. *The Australian* July 15: 9.

Bita, N. (1996c). Hill Loses Fight Against Gas Emission Targets. *The Weekend Australian* July 20–21: 5.

Bita, N. (1996d). Ministers Extend Freeze on Irrigation. *The Weekend Australian* June 29–30: 12.

Black, H. (1996). Buckyballs Make a Point. *New Scientist* October 12: 19.

Bloom, A. (1987). *The Closing of the American Mind: How Higher Education has Failed Democracy and Impoverished the Souls of Today's Students.* London: Penguin.

Bonyhady, T. (1995). Cracks in the Canvas. *The Sydney Morning Herald* September 23: 9.

Boulding, E. (1988). *Building a Global Civic Culture: Education for an Interdependent World.* Syracuse, New York: Syracuse University Press.

Bouma, J., Pearman, G.I. and Manning, M.R. (1996). *Greenhouse: Coping with Climate Change.* Collingwood, Victoria: CSIRO Publishing.

Brackett, D. W. (1996). *Holy Terror: Armageddon in Tokyo* New York: Weatherhill.

Brake, R. (1996). Return to Sender, Address Unknown. *New Scientist* September 21: 8.

Brandon, C. and Ramankutty, R. (1993) *Toward an Environmental Strategy for Asia*. Washington D.C.: The World Bank.

Brandt, R. B. (1989). Morality and Its Critics. *American Philosophical Quarterly* 26:89–100.

Brice, C. (1996). Scientist Top in Literature. *The Advertiser* (Adelaide) March 4: 8.

Brimelow, P. (1995). *Alien Nation: Common Sense About America's Immigration Disaster*. New York: Random House.

Bromby, R. (1997). Healthier Prognosis For Grain in China. *The Australian* February 25: 22.

Brown, C. (1995a). International Theory and International Society: The Viability of the Middle Way? *Review of International Studies* 21: 183–96.

Brown, L. R. (1995b). *Who Will Feed China? Wake-Up Call for a Small Planet*. New York: W. W. Norton.

Brown, L. R. (1996). The Acceleration of History. In: Brown, L. et al., *State of the World 1996*. London: Earthscan: 3–20.

Brown, L. R. and Kane, H. (1995). *Full House: Reassessing the Earth's Population Carrying Capacity*. London: Earthscan.

Brown, N. (1989). Climate, Ecology and International Security. *Survival* 31: 519–32.

Browne, D. (1990). Ethics Without Morality. *Australasian Journal of Philosophy* 68: 395–412.

Brzezinski, Z. (1993). *Out of Control: Global Turmoil on the Eve of the 21st Century*. New York: Charles Scribner's Sons.

Bureau of Industry Economics (1996). *Prospects for Australian Industry Involvement in Greenhouse Gas Abatement Overseas*. Canberra: Australian Government Publishing Service.

Burke, B. M. (1996). Managed Growth and Optimum Population: Irreconcilable Concepts. *Population and Environment* 17: 537–44.

Burnham, J. (1965). *Suicide of the West: An Essay on the Meaning and Destiny of Liberalism*. London: Jonathan Cape.

Button, J. (1993). Western Cracks Widen as 'Illegals' Pour In. *The Sydney Morning Herald* June 16: 19.

Calleo, D. P. (1994). America's Federal Nation State: A Crisis of Post-Imperial Viability? *Political Studies* 42: 16–33.

Calterall, C. and Kingston, M. (1993). *Remnant Bushland of South East Queensland in the 1990s: Its Distribution, Loss, Ecological Consequences and Future Prospects*. Brisbane: Institute of Applied Environmental Research, Griffith University and Brisbane City Council.

Camilleri, J. and Falk, J. (1992a). *The End of Sovereignty? The Politics of a Shrinking and Fragmenting World*. Aldershot: Edward Elgar.

Campbell, D. (1992a). *Writing Security*. Manchester: Manchester University Press.

Campbell, W. (1992b). *Identity/Difference: Democratic Negotiations of Political Paradox*. Ithaca, New York: Cornell University Press.

Canterbery, E. R. (1987). *The Making of Economics*. Belmont, California: Wadsworth.

Carlsen, E., Giwercman, A., Keiding, N., and Skakkebaek, N. E. (1992). Evidence for Decreasing Quality of Semen During Past 50 Years. *British Medical Journal* 305: 609–13.

Carroll, J. (1993). *Humanism: The Wreck of Western Culture*. London: Fontana Press.

Carson, T. L. (1985). Relativism and Nihilism. *Philosophia* 15: 1–23.

Carter, B. (1983). The Anthropic Principle and Its Implications for Biologic Philosophical Transactions of the Royal Society of London. S 346–63.

Casey, M. (1996). Squad Targets Terrorism in Cyberspace. *The Advert* June 7: 15.

Castles, S. and Miller, M. J. (1993). *The Age of Migration: Internati Movements in the Modern World*. London: Macmillan.

Cater, N. (1995). Cyanide Fishing 'Killing Barrier Reef.' *The Adve* January 30: 3.

Ceresa, M. (1997). Drunks Fuel Tension: Stone. *The Weekend Australi*

Chamberlin, P. (1995). Grim River Report Brings Water Ban. *The Age*

Chandler, J. (1995). The Bridge and Liberal Principles. (Letter) *Th* September: 45.

Charlesworth, M. (1993). *Bioethics in a Liberal Society*. Car University Press.

Chester, G. (1993). *Berserk! Motiveless Random Massacres*. Lond Books.

Chilvers, C., Pike, M. C., Forman, D., Fogelman, K. and Wads Apparent Doubling of Frequency of Undescended Testis in 1962–81. *The Lancet* August 11: 330–32.

Cioran, E. M. (1975). *A Short History of Decay*. New York: Press.

Clark, D. (1995). Australia's Great Immigration Debate. *Aust* September 6: 28–29.

Clark, S. L. and Graham, D. R. (1995). The Russian Federa *Orbis* 39: 329–51.

Cochran, M. (1995). Postmodernism, Ethics and International *International Studies* 21: 237–50.

Cocks, D. (1992). *Use With Care: Managing Australia's Twenty-First Century*. Kensington, New South University Press.

Cocks, D. (1996). *People Policy: Australia's Population C* New South Wales Press.

Cocks, D., Foran, B. and Hamilton, N. (1995). *The Future* Futures Program, CSIRO Division of Wildlife a

Coghlan, A. (1996a). Doomsday has been Postponed. *Nev*

Coghlan, A. (1996b). Hopping Electron Promises S September 28: 24.

Cohen, B. (1997). The Media and Hindmarsh Islan *Australian* March 26: 13.

Cohen, J. E. (1995). *How Many People Can the Ea* Norton.

Colander, D. (1991). *Why Aren't Economists as Imp the State of Economics*. Armonk, New York

Colborn, R., Myers, J. P., and Dumanoski, D. (*Threatening Our Fertility, Intelligence, Story*. Boston: Little, Brown and Compan

Cole, L. A. (1997). *The Eleventh Plague: The Warfare*. New York: W. H. Freeman.

Co
Co

Cou
Cox

Crav

Cribb
Cribb
Cribb
Cribb

Cribb,
Cribb,

Cribb,
Cribb,

Cribb,

Cribb, J

Cribb, J.

Cribb, J.
Cribb, J.

Cribb, J.

Cribb, J.

Cribb, J.

Cribb, J. (19

Cribb, J. (1995h). Tap Water Fails to Meet Safety Standards. *The Australian* February 6: 6.

Cribb, J. (1996a). World Fish Stocks May Never Recover: Scientist. *The Australian* May 8: 6.

Cribb, J. (1996b). Water View Goes Against the Flow. *The Australian* June 6: 2.

Cribb, J. (1996c). Cotton Farm Will Ruin Historic Waterway, Biologist Warns. *The Weekend Australian* May 18–19: 10.

Crome, F., Foran, B., and Moore, L. (1994). Linkages Between Australia's Population and its Biodiversity Loss. *People and Place* 2: 11–14.

Crown, J. (1986). *Australia: The Terrorist Connection*. South Melbourne: Sun Books/Macmillan.

Da Silva, W. (1996). Long Dry Spells, Outlook Gloomy. *New Scientist* October 12: 9.

Daily, G. C. and Ehrlich, P. R. (1992). Population, Sustainability, and the Earth's Carrying Capacity. *BioScience* 42 November: 761–71.

Daily, G. C., Ehrlich, A. H., and Ehrlich, P. R. (1994). Optimum Human Population Size. *Population and Environment* 15: 469–75.

Daly, H. E. (1991). Growth, International Trade and Destruction of Community. *The Social Contract* Fall: 24–27.

Daly, H. E. (1993). The Perils of Free Trade. *Scientific American* 269, November: 24–29.

Daly, H. E. and Cobb, J. (1989). *For the Common Good: Redirecting the Economy Toward Community, the Environment, and a Sustainable Future*. Boston: Beacon Press.

Davidson, J. D. and Rees-Mogg, W. (1989). *Blood in the Streets: Investment Profits in a World Gone Mad*. London: Sidgwick and Jackson.

Davidson, J. D. and Rees-Mogg, W. (1992). *The Great Reckoning: How the World Will Change in the Depression of the 1990s*. London: Sidgwick and Jackson, 1992.

Davidson, P. and Davidson, G. (1988). *Economics for a Civilized Society*. New York: W.W. Norton.

Davies, P. (1994). *The Last Three Minutes*. New York: Basic Books.

Davies, P. (1995). *About Time: Einstein's Unfinished Revolution*. London: Penguin Books.

Davis, J. B. (1992). Atomism, Identity Criteria, and Impossibility Logic. *Methodus* 4: 83–87.

Davis, M. (1974). Avoiding the Voter's Paradox Democratically. *Theory and Decision* 5: 295–311.

Dayton, L. (1995). Humans Changing the Planet. *The Sydney Morning Herald* March 25: 10.

Dayton, L. (1996). Australia Warned on Climate Change. *The Sydney Morning Herald* July 22: 3.

Dayton, L. (1996a). Feeding a Hungry World. *The Sydney Morning Herald* June 3: 15.

Dayton, L. (1996b). World Starvation Crisis Within 10 Years. *The Sydney Morning Herald* May 29: 6.

Debreczeny, M. P., Svec, W. A. Marsh, E. M., and Wasielewski, M. R. (1996). Femtosecond Optical Control of Charge Shift within Electron Donor - Acceptor Arrays: An Approach to Molecular Switches. *Journal of the American Chemical Society* 118: 8174–75.

Delgado, R. (1996). *The Coming Race War? And Other Apocalyptic Tales of America After Affirmative Action and Welfare*. New York and London: New York University Press.

DeLong, H. (1991). *A Refutation of Arrow's Theorem.* Lanham, New York, and London: University Press of America.

Delors, J. (1995). As Japan and America Explode, Europe Will Endure. *New Perspectives Quarterly* 12: 24–27.

Denholm, M. (1996). Warmer climate inevitable, despite action. *The Advertiser* (Adelaide) June 1: 5.

Der Derian, J. and Shapiro, M., eds. (1989). *International/Intertexual Relations: Postmodern Readings of World Politics.* Lexington, Massachusetts: Lexington Books.

De Silva, K. M. and May, R. I., eds. (1991). *Internationalization of Ethnic Conflict.* London: Pinter Publishers.

Devine, F. (1996). Credibility Gap that Can't be Bridged. *The Australian* September 16: 11.

Di Zerega, G. (1994). Federalism, Self-Organization and the Dissolution of the State. *Telos* 100: 57–86.

Donagan, A. (1965). Mr. Hare and the Conscientious Nazi. *Philosophical Studies* 16: 8–12.

Douthwaite, R. (1992). *The Growth Illusion: How Economic Growth has Enriched the Few, Impoverished the Many, and Endangered the Planet.* Devon: A Resurgence Book/Green Books.

Dovers, S., Norton, T., Hughes, I., and Day, L. (1992). *Population Growth and Australian Regional Environments.* Canberra: Bureau of Immigration Research, Australian Government Publishing Service.

Downing, L. and Thigpen, R. (1984). After *Telos*: the Implications of MacIntyre's Attempt to Restore the Concept in *After Virtue. Social Theory and Practice* 10:39–54.

Downton, P. F. and Munn, D. (1996). *Urban Ecology Annotated Bibliography.* 2nd edition. Adelaide: Centre for Urban Ecology.

Dowrick, S. (1995). Economic Growth: Recent History and Prospects. In: Kriesler, P., ed. *The Australian Economy—The Essential Guide.* St Leonards, New South Wales: Allen and Unwin: 15–35.

Drexler, K. E. (1990). *Engines of Creation.* London: Fourth Estate.

Drexler, K. E., Peterson, C., and Pergamit, G. (1991). *Unbounding the Future: The Nanotechnology Revolution.* New York: William Morrow.

Drucker, P. F. (1993). *Post-Capitalist Society.* London: Butterworth/Heinemann.

Dunn, J. (1994). Introduction: Crisis of the Nation State. *Political Studies* 42: 3–15.

Dusevic, T. (1994). The Number's Up. *The Australian* December 6: 9.

Dusevic, T. (1995). Premier Tilts Population Debate in Wrong Direction. *The Weekend Australian* May 27–28: 7.

Dwyer, M. (1995). Australia at Odds on Greenhouse Target. *Australian Financial Review* April 21: 16.

Earl, G. (1997). Rise of Indonesian Islam a Question of Culture. *Australian Financial Review* February 12: 11.

Edwards, R. (1996). A Tank of the Cold Stuff. *New Scientist* November 23: 40–43.

Ehrlich, P. R., Ehrlich, A. H., and Daily, G. C. (1993). Food Security, Population, and Environment. *Population and Development Review* 19: 1–33.

Elegant, R. (1997). Violence Looms in Deng's Absence. *The Australian* March 19: 11.

Elliot, L. (1996). The Return of the Feudal Barons. *Guardian Weekly* June 30: 14.

Emerson, R. (1960). *From Empire to Nation.* Boston: Beacon Press.

Erdem, S. (1996). UN Warns World of Big Dry to Come. *The Sydney Morning Herald* June 5: 14.

Este, J. and Stapleton, J. (1996). Storm Brews on Peaceful Waters. *The Weekend Australian* July 20–21: 8.

Estlund, D. M. (1989). The Persistent Puzzle of the Minority Democrat. *American Philosophical Quarterly* 26: 143–51.

Etzioni, A. and Lawrence, P. (1991). *Socioeconomics: Toward a New Synthesis.* Armonk, New York: M. E. Sharpe.

Fagan, D. and Carruthers, F. (1997). Graziers Fear Wik Ruling Will Devalue Properties. *The Australian* January 6: 3.

Farah, D. and Robberson, T. (1995). U.S.-Style Gangs Build Free Trade in Crime. *Guardian Weekly* September 10: 19.

Farinella, P. and Davis, D. R. (1996). Short-Period Comets-Primordial Bodies or Collisional Fragments. *Science* 273: 938–41.

Ferber, M. and Nelson, J. (1993). *Beyond Economic Man: Feminist Theory and Economics.* Chicago: University of Chicago Press.

Ferejohn, J. A. and Fiorina, M. P. (1974). The Paradox of Not Voting: A Decision Theoretic Analysis. *American Political Science Review* 68: 525–36.

Feyerabend, P. (1978). *Science in a Free Society.* London: New Left Books.

Fife-Yeoman, J. (1995). Serial Killing to Rise: Ex-FBI Man. *The Australian* October 23: 3.

Fincher, R. (1991). *Immigration, Urban Infrastructure and the Environment.* Canberra: Bureau of Immigration Research, Australian Government Publishing Service.

Fingleton, E. (1995). Japan's Invisible Leviathan. *Foreign Affairs* 74: 69–85.

Fishburn, P. C. (1974). Paradoxes of Voting. *American Political Science Review* 68: 537–46.

Flannery, T. (1994). *The Future Eaters: An Ecological History of the Australasian Lands and People.* Port Melbourne: Reed Books.

Flannery, T. (1995). Migrant Policy. *The Sydney Morning Herald* December 7: 12.

Fleay, B. J. (1995). *The Decline of the Age of Oil.* Annandale, New South Wales: Pluto Press.

Fleay, B. J. (1996). World Slips Consciously into Black Hole of Oil Deprivation. *The Australian* July 19: 30.

Fleming, T. (1994). The Federal Principle. *Telos* 17–36.

Fletcher, J. (1991). Chronic Famine and the Immorality of Food Aid: A Bow to Garrett Hardin. *Population and Environment* 12: 331–38.

Flynn, J. R. (1974). The Unresolvability of Ethical Disputes. *Philosophical Quarterly* 24: 337–48.

Foot, P. (1978). *Virtues and Vices.* Oxford: Blackwell.

Foran, B. (1996). The Human Species: Me and My Lifestyle. Canberra: Paper given at ANZAAS Conference.

Foran, B. and Poldy, F. (1996). The Modern City and Its Life Support: City Footprints and City Futures. Melbourne: Paper given at the seventh International Housing and Home Conference, October 20–24.

Foreshew, J. (1996). Abalone Link to Crime Gangs. *The Weekend Australian* May 25–26: 5.

Franchetti, M. and Smith, D. (1997). Out of Order. *The Australian* February 19: 23.

Francis, S. (1994). The Choice is Your Country or Their GATT. *The Washington Times* June 28: A21.

Friedland, E. I. and Cumbala, S. J. (1973). Process and Paradox: The Significance of Arrow's Theorem. *Theory and Decision* 4: 51–64.

Friedman, M. (1995). *What Went Wrong? The Creation and Collapse of the Black-Jewish Alliance.* New York: The Free Press.

Fries, P. (1995). Mining Industry Must Lift Environmental Game. *The Weekend Australian* August 5–6: 11.

George, J. (1994). *Discourses of Global Politics:A Critical (Re)Introduction to International Relations.* Boulder, Colorado: Lynne Rienner Publishers.

George, R. P. (1989). Moral Particularism, Thomism and Traditions. *Review of Metaphysics* 42: 593–605.

Gerrans, P. (1995). Colonising Nationalism. *Political Theory Newsletter* 7: 35–41.

Gever, J., Kaufman, R., Skole, D., and Vörösmarty, C. (1991). *Beyond Oil* Boulder, Colorado: University Press of Colorado.

Giampietro, M., Bukkens, S.G.F., and Pimental, D. (1992). Limits to Population Size: Three Scenarios of Energy Interaction Between Human Society and Ecosystem. *Population and Environment* 14: 109–31.

Gibbard, A. (1973). Manipulation of Voting Schemes: A General Result. *Econometrica* 41: 587–602.

Gibbs, N. (1996). Tracking Down the Unabomber. *Time* (Australia) April 15: 24–30.

Giddens, A. (1985). *The Nation-State and Violence.* Cambridge: Polity Press.

Giddens, A. (1990). *The Consequences of Modernity.* Stanford, California: Stanford University Press.

Gifford, R. M., Kalma, J. D., Aston, A. R., and Millington, R. J. (1975). Biophysical Contrast in Australian Food Production: Implications for Population Policy. *Search* 6: 212–23.

Gilchrist, G. (1996a). Deadly Dust: Pollution Watchdogs Accused. *The Sydney Morning Herald* February 13: 1.

Gilchrist, G. (1996b). Scientists Unearth a Growing Problem. *The Sydney Morning Herald* July 11: 3.

Gleick, J. (1987). *Chaos: Making a New Science.* London: Cardinal.

Gleick, P. (1989). The Implications of Global Climatic Changes for International Security. *Climatic Change* 15: 309–25.

Glendinning, C. (1990). *When Technology Wounds: The Human Consequences of Progress.* New York: Morrow.

Goldman, A. H. (1991). *Empirical Knowledge.* Berkeley: University of California Press.

Goldrick, P. M. and Potter, E. F. (1982). The Irrationality of Immorality: An Answer to Professor Foot. *Modern Schoolman* 59: 195–206.

Goldsmith, J. (1994). *The Trap.* London: Macmillan.

Goldsmith, J. (1995a). *The Response.* London: Macmillan.

Goldsmith, J. (1995b). Global Free Trade: Recipe for a Lumpenplanet. *New Perspectives Quarterly* 12, Winter: 39–41.

Goldstick, D. (1973). An Alleged Paradox in the Theory of Democracy. *Philosophy and Public Affairs* 2: 181–89.

Gorman, J. L. (1978). A Problem in the Justification of Democracy. *Analysis* 38:46–50.

Gottliebsen, R. (1996). China and World Population are the Dominant Issues. *Business Review Weekly* March 4: 41.

Gowan, P. (1995). Neo-Liberal Theory and Practice for Eastern Europe. *New Left Review* 213: 3–60.

Graham, K. (1975–76). Democracy, Paradox and the Real World. *The Aristotelian Society* 76: 227–45.

Grant, M. (1916). *The Passing of the Great Race: Or the Racial Basis of European History.* New York: Charles Scribner's Sons.

Gray, J. (1995). *Enlightenment's Wake: Politics and Culture at the Close of the Modern Age.* London and New York: Routledge.

Griffith, T. (1996). Thousands Flee Savage Inferno in Monrovia. *The Australian* May 7: 6.

Gumbel, A. (1997). Albania Enters the Twilight Zone. *The Independent* March 4: 1.

Gurr, T. R. (1985). On the Political Consequences of Scarcity and Economic Decline. *International Studies Quarterly* 29: 51–75.

Gutmann, A. (1985). Communitarian Critics of Liberalism. *Philosophy and Public Affairs* 14: 308–22.

Hailstone, B. (1996). Tumour Link to Algae Feared. *The Advertiser* May 11: 14.

Haksar, V. (1976). The Alleged Paradox of Democracy. *Analysis* 37: 10–14.

Hamilton, E. (1959) *Mythology.* New York and Toronto: A Mentor Book/The New American Library.

Hamilton, N. and Cocks, D. (1994). Australia's Coastal Population: Environmental Impacts Today and Tomorrow. Melbourne: Paper presented at the "Mobility in Australia" Workshop held by the Australian Population Association, Melbourne University, November.

Hammond, P. (1997). Bedroom May Not be for Mating in Future. *The Advertiser* (Adelaide) June 5:11.

Hanson, P. (1997). *The Truth: On Asian Immigration, The Aboriginal Question, The Gun Debate and the Future of Australia.* Canberra: Parliament House, House of Representatives, Pauline Hanson, Member for Oxley.

Hansson, S. O. (1993). A Resolution of Wollheim's Paradox. *Dialogue* 32: 681–87.

Haran, P. (1995). Armed Gang Forces Pursuit Car Off Road. *The Sunday Mail* (Adelaide) August 20: 5.

Hardin, G. (1985). Human Ecology: The Subversive Conservative Science. *American Zoologist.* 25: 469–76.

Hardin, G. (1986). Lifeboat Ethics: A Radical Approach. In: Forbes, M. H. and Merrill, L. J., eds. *Global Hunger: A Look at the Problem and Potential Solutions.* Evansville: University of Evansville Press: 139–48.

Hardin, G. (1993). *Living Within Limits: Ecology, Economics, and Population Taboos.* New York and Oxford: Oxford University Press.

Hardin, G. (1995). *The Immigration Dilemma: Avoiding the Tragedy of the Commons.* Washington D. C.: Federation for American Immigration Reform.

Hardison, O. B. (1989). *Disappearing Through the Skylight.* New York: Viking/Penguin.

Harman, G. (1989). Is There a Single True Morality? In: Krausz, M., ed. *Relativism: Interpretation and Confrontation.* Notre Dame, Indiana: University of Notre Dame Press: 363–86.

Harries, O. (1993). The Collapse of "The West." *Foreign Affairs* 72, September/October: 41–53.

Harries, O. (1995). Realism in a New Era. *Quadrant* April: 11–18.

Harris, A. W. (1995). Destructive Debris. *Nature* 374: 212–13.

Harris, F. C. (1994). Something Within: Religion as a Mobilizer of African-American Political Activism. *The Journal of Politics.* 56: 42–68.

Harris, T. (1995). States Unite to Save Murray-Darling. *The Weekend Australian* July 1–2: 3.

Harsanyi, J. C. (1975). Can the Maximin Principle Serve as a Basis for Morality? A Critique of John Rawls's Theory. *American Political Science Review* 69: 594–606.

Harvey, R. (1995). *The Return of the Strong: The Drift to Global Disorder.* London: Macmillan.

Hawes, R. (1995). BHP Risks Contempt in Row on Ok Tedi. *The Australian* August 30: 2.

Hawthorn, G. (1994). The Crisis of Southern States. *Political Studies* 42: 130–45.

Hayes, D. (1990). *Behind the Silicon Curtain: The Seductions of Work in a Lonely Era.* Montréal and New York: Black Rose Books.

Heath, J. R. (1995). The Chemistry of Size and Order on the Nanometer Scale. *Science* 270: 1315–16.

Heilbroner, R. and Milberg, W. (1995). *The Crisis of Vision in Modern Economic Thought.* Cambridge: Cambridge Unversity Press.

Hern, W. M. (1990). Why Are There So Many of Us? Description and Diagnosis of a Planetary Ecopathological Process. *Population and Environment* 12: 9–39.

Higgins, E. (1996). Anarchy Threatens Unless Troops Remain. *The Australian* September 16: 7.

Hiscock, G. (1996). Traffic Congestion Exhausts Patience of Bangkok Rulers. *The Australian* June 14: 25.

Hittinger, R. (189). After MacIntyre: Natural Law Theory, Virtue Ethics, and Eudaimonia. *International Philosophical Quarterly* 29: 449–61.

Hocutt, M. (1986). Must Relativists Tolerate Evil? *The Philosophical Forum* 17: 188–200.

Hocutt, M. (1994). Relativism and Moral Judgements: A Reply to Sullivan. *Philosophia* 24: 203–10.

Hodgson, G. M. (1988). *Economics and Institutions: A Manifesto for Modern Institutional Economics.* Philadelphia: University of Pennsylvania Press.

Hogan, H. (1996). Invasion of the Micromachines. *New Scientist* June 29: 28–33.

Homer-Dixon, T. F. (1991). On the Threshold: Environomental Changes as Causes of Acute Conflict. *International Security* 16: 76–116.

Homer-Dixon, T. F., Boutwell, J. H., and Rathjens, G. W. (1993). Environmental Change and Violent Conflict. *Scientific American* 268, February: 16–23.

Homer-Dixon, T. F. (1995). The Ingenuity Gap: Can Poor Countries Adapt to Resource Scarcity? *Population and Development Review* 21:587– 612.

Honderich, T. (1974). A Difficulty with Democracy. *Philosophy and Public Affairs* 3: 221–26.

Hont, I. (1994). The Permanent Crisis of a Divided Mankind: 'Contemporary Crisis of the Nation State' in Historical Perspective. *Political Studies* 42: 166–231.

Horgan, J. (1996). *The End of Science: Facing the Limits of Knowledge in the Twilight of the Scientific Age.* Reading, Massachusetts: Helix Books, Addison-Wesley.

Horton, J. and Mendus, S., eds. (1994). *After MacIntyre: Critical Perspectives on the Work of Alasdair MacIntyre.* Cambridge: Polity Press.

House of Representatives. (Parliament of the Commonwealth of Australia) Standing Committee for Long Term Strategies (1994a). *Australia's Population 'Carrying Capacity': One Nation—Two Ecologies.* Canberra: Australian Government Publishing Service.

House of Representatives. (Parliament of the Commonwealth of Australia) Standing Committee for Long term Strategies (1994b). *Submissions to the Committee's*

Inquiry into Australia's Population Carrying Capacity, volumes 1–5. Canberra: Australian Governmnt Publishing Service.

Howard, M. (1995). Ethnic Conflict and International Security. *Nations and Nationalism* 1: 285–95.

Hoy, A. (1996). Mismanagement Puts Fisheries at Risk: Audit. *The Sydney Morning Herald* June 26: 10.

Hueglin, T. O. (1994). Federalism, Subsidiarity and the European Tradition: Some Clarifications. *Telos* 100: 37–55.

Huntington, S. P. (1996). *The Clash of Civilizations and the Remaking of World Order.* New York: Simon and Schuster.

Hurrell, A. (1994). A Crisis of Ecological Viability? Global Environmental Change and The Nation State. *Political Studies* 42: 146–65.

Hurrell, A. (1995). Explaining the Resurgence of Regionalism in World Politics. *Review of International Studies* 21: 331–58.

Hutcheon, S. (1996). Pollution Crisis as Economy Goes into Overdrive. *The Sydney Morning Herald* June 5: 15.

Hutchings, G. (1996). Thousands Executed as Crime Sweeps Country. *The Sydney Morning Herald* May 8: 12.

Hutson, J. M, Baker, M., Terada, M., Zhou, B., and Paxton, G. (1994). Hormonal Control of Testicular Descent and the Cause of Cryptorchidism. *Reproductive Fertility and Development* 6: 151–56.

Ignatieff, M. (1993). *Blood and Belonging: Journeys into the New Nationalism.* Toronto: Penguin Viking.

Ikenberry, G. J. (1996). The Myth of Post-War Chaos. *Foreign Affairs* 75, May/June: 79–91.

Inayatullah, N. and Blaney, D. L. (1995). Realizing Sovereignty. *Review of International Studies* 21: 3–20.

Industry Commission Report (Australia) (1995). *The Growth and Revenue Implications of the Hilmer Reforms* Canberra: Industry Commission.

Isaacs, H. R. (1989). *Idols of the Tribe: Group Identity and Political Change.* Cambridge, Massachusetts: Harvard University Press.

Isbester, K. (1996) Understanding State Disintegration: The Case of Nicaragua. *Journal of Social, Political and Economic Studies* 21: 455–76.

Jackson, T. (1997). Build the State, Destroy the Nation. *American Renaissance* 8, 3: 8–10.

James, C. and Weir, L. (1996). Environment Fear on Tuna Farm Vandalism. *The Advertiser* August 10: 5.

Jinman, R. (1996). Date with Digital Disaster. *The Australian* July 2: 11.

Johns, G. (1997). Labor: Back to Work. *The Sydney Morning Herald* March 4: 15.

Johnstone, F. (1992). Quebeckers, Mohawks and Zulus: Liberal Federalism and Fair Trade. *Telos* 93: 2–20.

Juergensmeyer, M. (1995). The New Religious State. *Comparative Politics* 27: 379–91.

Kagan, S. (1989). *The Limits of Morality.* Oxford: Clarendon Press.

Kaiser, J. (1995). Making a New Ruler for the Nanoworld. *Science* 270: 1920.

Kalai, E. and Schmeidler, D. (1977). Aggregation Procedure for Cardinal Preferences: A Formulation and Proof of Samuelson's Impossibility Conjecture. *Econometrica* 45: 1431–38.

Kaplan, D. E. and Marshall, A. (1996). *The Cult at the End of the World: The Incredible Story of Aum.* London: Hutchinson.

Kaplan, R. D. (1994). The Coming Anarchy: How Scarcity, Crime, Overpopulation, Tribalism, and Disease are Rapidly Destroying the Social Fabric of Our Planet. *The Atlantic Monthly.* February: 44–76.

Kaplan, R. D.(1996a). *The Ends of the Earth: A Journey at the Dawn of the 21st Century.* New York: Random House.

Kaplan, R. D. (1996b). Fort Leavenworth and the Eclipse of Nationhood. *The Atlantic Monthly.* September: 75–90.

Kapstein, E. (1996). Workers and The World Economy. *Foreign Affairs* 75: 16–37.

Kaviraj, S. (1994). Crisis of the Nation-State in India. *Political Studies* 42: 115–29.

Kavka, G. S. (1991). Is Individual Choice Less Problematic than Collective Choice? *Economics and Philosophy* 7: 143–65.

Kearney, R. (1987). Ethics and the Postmodern Imagination. *Thought* 62: 39–58.

Keiding, N., Giwercman, A., Carlsen, F., and Skakkebaek, N. E. (1994). Falling Sperm Quality. *British Medical Journal* 309: 131.

Kelly, J. S. (1976). The Impossibility of a Just Liberal. *Economica* 43: 67–75.

Kelly, J. S. (1989a). Interjacency. *Social Choice and Welfare* 6: 331–335.

Kelly, J. S. (1989b). The Ostrogorski Paradox. *Social Choice and Welfare* 6:71–76.

Kelly, P. (1997). The New Battle of Britain. *The Weekend Australian* (Review) March1–2: 1,6.

Kemp, M. C., and Ng, Y-K. (1976). On the Existence of Social Welfare Functions, Social Orderings and Social Decision Functions. *Economica* 43: 59–66.

Kemp, M. C. and Ng, Y-K. (1977). More on Social Welfare Functions: the Incompatibility of Individualism and Ordinalism. *Economica* 44: 89–90.

Kemp, M. C. and Ng, Y-K. (1982). The Incompatibility of Individualism and Ordinalism. *Mathematical Social Sciences* 3: 33–37.

Kennedy, D. (1995). GATTastrophe. *Habitat Australia* April: 42–43.

Kennett, J. (1992). Speech to the Italian Chamber of Commerce. Office of the Premier of Victoria, Australia; August.

Kennedy, P. (1993). *Preparing for the Twenty-First Century.* New York: Random House.

Kerin, J. (1996). Tuna Industry Probe Urgent: Democrats. *The Australian* August 12: 4.

Kirkpatrick, J. J. (1993). The Modernizing Imperative: Tradition and Change. *Foreign Affairs* 72, September/ October: 22–24.

Kitcher, P. (1993). *The Advancement of Science: Science Without Legend, Objectivity Without Illusions.* Oxford: Oxford University Press.

Kleinburg, S. S. (1991). *Politics and Philosophy: The Necessity and Limitations of Rational Argument.* Oxford: Basil Blackwell.

Kleiner, K. (1996a). Long-Lived Pollutants Threaten the Great Lakes. *New Scientist* July 13: 5.

Kleiner, K. (1996b). Will Russia's Criminal Underworld Go Nuclear? *New Scientist* July 6: 10.

Krauthammer, C. (1995). Quebec and the Death of Diversity. *Time* (Australia) November 13: 96.

Kremer, P. (1994). The Lucky Country Counts its Visitors. *Guardian Weekly.* December 18: 17.

Krieger, M. H. (1987). The Possibility of Doom. *Technology in Society* 9: 181–90.

Krieger, M. H. (1989). *Marginalism and Discontinuity.* New York: Russell Sage Foundation.

Krieger, M. H. (1995). Could the Probability of Doom be Zero or One? *Journal of Philosophy* 92: 382–87.

Kuttner, R. (1991). *The End of Laissez-Faire: National Purpose and the Global Economy After the Cold War*. New York: A. Knopf.

Lamont, L. (1994). *Breakup: The Coming End of Canada and the Stakes for America*. New York: W. W. Norton.

Lange, T. and Hines, C. (1993). *The New Protectionism: Protecting the Future Against Free Trade*. London: Earthscan.

Larmore, C. (1989). Review of *Whose Justice? Which Rationality? Journal of Philosophy* 86: 437–42.

Lavers, P. J. (1995). BHP Unfairly Blamed Over PNG. *The Australian* September 13: 16.

Le Grand, C. (1995). Little Fingers Sew as Social Fabric Unravels. *The Weekend Australian* December 9–10: 1,4.

Leahy, M.P.T. (1977). Lies, Damned Lies, and Miss Anscombe. *Analysis* 37: 80–81.

Lepsius, M. R. (1992). Beyond the Nation-State: The Multinational State as the Model for the European Community. *Telos* 91: 57–76.

Leslie, J. (1983). Why Not Let Life Become Extinct? *Philosophy* 58: 329–38.

Leslie, J. (1989). *Universes*. London and New York: Routledge.

Leslie, J. (1992). Time and the Anthropic Principle. *Mind* 101: 521–40.

Leslie, J. (1994). Testing the Doomsday Argument. *Journal of Applied Philosophy* 11: 31–44.

Leslie, J. (1996). *The End of the World: The Science and Ethics of Human Extinction*. London and New York: Routledge.

Levidow, L. and Robins, K., eds. (1989). *Cyborg Worlds: The Military Information Society*. London: Free Association Books.

Levine, A. (1978). A Conceptual Problem for Liberal Democracy. *Journal of Philosophy* 75: 302–08.

Levine, A. (1981). *Liberal Democracy: A Critique of Its Theory*. New York: Columbia University Press.

Levine, R. A. (1996). The Economic Consequences of Mr. Clinton. *The Atlantic Monthly* 278, July: 60–65.

Lorenz, K. (1989). *The Waning of Humaneness*. London: Unwin Paperbacks.

Lovelock, J. (1979). *Gaia: A New Look at Life on Earth*. Oxford: Oxford University Press.

Lovelock, J. (1988). *The Ages of Gaia: A Biography of Our Living Earth*. London: Norton and Company.

Lowry, B. (1996). *The Armed Forces of Indonesia*. St. Leonards, New South Wales: Allen and Unwin.

Lynn, R. (1996). *Dysgenics: Genetic Deterioration in Modern Populations*. Westport Connecticut: Praeger.

Lyons, G., Moore, E., and Smith, J. W. (1995). *Is the End Nigh? Internationalism, Global Chaos and the Destruction of the Earth*. Aldershot: Avebury.

Lyons, J. (1994). Stars and Strife: The Lessons for Australia in the Crumbling of America. *The Weekend Australian Review* July 2–3: 1–2.

MacIntyre A. (1981). *After Virtue: A Study in Moral Theory*. London: Duckworth.

MacIntyre, A. (1988). *Whose Justice? Which Rationality?* Notre Dame, Indiana: University of Notre Dame Press.

MacIntyre, A. (1990). *Three Rival Versions of Moral Inquiry: Encyclopaedia, Genealogy and Tradition*. London: Duckworth.

MacIntyre, F. (1996). Doomsday Doubts. *New Scientist* November 2: 54.

MacKay, A. F. (1980). Impossibility and Infinity. *Ethics*. 90: 367–82.

MacKay, H. (1993). *Reinventing Australia: The Mind and Mood of Australia in the 90s.* Sydney: Angus and Robertson.

MacLachlan, A. (1995). Some Comments on *Colonising Nationalism. Political Theory Newsletter* 7: 56–59.

Maddox, B. (1995). Tales of Doom Backfire on Greens. *The Australian* April 5: 8.

Mahbubani, K. (1993). The Dangers of Decadence: What the Rest Can Teach the West. *Foreign Affairs* 72, September/October: 10–14.

Mahnaimi, U. and Adams, J. (1996). Iran Ready to Unleash Germ Warfare: US. *The Australian* August 12: 6.

Malawski, M. and Zhou, L. (1994). A Note on Social Choice Theory Without the Pareto Principle. *Social Choice and Welfare* 11: 103–7.

Malone, A. (1997). Death Rains Down on the Innocent. *The Australian* March 17: 6.

Manzo, K. (1995). The Practice and Promise of Nationalism. *Political Theory Newsletter* 7: 42–47.

Marshall, A. (1997) Behind the Lines. *The Australian Magazine* April 5–6: 20–26.

Mates, E. (1973). Paradox Lost—Majority Rule Regained. *Ethics* 84: 48–50.

Matthews, R. (1996). 'Unbreakable' Code Cracked Wide Open. *New Scientist* November 9: 8.

Matthews, R. (1996). Smash Hits. *The Sydney Morning Herald* July 30: 15.

Maxwell, M. (1990). *Morality Among Nations: An Evolutionary View.* Albany, State University of New York Press.

May, K. O. (1952). A Set of Independent, Necessary and Sufficient Conditions For Simple Majority Decision. *Econometrica* 20: 680–84.

Mazur, A. (1994). How Does Population Growth Contribute to Rising Energy Consumption in America? *Population and Environment* 15: 371–78.

McConkey, M. (1992). Individuals, Communities and Federalism—Reply to Johnstone. *Telos* 93: 21–26.

McConnell, R. A. (1996). Review of *Is the End Nigh? Population and Environment* 18: 82–100.

McGregor, R. (1996a). Beijing Propaganda Blast Defends its Growing Appetite. *The Australian* May 8: 11.

McGregor, R. (1996b). China to Invest in Our Food Industry. *The Australian* June 3: 18.

McInerney, D. (1995). Nations Before Nationalism? A Response to *Colonising Nationalism. Political Theory Newsletter* 7: 48–55.

McIntosh, T. (1996). No-One is Safe from the Info Gangsters. *The Australian* December 3: 52–53.

McKenzie, S. (1997). Riots as People Rally for General. *Herald Sun* March 20: 4.

McLean, L. (1994). Forest Image Wins Prestigious Art Award. *The Australian* December 16: 4.

McLean, L. (1995). Stand on Gas Targets Threatens Relations. *The Australian* April 10: 6.

McMichael, A. J. (1993). *Planetary Overload: Global Environmental Change and the Health of the Human Species.* Cambridge: Cambridge University Press.

McMullen, W. A. (1972). Censorship and Participatory Democracy: A Paradox. *Analysis* 32: 207–8.

McNeill, W. H. (1976). *Plagues and Peoples.* Harmondsworth: Penguin.

McNeill, W. H. (1986). *Polyethnicity and National Unity in World History.* Toronto: University of Toronto Press.

McNicoll, D. (1993). Red Tape 'Choking our Coast.' *The Australian* December 9: 4.

Meade, A. and Fife-Yeoman, J. (1997). Food Terrorism. *The Weekend Australian* February 15–16: 23.

Meade, K. (1995). Wetlands Sucked Dry by Irrigation. *The Weekend Australian* September 16–17: 10.

Meadows, D. H., Meadows, D. L., Randers, J., and Behrens, W. W. (1972). *The Limits to Growth.* New York: Universe Books.

Medlin, B. (1992). *Human Nature Human Survival.* Bedford Park, South Australia: Board of Research, The Flinders University of South Australia.

Michael, P., Farinella, P., and Froeschlé, C. (1996). Orbital Evolution of the Asteroid Eros and Implications for Collision with the Earth. *Nature* 380: 689–91.

Middleton, K. and Pegler, T. (1995). Fury on Carr Migrant Call. *The Age* May 25: 7.

Milbank, D. (1994). In His Solitude a Finnish Thinker Posits Cataclysms. *The Wall Street Journal* May 20: A1, A6.

Milbrath, L. W. (1989). *Envisioning a Sustainable Society: Learning Our Way Out.* Albany: State University of New York Press.

Mish'alani, J. K. (1982). The Limits of Moral Community and the Limits of Moral Thought. *Journal of Value Inquiry* 16: 131–41.

Moffett, G. D. (1994). *Critical Masses: The Global Population Challenge.* New York:Viking Press.

Moorhouse, F. (1996). The Internet—Threats to the Book and to All Civilised Values and Decent People—An Inquiry. *The Adelaide Review* September: 19.

Morgan, H. (1994). Algae Stops Town's Usual Water Supply. *The Advertiser* (Adelaide) February 23: 9.

Morgan, H. and Papps, N. (1996). Abalone Poachers Fund Drug Trade. *The Advertiser* (Adelaide) May 13: 1.

Moynihan, D. P. (1993). *Pandaemonium: Ethnicity in International Politics.* Oxford: University Press.

Murphy, P., Burnley, I., Harding, H., Weisner, D., and Young, Y. (1990). *Impact of Immigration* on *Urban Infrastruture.* Canberra: Australian Government Publishing Service.

Murray-Darling Basin Commission (1995). *An Audit of Water Use in the Murray-Darling Basin.* Canberra: Murray-Darling Ministerial Council.

Myers, N. (1989). Environment and Security. *Foreign Policy* 74: 23–41.

Myers, N. and Kent, J. (1995). *Environmental Exodus: An Emergent Crisis in the Global Arena.* Washington D. C.: Climate Institute.

Nagel, T. (1986). *The View from Nowhere.* New York: Oxford University Press.

Nathan, N.M.L. (1971). On the Justification of Democracy. *Monist* 55: 89–120.

Nathan, N.M.L. (1989). Democracy and Impartiality. *Analysis* 49: 65–70.

Nelan, B. W. (1995). The Price of Fanaticism. *Time* (Australia) April 3: 32–35.

Nelson, W. N. (1980). *On Justifying Democracy.* London: Routledge and Kegan Paul.

Nermuth, M. (1992). Two-Stage Discrete Aggregation: The Ostrogorski Paradox and Related Phenomena. *Social Choice and Welfare* 9: 99–116.

Newton-Smith, W. H. (1981). *The Rationality of Science.* Boston: Routledge and Kegan Paul.

Ng, Y-K. (1981). Bentham or Nash? On the Acceptable Form of Social Welfare Functions. *The Economic Record* 57: 238–50.

Nicholas, D. (1996). Weep for the Darling River. *The Sydney Morning Herald* April 3: 12.

Nielsen, K. (1984). Why Should I be Moral? Revisited. *American Philosophical Quarterly* 21: 81–91.

Nielsen, K. (1989). *Why be Moral?* Buffalo, New York: Prometheus Books.

Nino, C. S. (1989). The Communitarian Challenge to Liberal Rights. *Law and Philosophy* 8: 37–52.

Nissani, M. (1996). The Greenhouse Effect: An Interdisciplinary Perspective. *Population and Environment* 17: 459–89.

North, D. (1992). Democratic Governments: Why They Cannot Cope With Illegal Immigration. *The Social Contract* Spring: 153–58.

Norton, T., Dovers, S., Nix, H., and Elias, D. (1994). *An Overview of Research on the Links between Human Population and the Environment.* Canberra: Bureau of Immigration and Population Research, Australian Government Publishing Service.

Nuckolls, J. H. (1995). Post-Cold War Nuclear Danger: Proliferation and Terrorism. *Science* 267: 1112–14.

Nuttall, N. (1995). Europe's Flood Disaster to Fuel Debate on Global Warming. *The Australian* February 2: 9.

Oaten, C. (1996). How Migrants Help. *The Advertiser* (Adelaide) October 29: 23.

O'Callaghan, M-L and Scott, L. (1997). Chan Backs Off Mercenaries. *The Australian* March 20: 1.

Ohmae, K. (1990). *The Borderless World: Power and Strategy in the Interlinked Economy.* London: HarperCollins Publishers.

Ohmae, K. (1995). *The End of the Nation State: The Rise of Regional Economies.* New York: The Free Press.

Oliver, R. P. (1981). *America's Decline: The Education of a Conservative.* London: Londinium Press.

O'Neill, R. (1995). UN Chief Warns on Growth of Separatism. *The Australian* April 27: 4.

Ophuls, W. and Boyan, A. S. (1992). *Ecology and the Politics of Scarcity Revisited: The Unraveling of the American Dream.* New York: W. H. Freeman.

Oppenheimer, A. (1996). *Bordering on Chaos: Guerrillas, Stockbrokers, Politicians, and Mexico's Road to Prosperity.* Boston: Little, Brown and Co.

Osborne, D. K. (1976). Irrelevant Alternatives and Social Welfare. *Econometrica* 44: 1001–15.

Owen, E. (1996). Inequality May Shatter Spain. *The Weekend Australian* April 6–7: 11.

Palley, T. I. (1996). The Forces Making for an Economic Collapse. *The Atlantic Monthly* 278, July: 44–58.

Palmer, N. D. (1991). *The New Regionalism in Asia and the Pacific.* Lexington: Lexington Books.

Papps, N. (1996). Asian Crime Sweep Nets 38 on Drug Counts. *The Advertiser* (Adelaide) April 17: 3.

Parks, R. P. (1976). An Impossibility Theorem for Fixed Preferences: A Dictatorial Bergson-Samuelson Welfare Function. *Review of Economic Studies* 42: 447–50.

Parry, M. L. and Rosenzweig, C. (1993). Food Supply and Risk of Hunger. *The Lancet*: 1345–47.

Parsons, T. (1970). *The Social System.* London: Routledge and Kegan Paul.

Passey, D. (1995). Water Laws Spell Ruin for Farmers. *The Sydney Morning Herald* September 9: 7.

Patel, T. (1996a). Power Station Failure Adds to Delhi's Woes. *New Scientist* October 12: 8.

Patel, T. (1996b). Will India Starve if Rains Fail? *New Scientist* October 19: 10.

Pauly, L. W. (1995). Capital Mobility, State Autonomy and Political Legitimacy. *Journal of International Affairs* 48: 369–88.

Pearce, F. (1992). Grain Yields Tumble in a Greenhouse World. *New Scientist* April 18:4.

Pearce, F. (1995). Fiddling While Earth Warms. *New Scientist* March 25: 14–15.

Pearce, F. (1996). Hormones Blamed for Sex-Change Fish. *New Scientist* November 16: 7.

Pearce, F. (1996a). Urban Apocalypse Postponed? *New Scientist* June 1: 4.

Pearce, F. (1996b). Africa Overtakes Europe as World Birth Rate Slows. *New Scientist* December 14: 6.

Pearce, F. (1996c). Deserts on Our Doorstep. *New Scientist* July 6: 12–13.

Pearce, F. (1997). Thirsty Meals that Suck the World Dry. *New Scientist* February 1: 7.

Pearce, R. (1996). Quantum Hologram Says it With Atoms. *New Scientist* August 17: 19.

Pearson, G. (1996). Is this the Way the World Ends? *New Scientist* November 9: 42–43.

Pennock, J. R. (1974). Democracy is *Not* Paradoxical: Comment. *Political Theory* 2: 88–93.

Perelman, L. J. (1980). Speculations on the Transition to Sustainable Energy. *Ethics* 90: 392–416.

Philpott, D. (1995). Sovereignty: An Introduction and Brief History. *Journal of International Affairs* 48: 353–68.

Piccone, P. (1992). The Case Against Liberal Federalism and Protectionism—Reply to Johnstone. *Telos* 93: 27–42.

Piccone, P. (1995). Postmodern Populism. *Telos* 103: 45–86.

Piccone, P. and Ulmen, G. (1994). Re-Thinking Federalism. *Telos* 100: 3–16.

Piccone, P. and Ulmen, G. (1995). Populism and the New Politics. *Telos* 103: 3–8.

Pick, H. (1993). World Refugee Crisis Spinning Out of Control, UN Warns. *The Guardian Weekly* November 21: 1, 3.

Pimental, D., Harman, R., Pacenza, M., Pecarsky, J., and Pimental, M. (1994). Natural Resources and an Optimum Human Population. *Population and Environment* 15: 347–69.

Pitt, H. and Dayton, L. (1996). Sydney Smog Toll Doubles Road Dead. *The Sydney Morning Herald* June 3: 1, 2.

Pollak, R. A. (1979). Bergson-Samuelson Social Welfare Functions and the Theory of Social Choice. *Quarterly Journal of Economics* 93: 73–90.

Poole, R. (1991). *Morality and Modernity*. London: Routledge.

Poole, R. (1995). How European is Nationalism? A Response to Philip Gerrans. *Political Theory Newsletter* 7: 60–66.

Population Issues Committee (1991). *Population Issues and Australia's Future: Environment, Economy and Society* (Final Report). Canberra: Australian Government Publishing Service.

Possingham, H. (1996). Human Impact on Biodiversity in Australia. Adelaide: Talk given to Australians for an Ecologically Sustainable Population, Adelaide, June 12.

Press Association (1997). Return of Giant Comet to Bring a New 'Dark Age.' *The Advertiser* (Adelaide) April 1: 17.

Price, D. (1995). Energy and Human Evolution. *Population and Environment* 16: 301–19.

Pringle, J. (1997). Chinese Paint Grim Picture of North Korea's Desperation. *The Australian* March 20: 8.

Quiggin, J. (1995). The Growth Consequences of Hilmer and Related Reforms (Unpublished paper). Townsville: James Cook University.

Quigley, P. (1990). *Armed and Female*. New York: St. Martin's Paperbacks.

Rae, D. W. and Daudt, H. (1976). The Ostrogorski Paradox: A Peculiarity of Compound Majority Decision. *European Journal of Political Research* 4: 391–98.

Rasmussen, D. B. (1990). Liberalism and Natural End Ethics. *American Philosophical Quarterly* 27: 153–61.

Raspail, J. (1975). *The Camp of the Saints*. London: Sphere Books.

Raspail, J. (1995). *The Camp of the Saints*. Petoskey, Michigan: The Social Contract Press.

Rawlins, G.J.E. (1996). *Moths to the Flame: The Seductions of Computer Technology*. Cambridge, Massachusetts and London: MIT Press/ A Bradford Book.

Rees, W. E.(1996). Revisiting Carrying Capacity: Area-Based Indicators of Sustainability. *Population and Environment* 17: 195–215.

Rees-Mogg, W. (1992). The Sheriff Fiddles While the Town Burns. *The Independent* May 4: 17.

Reeve, S., Adams, J. and Davison, J. (1996). Countdown to Armageddon. *The Australian* June 25: 53.

Regis, E. (1992). *Great Mambo Chicken and The Transhuman Condition: Science Slightly Over the Edge*. London: Penguin.

Report by the Independent Committee of Inquiry (1993). *National Competition Policy*. Canberra: Australian Government Publishing Service.

Resources Assessment Commission (RAC). (1993). *Coastal Zone Inquiry: Final Report*. Canberra: Australian Government Publishing Service.

Richardson, M. (1995). ASEAN Arms Buildup Sparks Concern. *The Weekend Australian* December 9–10: 14.

Richardson, M. (1996a). Timely Grain. *The Australian* July 12: 25.

Richardson, M. (1996b). Asia Looks Further Afield to Satisfy Growing Oil Demand. *The Australian* August 29: 25.

Richter, D. (1995). The Incoherence of the Moral 'Ought.' *Philosophy* 70: 69–85.

Rifkin, J. (1995). *The End of Work: The Decline of the Global Labor Force and the Dawn of the Post-Market Era*. New York: J. P. Tarcher/G. P. Putnam's Sons.

Rimmer, S. J. (1991). *The Cost of Multiculturalism*. Bedford Park, South Australia: Flinders Press.

Roberts, K.W.S. (1980). Social Choice Theory: The Single-Profile and Multi-Profile Approaches. *Review of Economic Studies* 47: 441–50.

Robins, N. and Pye-Smith, C. (1997). The Ecology of Violence. *New Scientist* March 8: 12–13.

Rorty, R. (1979). *Philosophy and the Mirror of Nature*. Princeton, New Jersey: Princeton University Press.

Routley, R. (1979). Repairing Proofs of Arrow's General Impossibility Theorem and Enlarging the Scope of the Theorem. *Notre Dame Journal of Formal Logic* 20: 879–90.

Routley, R. (1980). On the Impossibility of an Orthodox Social Theory and of an Orthodox Solution to Environmental Problems. *Logique et Analyse* 23: 145–66.

Rowan, C. T. (1996). *The Coming Race War in America: A Wake-Up Call*. Boston: Little, Brown and Co.

Ruggie, J.G. (1993).Territoriality and Beyond: Problematizing Modernity in International Relations. *International Organization* 47: 139–74.

Ruggie, J. G. (1994). Trade, Protectionism, and the Future of Welfare Capitalism. *Journal of International Affairs* 48: 1–11.

Rush, N. (1994). What Was Socialism . . . and Why We Will All Miss It So Much. *The Nation* January 24: 92.

Ryan, S. (1995). Environment Summit Faces Hot Debate. *The Australian* March 28: 13.

Sale, K. (1980). *Human Scale*. London: Secker and Warburg.

Sale, K. (1985). *Dwellers in the Land: The Bioregional Vision*. San Francisco: Sierra Club Books.

Sanger, D. (1996). Trapped: How a US Sting Caught the Chinese Arms Smugglers. *The Sydney Morning Herald* May 25: 23.

Satterthwaite, M. (1975). Strategy-Proofness and Arrow's Conditions: Existence and Correspondence Theorems for Voting Procedures and Social Welfare Functions. *Journal of Economic Theory* 10: 187–217.

Savage, M. T. (1994). *The Millennial Project: Colonizing the Galaxy in Eight Easy Steps*. Boston: Little, Brown and Company.

Schmidt, K. (1996). Bend it, Shake it . . . *New Scientist* August 31: 22–23.

Schofield, J. (1996). *Silent Over Africa: Stories of War and Genocide*. Sydney: HarperCollins Publishers.

Schwartz, T. (1970). On the Possibility of Rational Policy Evaluation. *Theory and Decision* 1: 89–106.

Schwartz, T. (1995). The Paradox of Representation. *Journal of Politics* 57: 309–23.

Scott, L. (1994). The Real Culprits in Mangrove Destruction. *The Weekend Australian* December 3–4: 10.

Sen, A. (1970). The Impossibility of a Paretian Liberal. *Journal of Political Economy* 78: 152–57.

Sen, A. (1983). Liberty and Social Choice. *Journal of Philosophy* 80: 5–28.

Sen, A. (1994). Population: Delusion and Reality. *New York Review of Books* 41: 62–71.

Shapere, D. (1984). *Reason and the Growth of Knowledge*. Dordrecht: D. Reidel.

Sharpe, R. E. and Skakkebaek, N. E. (1993). Are Oestrogens Involved in Falling Sperm Counts and Disorders of the Male Reproductive Tract? *The Lancet* 341: 1392–95.

Shawcross, W. (1994). A New Dark Age? *The Weekend Australian* (Focus) August 20–21: 23–24.

Shearman, D., Gaughwin, M., Sauer-Thompson, G. and Smith, J. W. (forthcoming). *Green or Gone?* Adelaide: University of Adelaide, Department of Medicine (Forthcoming).

Sheehan, P. (1995). Four Stories the US Media Refuse to Tell:1. The Race War of Black Against White. *The Sydney Morning Herald* (Spectrum) May 20: 1A.

Shelley, L. I. (1995). Transnational Organized Crime: An Imminent Threat to the Nation-State. *Journal of International Affairs* 48: 463–89.

Short, J. (1996). 71 percent Say Migrant Intake Too High. *The Australian* October 4: 1.

Short, R. (1994). Australia: A Full House. *People and Place* 2:1–5.

Shuja, S. M. (1995) New World Order and Its Implications on the Korean Peninsula. *Australia and World Affairs* 24: 26–32.

Simon, J. and Zinsmeister, K. (1995). How Population Growth Affects Human Progress. In: M. Cromartie, ed. *The Nine Lives of Population Control*. Grand Rapids, Michigan: W. B. Eerdmans: 61–79.

Simonion, H. (1995). High Power Alliance Seeks Climate Action. *The Australian* March 28: 13.

Singer, P. (1994). *Rethinking Life and Death: The Collapse of Our Traditional Ethics*. Melbourne: Text Publishing Company.

Singleton, J. (1981). Moral Theories and Tests of Adequacy. *Philosophical Quarterly* 31: 31–46.

Slattery, L. (1996). The Tribes of Europe. *The Weekend Australian* (Review) November 30–December 1: 1, 4.

Smil, V. (1993). *China's Environmental Crisis: An Inquiry into the Limits of National Development.* New York: M. E. Sharpe.

Smil, V. (1996a). *Environmental Problems in China: Estimates of Economic Cost.* Honolulu: East West Center.

Smil, V. (1996b). Is There Enough Chinese Food? *The New York Review of Books* February 1: 32–34.

Smith, A. (1986). History and Liberty: Dilemmas of Loyalty in Western Democracies. *Ethnic and Racial Studies* 9: 43–65.

Smith, D. and Sheridan, M. (1997) Tigers Lose Their Bite. *The Australian* January 14: 28.

Smith, J.W.(1991).*The HighTech Fix: Sustainable Ecology orTechnocratic Megaprojects for the 21st Century?* Aldershot: Avebury.

Smith, J. W., ed. (1991). *Immigration, Population and Sustainable Environments: The Limits to Australia's Growth.* Bedford Park, Adelaide: Flinders Press.

Smith, J. W., Lyons, G., and Sauer-Thompson, G. (1997). *Healing a Wounded World: Economics, Ecology and Health for a Sustainable Life.* Westport, Connecticut and London: Praeger.

Smith, J. W., Lyons, G., and Sauer-Thompson, G. (forthcoming). *The Bankruptcy of Economics: Ecology, Economics and the Sustainability of the Earth.* London: Macmillan.

Sober, D. (1972). Wolff's Logical Anarchism. *Ethics* 82: 173–76.

Soros, G. (1997). Why the Free Market is a Danger to Democracy. *The Weekend Australian* March 8–9: 26–27.

Spengler, O. (1926). *The Decline of the West vol. 1: Form and Actuality.* New York: Alfred A. Knopf.

Stahl, C., Ball, R., Inglis, C., and Gutman, P. (1993). *Global Population Movements and their Implications for Australia.* Canberra: Bureau of Immigration and Population Research, Australian Government Publishing Service.

Stapleton, J. (1995). Water Wars. *The Australian* September 15: 13.

State of the Environment Advisory Council (SEAC). (1996). *Australia: State of the Environment.* Collingwood, Victoria: CSIRO Publishing.

Stauth, G. and Turner, B. S. (1988). Nostalgia, Postmodernism and the Critique of Mass Culture. *Theory, Culture and Society* 5: 509–26.

Stead, G. (1997). Gunman Vowed to Kill Zionists. *Herald Sun* February 27: 26.

Steinberg, D. (1973). The Voter's Paradox Regained. *Ethics* 83: 163–67.

Steketee, M. (1996). Risk of Nuclear Attack on Rise, Experts Warn. *The Australian* August 15: 3.

Sterling, C. (1994). *Crime Without Frontiers: The Worldwide Expansion of Organised Crime and the Pax Mafiosa.* London: Little, Brown and Co.

Stevens, M. (1995). BHP Heads Off Ok Tedi Legal Tilt With Big Payout. *The Weekend Australian,* September 5–6: 41.

Stewart, I. (1997). Mahathir Warns of Migrant Flood. *The Australian* May 7: 10.

Stock, G. (1993). *Metaman: Humans, Machines, and the Birth of a Global Super-Organism.* London and New York: Bantam Books.

Stokstad, E. (1996). Rare Birds Ravaged by Mystery Poison. *New Scientist* July 13: 5.

Stoll, C. (1995). *Silicon Snake Oil: Second Thoughts on the Information Highway.* London: Pan Books.

Stott, D. (1995). Emission Rules Will Cost $14 bn. *The Sydney Morning Herald* December 2: 6.

Sturgiss, R. (1995). *Climate Change: Interpreting and Measuring Emission Targets.* Treasury Research Paper No. 9. Canberra: Australian Government Publishing Service.

Sugden, R. (1991). Rational Choice: A Survey of Contributions from Economics and Philosophy. *Economic Journal* 101: 751–85.

Sullivan, S. J. (1994). Relativism, Evil, and Disagreement: A Reply to Hocutt. *Philosophia* 24: 191–201.

Sunday Times Insight Team (1996). Banks pay a Huge Ransom to "Cyber Terrorists." *The Australian* June 4: 33, 40.

Sweet, M. and Beale, B. (1996). Australia's Deadly Air Pollution: Unsafe At Any Level. *The Sydney Morning Herald* May 27: 1.

Switzer, P. (1996). Budget to Stave Off Perils of Pauline. *The Weekend Australian* September 14–15: 56.

Sylvester, C. (1994). *Feminist Theory and International Relations in a Postmodern Era.* Cambridge: Cambridge University Press.

Taguieff, P-A. (1995). Political Science Confronts Populism: From a Conceptual Mirage to a Real Problem. *Telos* 103: 9–43.

Tainter, J. A. (1988). *The Collapse of Complex Societies.* Cambridge: Cambridge University Press.

Tanton, J., McCormack, D., and Smith, J. W. (1996). *Immigration and the Social Contract: The Implosion of Western Societies.* Aldershot:Avebury.

Taylor, C. (1971). Interpretation and the Sciences of Man. *Review of Metaphysics* 25: 3–51.

Taylor, J. (1992). *Paved with Good Intentions.* New York: Carroll and Graf Publishers.

Taylor, P. (1993). *International Organization in the Modern World: The Regional and Global Process.* London: Pinter.

Tenner, E. (1996). *Why Things Bite Back: Technology and the Revenge of Unintended Consequences.* New York: Alfred A. Knopf.

Thompson, J. (1992). *Justice and World Order: A Philosophical Inquiry.* London and New York: Routledge.

Thurow, L. (1996). *The Future of Capitalism:How Today's Economic Forces Shape Tomorrow's World.* St. Leonards, New South Wales: Allen and Unwin.

Tilley, J. (1988). Inner Judgements and Moral Relativism. *Philosophia* 18: 171–90.

Tobias, M. (1994). *World War III: Population and Biosphere at the End of the Millennium.* Sante Fe, New Mexico: Bear and Company Publishing.

TOES (The Other Economic Summit) (1995). Newsletter. *TOES* 4: 13.

Toffler, A. and Toffler, H. (1970). *Future Shock.* New York: Bantam.

Toffler, A. and Toffler, H. (1980). *The Third Wave.* New York: Bantam.

Toffler, A. and Toffler, H. (1983). *Previews and Premises.* New York: William Morrow.

Toffler, A. and Toffler, H. (1990). *Powershift.* New York: Bantam.

Toffler, A. and Toffler, H. (1993). *War and Anti-War: Making Sense of Today's Global Chaos.* London: Warner Books/Little, Brown and Company.

Toffler, A. (1995). Third Wave Terrorism Rides the Tokyo Subway. *New Perspectives Quarterly* 12: 4–6.

Toohey, B. (1995). Free Trade and Global Harmony. *The Australian Financial Review* June 20: 15.

Tough, P., Blackwell, R., Dunlap, A., Gilder, G., Luttwak, E., and Reich, R. (1996). Does America Still Work? (Round Table Debate). *Harpers* May: 36–47.

Tourism Forecasting Council (1996). *The Fifth Report of the Tourism Forecasting Council.* Canberra: Commonwealth of Australia.

Toynbee, A. J. (1949). *A Study of History* (Abridgement of volumes 1–6 by D. C. Somervell). London: Oxford University Press.

Trainer, T. (1995). *The Conserver Society: Alternatives for Sustainability.* London and New Jersey: Zed Books.

Tully, J. (1994). The Crisis of Identification: The Case of Canada. *Political Studies* 42: 77–96.

Turner, J. (1995). Murray on its Death-Bed. *The Advertiser* (Adelaide) October 24: 13.

Umpleby, S. (1988). Will the Optimists Please Stand Up? *Population and Environment* 10: 122–32.

Umpleby, S. (1990). The Scientific Revolution in Demography. *Population and Environment* 11:159–74.

United Nations Population Fund. (1996). Press Release, May 29.

Vacca, R. (1973). *The Coming Dark Age.* New York: Doubleday.

Van Biema, D. (1995). Prophet of Poison. *Time* (Australia) April 3: 24–31.

Van Creveld, M. (1991). *On Future War.* London: Brassey's (UK).

Van Niekerk, M. (1996). Three Years to Avert the Computer Equivalent of Meltdown. *The Age* December 14: A17.

Varese, F. (1994). Is Sicily the Future of Russia? Private Protection and the Rise of the Russian Mafia. *European Journal of Sociology* 35: 224–58.

Von Foerster, H., Mora, P. M., and Amiot, L. W. (1960). Doomsday: Friday 13 November, A.D. 2026. *Science* 132: 1291–95.

Wagner, C. (1983). Anscombe's Paradox and the Rule of Three-Fourths. *Theory and Decision* 15: 303–8.

Wainwright, R. (1996). Bush, Farms Threatened by Illegal Tyre Dumping. *The Sydney Morning Herald* January 10: 5.

Walker, C. (1996) Pitched Battles in Jerusalem as Black Jews' Fury Boils Over. *The Australian* January 30: 13.

Walker, T. (1997a). Albanians Admit Chaos but Reject Outside Help. *The Australian* March 7: 9.

Walker, T. (1997b). Isolated Albania Descends into Anarchy. *The Weekend Australian* March 15–16: 14.

Wallace, W. (1994). Rescue or Retreat? The Nation State in Western Europe, 1945–93. *Political Studies* 42: 52–76.

Walter, J. (1996). *Tunnel Vision: The Failure of Political Imagination.* St. Leonards, New South Wales: Allen and Unwin.

Walters, P. (1995). West, Islam Clash on Human Rights, Democracy. *The Weekend Australian* April 1–2: 16.

Walters, P. (1997a). Tough-Talking Suharto Repeats Threat to Clobber Dissent, Unrest. *The Weekend Australian* March 8–9: 18.

Walters, P. (1997b). Headhunting Dayaks Bring Ethnic Cleansing to Indonesia. *The Australian* February 18: 1, 7.

Walters, P. (1997c). How the Military Will Evolve After Suharto. *The Australian* April 4: 15.

Walzer, M. (1990). The Communitarian Critique of Liberalism. *Political Theory* 18: 6–23.

Walzer, M. ed. (1995). *Toward Global Civil Society.* Providence, Rhode Island: Berghahn Books.

Wark, M. (1995). Black Thunder. *21C* 4: 46–52.

Wasson, B. (1995). Draw on Store of Lessons and Knowledge. *The Sydney Morning Herald* November 13: 6.

Watson, L. (1995). *Dark Nature: A Natural History of Evil.* London: Hodder and Stoughton.

Watson, R. A. (1977). Reason and Morality in a World of Limited Food. In: Ailen, W. and LaFollette H., eds. *World Hunger and Moral Obligations.* Englewood Cliff, New Jersey: Prentice-Hall: 116–23.

Watson, W. I. (1989). Review of *Whose Justice? Which Rationality? Philosophy* 64: 564–66.

Weeks, A. L. (1993). The Modernizing Imperative: Tradition and Change. *Foreign Affairs* 72, September/ October: 24–25.

Weiner, M. (1995). *Global Migration Crisis.* New York: HarperCollins.

Weiss, D. D. (1973). Wollheim's Paradox: Survey and Solution. *Political Theory* 1: 154–70.

Wellhofer, E. S. (1995). 'Things Fall Apart; the Center Cannot Hold': Cores, Peripheries and Peripheral Nationalism at the Core and Periphery of the World Economy. *Political Geography.* 14: 503–20.

Whitehead, A. N. (1962). *Science and The Modern World.* New York: Macmillan.

Williams, B. (1985). *Ethics and the Limits of Philosophy.* Cambridge: Harvard University Press.

Williams, P. and Woessner, P. N. (1996). The Real Threat of Nuclear Smuggling. *Scientific American* 274, January: 26–30.

Williams, W. D. (1993). Australian Inland Waters: A Limited Resource. *Australian Biologist* 6: 2–10.

Wilson, E. (1996). Low-Life Meets High-Tech: A Warning. *The Australian* October 15: 3.

Wilson, P. (1995). Ralph Nader Targets BHP Over Ok Tedi. *The Australian* September 7: 3.

Wilson, R. (1996). Publish and Perish. *The Australian* October 22: 47.

Wilson, R. B. (1972). Social Choice Theory Without the Pareto Principle. *Journal of Economic Theory* 5: 478–86.

Windsor, G. (1996). Capital Backlash as Blacks Claim City Land. *The Australian* December 2: 1.

Wiseman, J. C. (1995). NAFTAmath. *Arena Magazine* April–May: 25.

Wolf, S. (1982). Moral Saints. *Journal of Philosophy* 79: 419–38.

Wolff, J. (1994). Democratic Voting and the Mixed-Motivation Problem. *Analysis.* 54: 193–96.

Wolff, R. P. (1970). *In Defense of Anarchism.* New York: Harper and Row.

Wollheim, R. (1969). A Paradox in the Theory of Democracy. In: Laslett, P. and Runciman, W. G., eds. *Philosophy, Politics and Society* (2nd Series). Oxford: Basil Blackwell: 71–87.

Wong, D. (1990). MacIntyre and the Commensurability of Traditions. *Philosophical Books* 30: 7–14.

Wood, A. (1997). The Hidden Immigration Debate. *The Australian* February 18: 13.

Woodford, J. (1995a). Murray-Darling Water Use Limited. *The Sydney Morning Herald* July 1: 3.

Woodford, J. (1995b). Sydney Faces Water Crisis, Say Officials. *The Sydney Morning Herald* August 19: 1.

Woodford, J. (1995c). Rivers Run into Pollution Crisis. *The Sydney Morning Herald* November 13: 6.

Woodford, J. (1996a). Australia Shamed over Gas Emissions. *The Sydney Morning Herald* February 17: 3.

Woodford, J. (1996b). Our 'Bread Basket' is in Big Trouble. *The Sydney Morning Herald* June 5: 6.

Woodley, B. (1990). Wide, Brown Land Can't Cope With Rising Population, Say Scientists. *The Australian* June 26: 6.

Woods, D. (1992). The Crisis of the Italian Party-State and the Rise of the Lombard League. *Telos* 93: 111–26.

Wright, C. (1992). *Truth and Objectivity*. Cambridge, Massachusetts: Harvard University Press.

Yakal, K. (1996). WWW Meltdown. *The Australian* July 2: 51.

Zann, L. P. and Sutton D., eds. (1995). *State of the Marine Environment Report for Australia.* Townsville: Great Barrier Reef Marine Park Authority for the Department of the Environment, Sport and Territories Ocean Rescue 2000 Program.

Zemach, E. M. (1986). Truth and Beauty. *The Philosophical Forum* 18: 21–39.

Index

About the Authors

JOSEPH WAYNE SMITH is Senior Research Fellow at The University of Adelaide, Australia.

GRAHAM LYONS is a leading South Australian businessman, agriculturist, and environmentalist. He co-authored *Healing a Wounded World: Economics, Ecology, and Health for a Sustainable Life* (Praeger Publishers) with Dr. Smith in 1997.

EVONNE MOORE is a research assistant at The University of Adelaide.

ISBN 0-275-95600-8

9 780275 956004

HARDCOVER BAR CODE